CW01333340

CHAPELS IN THE VALLEY

CHAPELS IN THE VALLEY

A STUDY IN THE SOCIOLOGY OF WELSH NONCONFORMITY

D. BEN REES

THE FFYNNON PRESS

ISBN 0 902158 08 2
© D. Ben Rees 1975

All rights reserved. No part of this publication may be reproduced, stored in a retrieval system, or transmitted, in any form, or by any means, electronic, mechanical, photocopying, recording or otherwise, without prior permission of the Ffynnon Press.

Set in 10 on 12 point Baskerville and printed in 1975
by Gee & Son, Denbigh, for the publishers,
THE FFYNNON PRESS
PO Box 2, Upton, Wirral, Merseyside, L49 1SY.

Cyflwynedig i fy Rhieni am fy nysgu yn ffyrdd Ymneilltuaeth.

Presented to my Parents for teaching me in the ways of Nonconformity.

ACKNOWLEDGEMENT

The author and publishers thank the following for the illustrations appearing in this book :

Aerofilms Limited (Plate 1); National Coal Board (Plate 18); Aberdare Public Library (Plates 2, 3, 5 & 6); and Mr. Glyn Davies, Aberdare (Plates 4, 7, 8, 9, 10, 11, 12, 13, 14, 15, 16, 17, 19, 20, 21 & 22).

CONTENTS

	Page
ACKNOWLEDGEMENT	6
THE ILLUSTRATIONS	8
PREFACE	9
SOME LITERATURE ON THE SOCIOLOGY OF RELIGION	11
LIFE IN THE VALLEY	31
THE INVESTIGATION IN THE LIGHT OF OTHER SURVEYS	50
CHAPELS IN THE VALLEY	66
THE DEVELOPMENT OF INDUSTRY	124
INDUSTRY AND RELIGION	147
CONCLUSIONS AND THE WAY AHEAD	208
APPENDIX	215
REFERENCES	216
INDEX	219

ILLUSTRATIONS

1. Aerial view of Aberdare.
2. David Alfred Thomas (1856 - 1918).
3. Calfaria Welsh Baptist Chapel.
4. Mountain Ash.
5. J. Keir Hardie.
6. Dr. Thomas Price (1820 - 1888).
7. Victoria Square, Aberdare.
8. Co-operative Store, Aberdare.
9. Penrhiwceibr Workmen's Hall and Institute.
10. Bryn Seion Welsh Congregationalist Chapel, Cwmbach.
11. Abercynon Welfare Hall.
12. Aberdare from Graig Mountain.
13. Hen-dŷ-Cwrdd Unitarian Chapel, Trecynon.
14. View of Mountain Ash and Abercwmboi.
15. Hermon Presbyterian Church of Wales, Penrhiwceibr.
16. Mountain Ash from the Perthcelyn Road.
17. Ynysboeth Industrial Estate.
18. Penrhiwceibr Colliery.
19. Mountain Ash from Newtown Quarry.
20. Aberaman Public Hall and Grand Social Club.
21. A modern Social Club.
22. Hirwaun Trading Estate.

PREFACE

THIS study arose out of my experience as a Minister of Religion in the Aberdare Valley in South Wales, and I depended a great deal on the co-operation of people living in that valley. Their kindness and generosity are proverbial, and I knew of it first-hand. The valley has indelibly left its mark on my subsequent life, as I married a daughter of an Abercwmboi Baptist minister, and our first son was born in the Aberdare Hospital. We are kept informed by friends among the two congregations to which I ministered in Abercynon and Penrhiwceibr, and this book is at least an acknowledgement of their heroic witness against so many obstacles.

The research would never have been completed without the constant encouragement of my Supervisor, Professor G. F. Thomason, M.A., Ph.D., Head of the Department of Industrial Relations in the University College of South Wales and Monmouthshire, Cardiff. His knowledge of the South Wales scene is encyclopaedic, though he hails originally from the North of England. I should also say that this study was accepted for the M.Sc. (Econ.) degree in the University of Wales.

The work was written up and edited in Liverpool, and I am grateful for the encouragement given to me by acknowledged sociologists of religion, such as Professor David A. Martin. There is no doubt that Welsh Nonconformity needs more studies of this kind, and, in my opinion, the University of Wales, in conjunction with the Welsh Council of Churches, should immediately scientifically research an institution which is so inseparably tied up with the Welsh nation since the eighteenth century.

The work was typed for publication by Mrs. Joan Nicholas of Liverpool, a versatile and most competent person.

Lastly, I am indebted to my parents who taught me in the ways of a Welsh Nonconformist Chapel, and to my wife who has shouldered the burdens of a minister's wife (knowing full well as a minister's daughter what it meant), and I would like to take this opportunity of expressing my gratitude.

1

SOME LITERATURE ON THE SOCIOLOGY OF RELIGION

THIS book is concerned with the position of Welsh Nonconformist Chapels in the industrial Aberdare Valley in Glamorganshire in the nineteenth and twentieth century. It is a vast field, and our concern is with the industrial and social reasons for the apparent decline of Nonconformity.

We will have to look at the historical growth of both Nonconformity and the mining industry, and collate the factors together to substantiate the main proposition, that there has been a definite decline in membership and influence.

To do this, we have to define certain terms which will be used throughout and we will have to place this sociological attempt within the context of the work that has been accomplished in Sociology of Religion over the years.

Nonconformity is a word that can be traced to the seventeenth century, and it was first used in the Penal Acts following the Restoration (1660) and the Act of Uniformity (1662) to describe the "conventicles" (places of worship) of the Separatist congregations. Nonconformists are also called *dissenters,* a word first used of the Five 'Dissenting Brethren' at the Westminster Assembly of Divines in 1644-47. They are also called *Free Churchmen* since the formation of the Free Church Federal Council in the second half of the nineteenth century, a body which largely inspired Nonconformists in their social and educational work. The term is loosely applied in the Aberdare Valley as elsewhere in England and Wales to all Protestants dissenting from Anglicanism: Baptists, Congregationalists, Methodists, Presbyterians, Unitarians, and even such independent groups as the Society of Friends (Quakers), Elim

Four Square, the Plymouth Brethren, the Churches of Christ and the Salvation Army.

We will take the four main denominations, Baptists, Congregationalists, Methodists, and Presbyterians or Calvinistic Methodists, and those churches who worship in particular through the Welsh language. For comparative purposes we will include reference to Anglican Churches, Unitarians and even the Roman Catholic Church, to show that to some extent there has been a decline among *all* churches in the Aberdare Valley.

The historical account will bring out and underline the links between Nonconformity and the mining industry, and that it was from the Methodist, Congregationalist and Baptist Church meetings that the leaders of Chartism, the Labour Party, Trade Unions and the Liberal Party came in the nineteenth and early twentieth centuries. It was the Liberal Government of 1906-10 which was the most complete expression of the *Nonconformist conscience*. In the twentieth century after the 1926 General Strike and in the late 30's a general decline set in, a decline which was much later than in other parts of the country. Bishop Winnington-Ingram could write in 1896 about England :

" It isn't that the Church of God has lost the great towns, it has never had them ". And even before Bishop Winnington-Ingram's statement Lord Shaftesbury had observed in 1885 that " The parochial system is, no doubt, a beautiful thing in theory, and is of great value in small rural districts, but in the large towns it is a mere shadow and a name."

1885 and 1896 were the hey-day of Nonconformity in the Aberdare Valley, and it was not until after the Second World War that Bishop Winnington-Ingram's observation could be applied to the Welsh valley. What happened between 1896 and 1946 and between 1946 and 1970 is the vital question to be asked.

The question needs also an answer, and this is why Sociology of Religion can be of vital importance to the mission and the witness of the Free Churches. Sociology can be a pastoral tool, and E. R. Wickham has given a valuable introduction to this aspect in *Encounter with Modern Society* (London, 1964).

Nonconformity in Wales at present has very limited interest in sociology as a means of understanding society within which it operates, and to help the organisation to equip itself for its work in an urban society. Besides the *Blaendulais Centre,* an ecumenical group which occasionally produces a paper, and has also published a book, *The Church in a Mobile Society,* there has been no attempt to analyse and offer an answer to the problems of a church in an industrial society.[1]

This is not surprising, for before the 1960s the primary interests of sociology were political sociology and social stratification and community, and religion was allowed little more than a footnote to the political text, or a sidelong glance in the Community Survey.[2] Sometimes it received much better than a sidelong glance as in T. Brennan, E. Cooney and M. Pollin's study, *Social Change in South West Wales.* This was published in 1954, and will be referred to more than once in this book. Another Welsh attempt was A. D. Rees and Elwyn Davies, *Welsh Rural Communities,* published in 1960, which introduced an anthropological flavour. This was a welcome addition, and reminded one of the impressive tradition which has been the English contribution to Sociology. For example, a large part of the " data of sociology " in Spencer's *Principles of Sociology* was composed of religious phenomena of one kind or another; Tyler's *Primitive Culture* was, similarly, largely concerned with religious and quasi-religious ideas; and from these pioneers it is possible to trace a continuous line of development through to the evolutionary theories of religion held by Hobhouse and Westermarck, on the one hand, and to the detailed comparison of religion and science in the erudite volumes of Sir James Fraser on the other. Some sociologists, like J. A. Banks, believe that we need to look again at the work of Fraser, and especially the work of such social anthropologists as Evans-Pritchard, and his work among the tribes of Africa. Ronald Frankenberg did a social-anthropological study of the civil parish of Llansantffraid Glyn Ceiriog in Denbighshire on the border of Wales. It was published in 1957, *Village on*

---

[1] It must be noted in fairness to the Nonconformist denominations that they have collected statistics concerning membership of their chapels over the years, though here again there is carelessness in collating and very little interpretation. It is not often that comments are made on the figures except in an optimistic fashion.

[2] This was the case in Alwyn D. Rees's work on Llanfihangel-yng-Ngwynfa and Margaret Stacey in her account of Banbury, to cite two examples out of many.

the Border, and Frankenberg disguised the village in the parish under the name of Pentrediwaith.

The *Welsh Rural Communities,* besides its anthropological flavour, trod well-worn routes in the footsteps of Durkeim and Weber, and especially Max Weber. The same thing can be seen in many of the surveys between 1925 and 1960. When Richard Niebuhr's *The Social Sources of Denominationalism* was published in 1929, it looked back to the study of Ernst Troelstch. This brings us to the work of the "classical school" of the Sociology of Religion.

Ernst Troelstch's massive volume, *Die Soziallehren der Christlichen Kirchen und Gruppen,* published in Tubingen in Germany in 1912, was the great attempt at defining the Sociology of Religion.[3] Troelstch limited his investigation to the historico-sociological analysis of Christianity. The second important work of the "classical school" was Max Weber, *Protestant Ethic and the Spirit of Capitalism,* "one of the most important works ever published in sociology" (Berger, 1971, p. 204).

Both of these two volumes are of a general historical nature, and it is of no wonder that the German theologian Dietrich Bonhoeffer could reproach the Sociology of Religion. He said that Sociology of Religion "had studied almost only religious history in its general historical or political economic aspects" (Bonhoeffer, 1960, p. 14). It had no systematic sociological frame of reference. Troelstch and Weber had other ideas, and to them Religion was indispensable. It would not be an exaggeration to put it in this way, that in studying the relationship between Religion and Society to Troelstch and Weber Religion was of primary importance.

The next great figure is Joachim Wach, who looked upon Sociology of Religion as an integral and integrating factor in Society. Religion expressed itself in myth, dogma, cult and religious grouping. To Wach, in *Sociology of Religion* (Chicago, 1944), Religion had fomenting and integrating power. Wach's observations are of a general culture and historical nature, and there can be no talk of Sociology of Religion as an independent subdivision of Sociology.

[3] It is worth reading this work in translation: *The Social Teaching of the Christian Churches,* New York, 1931. The translation was done by O. Wyon.

The position in Sociology of Religion is different today, reflecting no doubt the changes that have taken place in the position and significance of Religion and Church in modern society. It is right to say that the whole procedure is much more objective. In the 60's Bryan Wilson carefully distinguished in *Sects and Society* between types of sects and challenged Niebuhr's notion that the sects usually developed into denominations compromising the pristine version during their second generation. David Martin of the London School of Economics put forward the idea that a denomination is a specific type of Christian body, broadly exemplified by the Free Churches, which does not necessarily begin in a sectarian form at all and which is characteristic of Anglo-American religious culture (Martin, 1970, p. 234).

The best work in this field was the symposium *Patterns of Sectarianism,* published in 1967 and edited by Bryan Wilson. This symposium largely consists of work done by Wilson's collaborators and students at Oxford and exemplifies what might be called institutional analysis — a statement of historical origins, the dynamics of development, mode and type of recruitment, mechanism of conservation, continuity and schism, characteristic problems of leadership and organisation.

Some of the continental sociologists of religion, like D. Goldschmidt, H. Schelsky, P. Smit and Friedrich Fürstenberg, have tried to get rid of the theme of the classical writers, like Troelstch, Weber and Wach, but they have not succeeded. P. H. Vrijhof, the Dutch sociologist, puts it in a nutshell:

"That the theme of classical Sociology of Religion has been put the other way round, but remains essentially the same" (Vrijhof, 1967, p. 34).

The influence of Joachim Wach has not been discarded, and the chief problem still is insufficient anchorage in general sociological theory. "It remains true that the sociology of religion is marginal in terms of the sociological enterprise proper (as distinguished from the ecclesiastical research enterprise discussed before), both in terms of its practise and in terms of its thought. Whatever may be the historical reasons for the segregation of the sociology of religion into a somewhat eccentric preserve, the implication is quite clear: religion is not a central concern for sociological theory or for the sociological analysis of contemporary society" (P. Berger and T. Luckmann, 1971, p. 64). On the whole, Sociology of Religion today is based on a dichotomy of religion and society, and the task is to define more clearly the relationship and the dependence of religious institutions on sociological factors. This will be a difficult task.

Joachim Wach is, as I have already mentioned, one of the most important figures in the Sociology of Religion. It is worth the effort to look at his standpoint, which will differ from our effort.

He believes that no extensive research can in any way disclose the nature and essence of religion itself (Wach, 1944, p. 4). Religion to Joachim Wach was a personal matter, a relationship between God and individual man. Therefore religion cannot be identified with finite concepts, rites or institutions. Religion is " that profoundest source from which all human existence is nourished and upon which it depends in all its aspects: man's communion with God " (Wach, 1944, p. 385). Wach gives a substantial role to religion, it is the power that binds people together in fellowship, it has the force of social integration.

Wach differs in many a way from Weber, yet both have an individual, idealistic standpoint. Their influence is still apparent in the field of Sociology of Religion, and, in general, recent workers in the Sociology of Religion continue to abstain from inquiry into the essence of religion. Milton Yinger confines himself (as we will to a large extent) to a functional definition:

" The Sociology of Religion is, broadly speaking, the scientific study of the ways in which society, culture and personality influence religion — influence its origin, its doctrines, its practices, the types of groups which express it, the kinds of leadership, etc. And, oppositely, it is the study of the ways in which religion affects society, culture and personality — the processes of social conservation and social change, the structure of normative systems, the satisfaction or frustration of personality needs, etc. One must keep continuously in mind the interactive nature of these various elements " (Yinger, 1957, p. 20f).

If religion by its very nature is regarded as an encounter with a supernatural power, the Sociology of Religion can do nothing else than concern itself with those aspects which can be perceived in the world. That does not mean that one should not find out man's beliefs and ideas on God, the Trinity, Jesus, Life after Death, and other theological subjects.

But the main section must be the interaction of Church or Chapel and Society, rural or urban. This is the trend of the last decade in the Sociology of Religion. This has meant the use of demography and sociography. Demographic work included such matters as interfaith marriage, divorce rates, church attendance and so on.

Sociography included a careful study of the geographical and social location of different denominations, and the varied use made of the rites and services of the Church. An example of enumerative and descriptive work is provided by John Highet's *The Churches in Scotland Today* (1950), and *The Scottish Churches* (1960). A recent remarkable survey is John D. Gray, *The Geography of Religion in England* (1971).

The primary impulse in charting the social anatomy of the Church came from France through the inspiration of Gabriel Le Bras. His work became known in England through F. Boulard's work, *An Introduction to Religious Sociology*, published in 1954. It is marked by a deep historical interest based on the assumption that patterns of institutional involvement and vitality remain in being over very long periods.

A bold and successful attempt within Protestantism was the work of Roger Mehl, *The Sociology of Protestantism* (1970).[4] Mehl has to admit that Sociology has not yet won full acceptance within Protestantism. This is much more true of the Free Churches and Nonconformity.

Parish studies are in general associated with the Bras/Boulard school; pioneer work was done by Joseph Fichter, *Southern Parish* (1951), and by Joan Brothers's *Church and School* (1964).

The establishment of historical perspective by the French and the clear crux provided by large-scale industrialism in the erosion of institutional vitality formed a background to the pioneer study in England by Edward Wickham, *Church and People in an*

---

[4] Translated by James H. Farley from the French, *Traité de sociologie du protestantisme*, published 1965 by Delachaux and Niestlé, Neuchâtel, Switzerland, and published by the S.C.M., London, in 1970.

Industrial City (1957). This chartered the way in which the churches had never really penetrated the urban masses, and also the revival of middle class religion in the second part of the nineteenth century. K. S. Inglis performed a similar task on a national scale in his *Churches and the Working Classes in Victorian England* (1963), though part of his preoccupation was the reaction of the churches to this situation, more particularly their own comment on it. David Martin brought together the main strands (historical background as well as research work being carried out) in *A Sociology of English Religion,* published in 1967. Such researches, Wickham, Inglis and Martin, established links with the 1891 Census and with the work of Abraham Hume, Charles Booth and R. Mudie Smith.

Studies were carried out of organisational change and the role of the minister and clergy. Leslie Paul's *The Deployment and Payment of the Clergy* (1964) combined organisational prescriptions with analysis of the position of the clergy. The tension and ministerial role has been looked upon in articles and theses. Eric Carlton looked upon candidates for the Baptist ministry and Francis Absalom on the Anglo-Catholic Priest: Aspects of Role Conflict[5] among many other efforts.

There are within the Sociology of Religion a number of specially marked out types of research. These will be briefly looked at.

1. *Religious Sociology*

The movement called "Religious Sociology" originated in 1931, when a French canon lawyer, Gabriel Le Bras, made a notable appeal for historians, archivists, clergy and the like to co-operate in an effort to understand the religious position in France. For some years Le Bras worked almost alone, producing numerous articles, and eventually collaboration came from Canon Fernand Boulard, who was responsible for collecting a great deal of material on religious observance in rural France. This was a practical effort, and was extended to other areas, outside France, within the Roman Catholic Church.

The studies at the beginning tended to be concerned with

---

[5] See *A Sociological Yearbook of Religion in Britain 4,* edited by Michael Hill, London, S.C.M. Press, 1971, pp. 46-61.

collecting background material, taking into account historical factors. A study might be concerned with a survey of those actually present in church on a particular Sunday, including information on the age, socio-economic background, occupational status and family structure and the like. These surveys have developed and grown, and the interpretation of the facts has contributed considerably to our knowledge of religious behaviour.

Centres have been established outside France, the most notable one being the *Belgian Centre de Recherches Socio-Religieuses,* now in Louvain, with several branches in Belgium. Protestant and Catholic institutes have been set up in the Netherlands. Other bodies have been formed throughout the continent of Europe, such as the *Conférence Internationale de Sociologie Religieuse,* which has been a body for research in the Sociology of Religion.

Religious sociology has become mor specialised, and an idea of the work being done can be gathered from the publications and bibliographies that have been prepared by J. Dellepoort, N. Greinacher and W. Menges. In Britain, however, Sociology of Religion is often entirely disregarded by professional sociologists. Joan Brothers has indicated some of the limitations of the study (Brothers, 1967, p. 17). The targets of criticism have been the repetition of surveys of the established pattern rather than studies embodying fresh directions in the aims and methods, the desire for the findings to be immediately available for pastoral decisions, and the superficiality of demographic analyses and their inadequacy in indicating the religious life of a community.

But although I would not call this research a religious sociology, I have used the work of the French-Canadian writer H. Carrier, S.J. His work was published in England in 1965 under the title of *The Sociology of Religious Belonging.* He calls the new approach the psycho-sociology of religion, and asks such questions: to what extent are our spiritual attitudes influenced by the groups (religious or secular) to which we are attached?

Carrier has three headings:

(i) Psycho-Sociological Study of Attitudes.
(ii) The Connections between our Attitudes and our Reference Groups.
(iii) Application to Socio-Religious Behaviour.

The application can be used in reference to the religious sentiment of the young; attitudes of the "modal" catholic; and religious conversion. It was Carrier who brought me to realise that the research would be futile without devoting some time and effort to the discipline of social psychology. It is true that there is overlapping in all this, and that social psychology may often be blurred and blend into other fields, but as Carrier and Kimball Young have shown, social psychology is concerned with attitudes, the relation between social structure and personality, and group processes.

The concept of an attitude is a very useful and important one; it implies a readiness to act in a consistent way over a range of issues. We cannot see an attitude, we can only infer it from its manifestations in what a person does and says. And one more concept is needed, because research has shown that attitudes themselves are combined into further groupings. Writers on attitudes have called these "ideologies", and "ideology" is used to stand for an organisation of opinions, attitudes and values — a way of thinking about Man and Society. It is strange to use the phrase Nonconformist ideology, but it is valid to do so.

It is the task of the social psychologist also to relate to another the social structure and personality, and to deal with group processes. Social psychology is concerned (as it should) with a strategic area for the meeting-points of sociology and psychology. The justification for studying these two great disciplines is obvious and the same argument applies to social psychology.

2. *Institutional Analysis*

Another important aspect of the sociological approach has been the empirical study of how institutions work. Religious institutions have been considered in this way, and this is especially true in the United States of America, where a general study of an area will usually include the analysis of religious communities. The best example of this is R. Lynd and H. M. Lynd's study of *Middletown: A Study in Modern American Culture,* New York, 1929, where we have four chapters devoted to Religion. Chapter 20 is on Dominant Religious Beliefs; Chapter 21 on Where and When Religious Rites are Carried On; Chapter 22 on Leaders and Participants in

Religious Rites, and Chapter 23 on Religious Observances. The United States has pioneered in this work, and reference has been made to one of the most prominent in the field, J. H. Fichter. What is important about J. H. Fichter's work is the way in which the observation and analysis of religious structures are accompanied by the development of theory. For instance, his typology of parishioners — nuclear, modal, marginal and dormant — has grown out of his empirical investigation of parochial life. Role theory has also been relied on in this kind of research, and the role of the priest or minister has become an important area for research. It is my contention that this is as true for a minister in the Nonconformist chapel as it is for a priest in the parochial system. Another major contribution of Fichter has been to demonstrate, through empirical research instead of the assertions other writers often make on the subject, that religious institutions are susceptible to sociological investigation without their ideologies being undermined.

Sociological analysis may reveal that beliefs can produce conflict in the life of a Welsh Congregationalist miner, or it may reveal that the behaviour of participants in a religious community has little relation to the values they profess. It cannot evaluate the ultimate truth or falsity of values, nor, indeed, is that its aim, but it can demonstrate that an ideology gives rise to certain characteristics or disadvantages in an institutional setting.

One weakness in Fichter's work is that he has not concerned himself with the role of ideas and beliefs as he has done with the operation of institutions. I will mention the role of ideas and beliefs, but the work of Fichter does provide a solid empirical foundation which is valuable.

3. *Religion and Society*

One of the limitations of institutional analysis in relation to religion has been the concentration upon religious communities as though they were self-contained units, to the neglect of relationships with the wider society, both formally in terms of official interaction of one institution with others and informally through the everyday contact of members with those outside the group. Too much emphasis upon the minutiae of organisation within a religious system can be responsible for disregarding the functions of religious institutions in the general society and the influence of membership of a religious group in ordinary living. It is this general weakness in the Sociology of Religion that is largely overcome by two American sociologists, Lenski and Herberg.

The theme of Herberg's analysis is the experience of minority groups as they become assimilated into the middle classes and are seen as acceptable within the American way of life. His analysis illustrates how religious beliefs can be absorbed by a community and made to fulfil functions unrelated to the religious sphere. Herberg deals with Protestantism, Catholicism and Judaism, and shows how identification with one of these three groups can be a passport to social acceptability. " Religious belonging has become a mode of defining one's American identity " (Herberg, 1967, p. 214). In a different context, Nonconformity can be looked upon as similar in the Welsh valleys to what we call *Y Ffordd Gymreig o Fyw*.

But there is also a difference. The religions mentioned in America have status in society, while the status of Nonconformity has largely disappeared in the mining valleys. " . . . Religion enjoys a high place in the American scheme of things, higher today, perhaps, than at any time in the past century. But it is a religion thoroughly secularised and homogenized, a religion — in general — that is little more than a civic religion of democracy, the religionization of the American Way " (Herberg, 1967, p. 215).

The order of things is entirely different in Welsh Nonconformity in the days of Dr. Thomas Price, Aberdare, and Rev. David Price, Siloa, Aberdare, in the middle of the nineteenth century. The congregation at Siloa in the middle of the nineteenth century overflowed the chapel. It was a mixed congregation according to the Rev. David Price's successor, the Rev. D. Silyn Evans, " Cynulleidfa gymysg fuasai — mynychwyr rheolaidd, dynion achlysurol, ' dynion dwad ' — rhai yn myned i rywle i dreulio noson, ac eraill mewn camgymeriad, yn bresennol " (It was a mixed congregation — the regular members, occasional members, visitors — some going anywhere to spend the evening, and others through mistake being present) (Evans, 1896, p. 70).

Nonconformity at that time had status, it is in the middle of the twentieth century that things have changed, and that Nonconformity does not attract the occasional members, visitors, or people who want to spend an evening. There are plenty of other organisations to cater for their wants, and Nonconformity has remained 'religious' and linguistic, in an age which has seen Protestantism in America being secularised into "a civic religion of democracy", to borrow W. Herberg's phrase.

Lenski's contribution has been to discover in his study of Detroit (see *The Religious Factor,* Garden City, 1961) how far beliefs and membership of a religious group were a factor in determining reactions to political, economic and social issues. His analysis reveals that religion is as strong an influence as social class in affecting behaviour. The findings of Lenski challenge the conceptual framework of many writers in the sociology of religion. Religion can be an important causal factor in social situations, and is an essential analytical tool without which they cannot be understood.

Religion, as Lenski has shown, can affect social behaviour in many an anticipated way; it has also a way of affecting behaviour in unintended ways. The influence of subgroups within religious communities enters into the question here. The complex subcultures which develop within religious communities can exert considerable influence upon general attitudes and behaviour and make religion a particularly powerful force in determining social behaviour.

Lenski has interesting conclusions, the most relevant one for us being the following in his analysis of the differences in family life between Catholics and Protestants.

" The more faithful Protestants were in their attendance at worship services, the weaker were the ties with their kin group " (Lenski, 1967, p. 227).

Gerhard Lenski has introduced a new dimension into the sociology of religion; he considers not only the content and form of ideologies, but also their relationship to actual situations.

4. *History and Sociology of Religion*

C. Wright Mills, in his last book, *Sociological Imagination,* made a plea for sociologists to take seriously the material of history. Le Bras used history to an advantage, and I will also attempt to do the same, for history provides endless material, and this is especially true of Welsh Nonconformity. Most of the ministers which Nonconformity had in its golden age had biographies written about them, usually written a few years after their death. The Welsh biography is a source of endless material that can be used to substantiate generalisations and to show that there was a close connection between the chapel and the community. It is also a source that has not been used for this purpose in the sociology of Welsh Nonconformity.

This was one reason why the Aberdare Valley in Glamorganshire was chosen as the site of study. There were many other reasons.

(1) We find in the Aberdare Valley that the location of the mines has been associated to a great extent with the location of the Nonconformist chapels. A Congregationalist minister, Rev. D. Silyn Evans, in his biography of Rev. David Price (1811 - 1878), has shown how the growth of their denomination in the Aberdare Valley developed hand in hand with the opening of the mines.

" Ar ddechreuad gweinidogaeth cyhoeddus Mr. Price yn Siloa, dechreuid yn ogystal i agor gweithfeydd mawrion yn y lle — gwaith yr Aberdare Coal Company, gwaith Mri. Williams a Lewis, gwaith Llety Shenkyn, gwaith Blaengwawr, gwaith Haearn Aberaman, gwaith y Werfa, gwaith Ysguborwen, ac amryw fân a mawr weithiau eraill." (At the beginning of the public ministry of Mr. Price in Siloa, a number of large works were opened — the colliery of the Aberdare Coal Company, the colliery of Messrs. Williams and Lewis, the colliery of Llety Shenkyn, the colliery at Blaengwawr, the iron works at Aberaman, the colliery at Werfa, the colliery at Ysguborwen, and a number of other large and small collieries) (Evans, 1896, p. 37).

(2) Both the mining industry and the Nonconformist chapels have seen change and decline. We are concerned to see if there is any relationship between the decline of Nonconformity and the run-down of the mining industry.

(3) My qualifications for attempting this survey seem to be:

(a) a personal sympathy with the cause of Welsh Nonconformity and the Aberdare mining community. I lived among the people of the valley for nearly seven years, and during that time was within Nonconformity as a minister of two Presbyterian churches in the lower end of the Aberdare Valley. (In my view, it is essential that sociological researchers, being bound to have personal prejudices, should endeavour honestly to think them out and state them.)

(b) a Welsh background, and possession of first-hand knowledge of Welsh culture, history and language. This enables one to read the vast amount of material relevant to the study which is to be found in the Welsh language, and to understand also the literature written in Welsh for the eisteddfodau held in the valley through the nineteenth and twentieth centuries.

Many of these Welsh Nonconformists published their poems, and a good instance of this was a bard who lived at Penrhiwceibr calling himself Ap Valant and who published a volume of poetry in 1885 under the title *Cyfeillach Awen* (Merthyr Tydfil). The volume is not important for the standard of its poetry; but it is important as a reflection of the Welsh Nonconformist mining community of the valley at the end of the last century.

Ap Valant was a *dyn dŵad*, an immigrant. We gathered that he hailed from the village of Llanafan in Cardiganshire. He has a poem in memory of a brother, Richard Valentine, who was born in Llanafan, but died at Mountain Ash in 1876 at the age of 34 (Ap Valant, 1885, pp. 109-111), and to a cousin from the same village who was killed in a colliery at Treherbert in 1880 at the age of 25.

Ap Valant was a miner and a radical. He has a poem on the state of the working class in South Wales in 1878, a satirical poem entitled 'Cydymdeimlad Cyfoethogion ein gwlad at Dlodion Deheudir Cymru yn 1878' (The Sympathy of the Rich People of our country towards the Poor People of South Wales in 1878).

He was also a Nonconformist in his religion. In his *englyn* to John Parry (Ioan Celyn) from Mountain Ash he pays tribute to him as an elder or deacon, " Blaenor a llenor call " (Ap Valant, 1885, p. 92), and this he does again in another poem in memory of the same man (Ap Valant, 1885, pp. 86-91).

He was a deacon in Bethania Congregationalist Church,

Mountain Ash. Ap Valant has also a poem to welcome a new minister to Penuel Chapel, Penrhiwceibr.

Ap Valant belonged also to the Welsh literary life, to the subgroup within Nonconformity which encouraged the eisteddfodau and literary societies of the chapels. In the introduction to the volume of poetry we come across five poets from the same areas besides others from the Rhondda and the Ogwr Valley (Ap Valant, 1885, pp. v-vi).[6]

I have looked at Ap Valant in detail, as he embodies the characteristics that I believe were part and parcel of the Nonconformist ideology, and as an indication that to truly appreciate and understand the Nonconformist attitude, which is called *y ffordd Gymreig o fyw,* one has to diagnose, read and analyse the literary and cultural life that has been in an unexpected way synonymous with Nonconformity. The chapel was the centre of this Welsh way of life (and remains, to some degree still, in parts of rural Wales), and to a Nonconformist, as a good Protestant, the chapel exists from the moment that " there exists a community which assembles to hear the word of God " (Mehl, 1970, p. 45).

This is one reason why Nonconformity had a predominance of chapel buildings in the valley compared with other traditions within Protestantism, such as the Anglican Church; and with the Roman Catholic Church. The Nonconformist chapels are to be seen in every village and town in the valley conurbation, which, in this respect, is typical of many other areas in the United Kingdom, e.g., industrial Lancashire and Yorkshire. It is typical in its composition and in its dilemma.

In the Aberdare Valley, as in many other parts of Britain, the Free Church picture is a bleak one. Not only have the numbers declined, but the social composition of those remaining and the influence they are able to exert has fallen dramatically.

" To visit those parts of the country where the chapels are most deeply embedded in the landscape and local history, to live in Methodist Yorkshire, or Baptist Wales, or Independent East Anglia, or Unitarian Lancashire is to recognise the real plight of Non-

---

[6] The Aberdare poets included Glan Duad, Mountain Ash; Rev. W. Thomas (Ceinfryn), Abercwmboi; Isaac Edmunds (Alaw Sylen), Abercwmboi; Harri ab Gwilym, Mountain Ash; and Erwyd from Penrhiwceibr.

conformity in the sixties. Anyone can point to shining exceptions in particular places, but over large tracts of country, behind the peeling facades and plaintive wayside pulpits, there is nothing left but a faithful ingrown remnant, whiling away its Pleasant Sunday Afternoons and its Women's Bright Hours in dingy rooms from which whole generations and classes and intelligence levels have long since fled " (Driver, 1962, pp. 16 and 17).

So wrote one of the most perceptive journalists of the 60's, Christopher Driver.

Anyone passing through the streets of the villages and towns of the Aberdare Valley is conscious that Driver is near the mark — in the many derelict or converted chapels. Once these were the centres for thriving Nonconformist communities; now they are garages, storehouses or workshops.

My knowledge of Nonconformity and the mining industry came not from biographies, literature, but from extensive study of those people who are still members of chapels and who are still working in the collieries of the valley, as well as a questionnaire. The following lines were followed:

Stage 1: meeting and conversing with members and sympathizers of Nonconformity.

Stage 2: meeting the miners and having interviews with retired miners and people who are at present engaged in the industry. And it was for the purpose of this research in January 1968 that I visited the Penrhiwceibr Colliery and we visited the men at the coal face. This was valuable and essential, so as to test the hypothesis that the changes in the realm of work-life have some causal relationship to the decline of Nonconformity.

It is in this context that reference will be made to the structural similarities between Nonconformity and the mining industry before mechanisation altered it, and following Trist *et al, Organizational Choice,* we will deal with the small team in the colliery and compare this with the small independent Nonconformist chapel.

The changes in the work-role of the miner and the run-down of the mining industry has meant an entirely new pattern of work relationship.

This brings me to *Stage 3,* that of the factory worker. Many of the factory workers who work in the new industries located in the Rhigos and the Ynysboeth Industrial Estates, which were prepared by the Government and local authorities to counteract the decline of the mining industry, are ex-miners, or people associated in some direct or indirect way with mining, e.g., miners' sons, or miners' wives.

This location of these new industries has meant commuting to work for these people, a new experience to a large extent, though there were miners in the twenties and thirties who commuted from the valley to Merthyr, Rhondda and the Neath Valleys. But the mining industry was located where the raw materials were, and in the main the miners would live in the terraced houses around the colliery. This is still very much the case at Penrhiwceibr and Abercynon.

The light industries situated at Rhigos and Ynysboeth are an entirely different set-up from that of the mining industry. Light industries are located in strategic positions, and they have to take into account raw material orientation, market orientation and what they call " geographically necessited " transport costs.

This is a new phase of the industrial revolution, and we cannot, and it is not possible to, see the relationship between the complex structure of factories and other industrial work situation with the more traditional structure of Nonconformity in a simple and direct way. Industrial change is very complex, and caused by a complex set of variables, and it can be that these changes have meant a change in religious attitudes and practice.

Stage 4: meeting and conversing with people who are Nonconformists. They have much in common — both have been brought up in the Nonconformist tradition, but one group worships through the medium of the Welsh language and the other through the medium of the English language.

Their forefathers were in the main immigrants to the mining industry of the Aberdare Valley. The first wave of immigrants were Welsh-speaking and Nonconformist in religion, and it was they, as miners often supported financially by the mine-owners, who were responsible for so many of the chapels that remain today. The second wave of immigrants included English Nonconformists, as well as many others who were Catholics, Anglicans, and of no persuasion — but in the main they were Irish and English immigrants. Many of the second wave of immigrants built chapels, but they were Zion and not Seion; it meant that these chapels had a different language and a different culture from the Welsh Nonconformist chapels.

Stage 5: meeting representatives of the police, local government, schools and voluntary organisations of formal and informal social control.

Stages 1-4 provide satisfactory material, which was strengthened by the questionnaire given to a cross-section of the community as well as the advantage gained by Stage 5, which meant in all a thorough, rigorous examination of the growth and decline of Welsh Nonconformity in an industrial mining valley.

In the winter of 1967 I formulated a questionnaire made up of 49 questions to find out how people reacted to and thought about Nonconformity in an industrial society. The questionnaire was divided into seven parts:

1. Neighbourhood.
2. Politics.
3. Religious Education.
4. Religion and Nonconformity.
5. Christian Belief and Christian Ethics.
6. Sunday Observance.
7. Industry, Work and Leisure.

The number of questionnaires distributed was 150, of which 72 were returned (48 per cent), a good response. This compares with samples chosen in other research work, as, for example, the thesis by E. Carlton on the Probationer Minister, when a sample of fifty was selected.

Two methods were chosen for the distribution of the questionnaire. The first was to ask a number of people if they would help in organising and distributing the questionnaire. Four organisations were asked: The St. John Ambulance, through their headquarters in Cardiff; the minister of Elim Pentecostal Church, Mountain Ash; Barclays Bank, Aberdare; and a Hirwaun Youth Club. These four organisations were chosen to ensure representative answers, for in this way the whole valley would be covered, through four different channels.

Out of 70 given to the St. John Ambulance, eleven were received back, a 15.7 per cent return, while the Rev. S. J. Brown had six out of fourteen returned, a 42.8 per cent response given to Elim Young People's Fellowship. The Rev. Dilwyn O. Jones, minister of Bethel Presbyterian Church of Wales, Hirwaun, had a better response, with all the questionnaires answered, out of the eleven sent to him.

The other method in this empirical investigation consisted of a series of meetings, in 'depth', with the following organisations : Bethlehem Presbyterian Church of Wales, Mountain Ash, Sisterhood; a Sunday School class at Tabernacle Presbyterian Church of Wales, Abercynon; two adult classes — Comparative Religion and Conversational Welsh — which were under my tuition at the Abercynon Adult Education Centre; and a Lodge meeting of the Penrhiwceibr National Union of Mineworkers. The meeting, which was a valuable dialogue in depth, is fully reported in this book and referred to in this chapter.

With these tools I embarked on the analysis, a historical account of the growth of the Nonconformist denominations in the Aberdare Valley, as well as a factual account of the rise and progress of the mining industry, and an objective study and discussion of the industrial and social factors which have coloured the life and witness of the main Nonconformist Churches as well as other branches of the Universal Church in one particular area of the South Wales coalfield. It is my conviction that :

"Historical and sociological analysis can be a modern mode of self-examination and the prelude to penitence, understanding and amendment of life. It also furnishes the Church with new tools, new measuring instruments, a map and compass for charting a strategy of mission. To reject the new instruments or to restrict their use to the 'social sciences' would be blasphemy whereby God is yet further banished to the shrinking area of the inexplicable and the arbitrary" (Wickham, 1962, p. 15).

2

LIFE IN THE VALLEY

1. *A description of the Aberdare Valley (from the standpoint of environment, mining industry and places of worship with the Welsh Free Churches).*

The county of Glamorgan in South Wales may be roughly divided into two parts — the northern hilly and mountainous area known as *Y Blaenau,* and the southern undulating plain along the seaboard of the Bristol Channel known as *Y Fro.* The valley that I propose to use for the purposes of this book is called the Aberdare Valley and is situated in the northern part of the county of Glamorgan towards its eastern boundary, and has the following structure.

The River Cynon rises a few miles beyond the boundaries of the Aberdare parish at a spot called *Llygad y Cynon* (Eye of the Cynon) in the parish of Penderyn, which is situated in Breconshire, and flows in a south-easterly direction through the old parish of Llanwynno, through the towns of Mountain Ash and Penrhiwceibr until it joins the River Taff at Abercynon. There is a distance of 12 miles from Hirwaun in the north to Abercynon in the south, and the valley is very much wider than the neighbouring narrow valley of the Rhondda Fach to the west and the Taff Valley to the east.

Aberdare Valley is a mining valley, industrialised and urbanised. It is difficult to describe the area geographically, though the valley reflects the history of the growth of the area. The concentric land use model of E. W. Burgess has no relevance (Burgess, 1927, p. 178). Burgess was concerned with America, and even if we take the work done in Britain by P. H. Mann, again we have no comparison. Mann takes the cities of Huddersfield, Nottingham and Sheffield, and in each he found an easily recognisable Central Business District compounded of the specialised functions of law, finance and the major shopping complex, with nationally known chain stores such as the British Home Stores, Marks and Spencer and Woolworth.

This is not true of the Aberdare Valley, which is a small conurbation, and the two towns of Aberdare and Mountain Ash serving as what Mann calls the Central Business District. Aberdare had its Town Hall, and so had Mountain Ash, and the offices of the Aberdare Urban District Council and the Mountain Ash Urban District Council were housed there until the amalgamation of both Councils in 1974. Both towns have their chain stores and supermarkets, while Aberdare is regarded as a shopping centre for a larger area than Mountain Ash. People living in Hirwaun and Penywaun are often tempted to shop at Neath or Merthyr Tydfil, while the people of Abercynon to a large degree prefer Pontypridd to Mountain Ash. The train service which runs through Abercynon from Merthyr to Cardiff is an added reason for the popularity of Pontypridd, and, like Aberdare, it has a market.

There is no lack of variety in Mountain Ash or Aberdare, and one finds, as at Aberdare, two Nonconformist chapels, a brand new library, the Town Hall, situated together, and while in cities there is a definite pattern, this is not the case in the Aberdare Valley.

The structure of the Aberdare Urban District is of a complicated nature, with working houses mingled among new bungalows and residential areas. We will offer the following structure.

2. *The Upper Reaches of the Valley*

From the structure we can see that the pattern of development has been near an industry, the coal-mines being the main industry in that respect, and the subsequent development being around the old settlements, often the old settlement dividing the village into two with the private-owned and residential areas being on one side, and the large Council estates being on the other side of the settlement.

The Aberdare Council has built extensively to the north of the town. Penywaun, Hirwaun, Llwydcoed and Cwmdare have been extended, and Penywaun has grown from a straggling hamlet into

Life in the Valleys

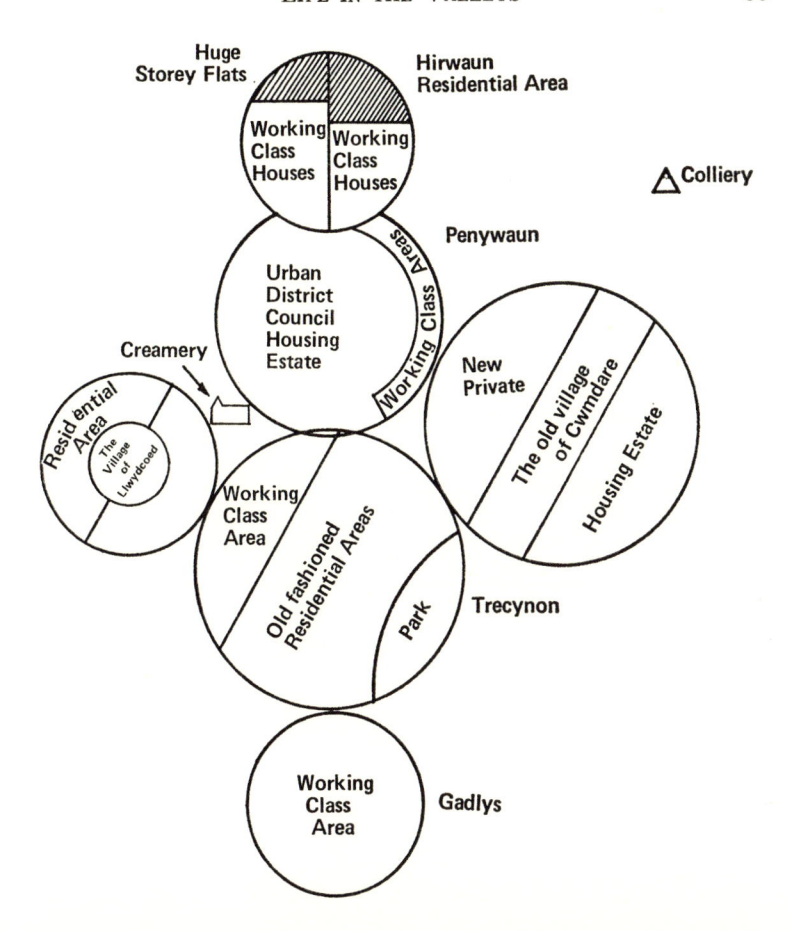

```
         Huge
      Storey Flats         Hirwaun
                           Residential Area
           Working  Working
           Class    Class                    △ Colliery
           Houses   Houses
                              Penywaun
             Urban
             District
             Council
  Creamery   Housing    New
             Estate     Private
                                 The old village of Cwmdare
  Residential Area
                                              Housing Estate
  The Village of Llwydcoed

           Working
           Class
           Area
                   Old fashioned
                   Residential Areas
                              Park  Trecynon


             Working
             Class      Gadlys
             Area
```

a large housing estate. Hirwaun has seen the erection of a number of huge flats, and the building, as we see, is still being carried on, largely by private firms, on the road to the Brecon Beacons (a favourite holiday spot for many of the Aberdare Valley people) between Hirwaun and Penderyn. The village of Penderyn came within the Cefncoed and Vaynor Urban District Council before 1974, but with regard to social and religious activities it is usually accepted as part of the Aberdare Valley.

Aberdare itself combines all the features except new buildings, and there is no land to be had for new housing estates. The town is static, and most of the houses were built in the Victorian and Edwardian eras.

We suggest the following structure for the town of Aberdare:

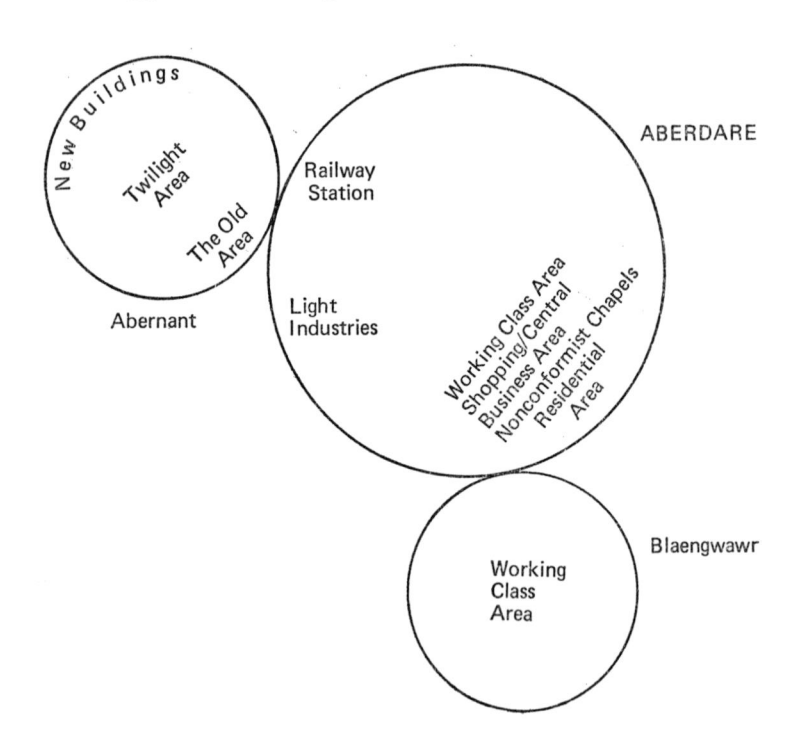

```
                                                          ABERDARE
   New Buildings
   Twilight Area         Railway
   The Old Area          Station

   Abernant              Light
                         Industries      Working Class Area
                                         Shopping/Central
                                         Business Area
                                         Nonconformist Chapels
                                         Residential Area

                                                          Blaengwawr
                              Working
                              Class
                              Area
```

Aberdare is a conglomeration of a Central Business Area, of working class streets, mingled with small industries, the railway station, and the residential area, which is around Monk Street, the road that leads out from the centre of the town to the Rhondda Fach. Monk Street has five Nonconformist chapels situated in it, and is often referred to by the local inhabitants as 'the most religious road in the valley'.

Abernant and Blaengwawr are very much solid working class areas, with Abernant being transformed and better-class houses being built instead of the terraced houses. It is a sector structure, and it has affected to a very large extent the community spirit of Abernant. Many of the older inhabitants have been moved to the housing estate or the council flats at Aberdare, and on Sundays they commute back to their Nonconformist chapels.

3. *Structure of the Middle Area of the Valley*

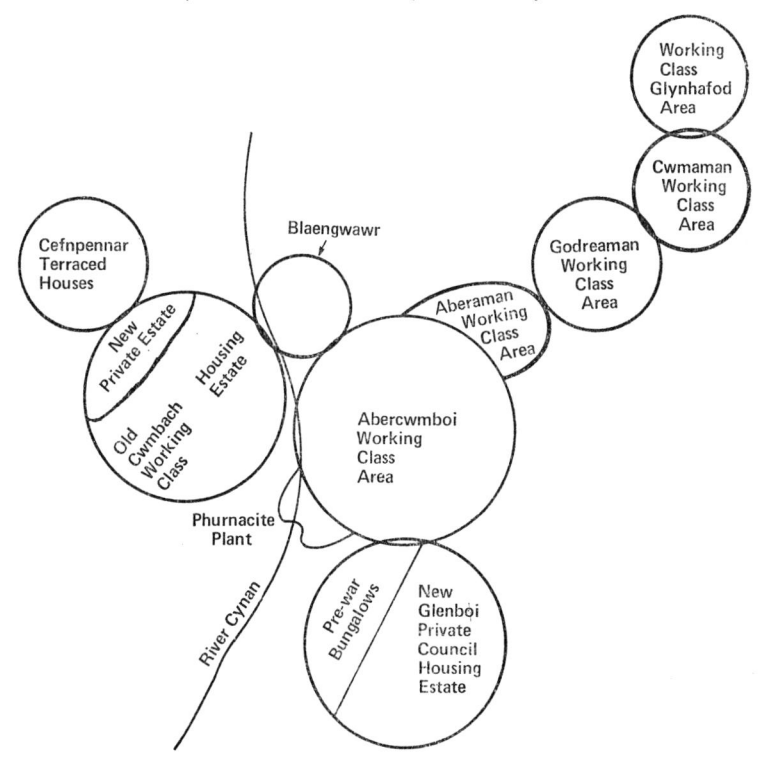

The middle area, which means, virtually, the villages of Aberaman, Godreaman, Cwmaman and Glynhafod, Abercwmboi and Cwmbach, is made up of the traditional terraces — a typical working class area, with layer upon layer of houses built up the Valley of Aman to Brynhafod and its colliery. Across the valley at Cwmbach we have a combination of new and old, of redevelopment on a small scale and the building of luxury bungalows that attract people from all parts of the valley. Glenboi serves the same purpose, a residential area which to some extent is severely handicapped by the presence of the huge Phurnacite plant at Abercwmboi. Cwmbach and Glenboi were the only available areas to the south of the town of Aberdare on the valley floor that had land available for building houses. Cwmpennar is a small hamlet, which is accessible by car from the town of Mountain Ash and not through Cwmbach.

4. *Structure of the Mountain Ash town*

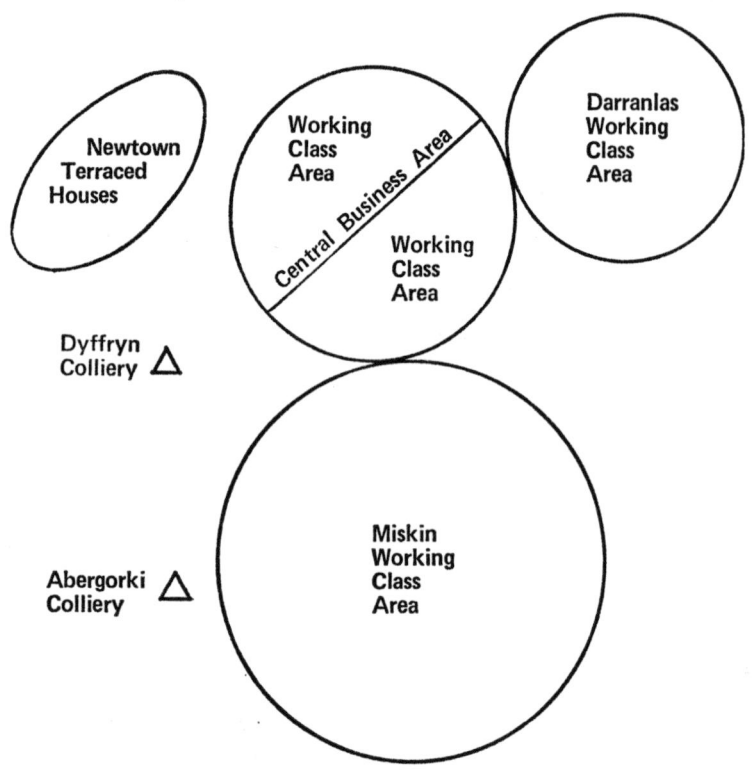

Mountain Ash is more a mining town than Aberdare; it has been literally built around the collieries. We have records that the area was a pleasant wooded valley, while Aberdare was slowly growing as a result of the iron industry at Hirwaun, Gadlys and Abernant.

The central business area is much more confined at Mountain Ash, and it straddles the main road for buses, for it is to be remembered that there is another road linking Aberdare-Mountain Ash and the lower reaches which is called the New Road, and it was built to follow the old Aberdare to Abercynon Canal. Miskin and Darranlas and Newtown are zones of small terraced houses, which depend to a large extent on Mountain Ash for their amenities. This area is also much more river-based than Aberdare and its base is commercial-industrial-working class area.

5. *Structure of the Lower Reaches of the Valley*

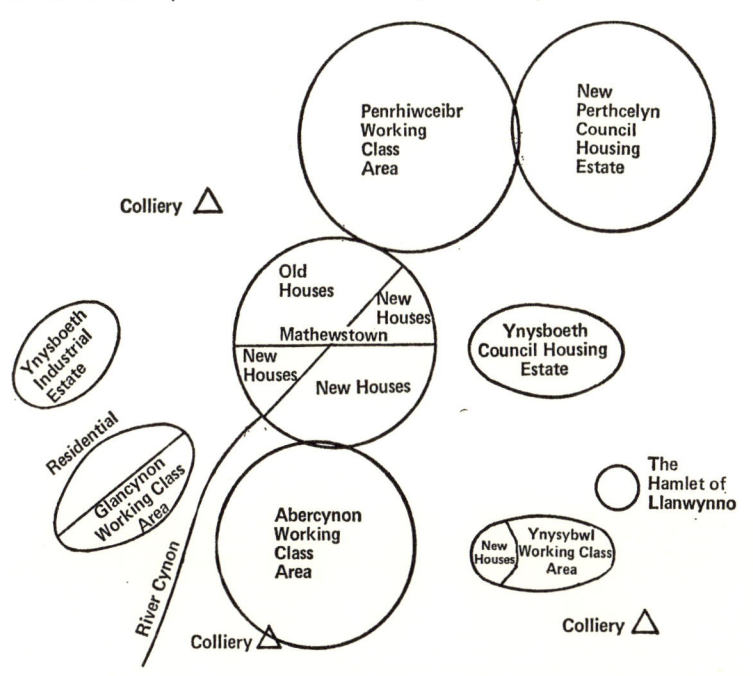

The lower end of the valley, more than any other part, depends upon the mining industry, and there are three collieries still in existence, one at Penrhiwceibr, another at Abercynon, and the third at Ynysybwl. All three towns are built around the collieries, but there has been extensive building done by the Mountain Ash Urban District Council since the Second World War.

The most interesting experiment was to build a large housing estate above Penrhiwceibr, called Perthcelyn. Its view is breathtaking, looking down over Penrhiwceibr and across the valley, but it lacks the amenities associated with the old traditional areas. It has one hotel, and no cinema or a chapel, and a flourishing Sunday School was held for a long time in one of the rooms of the hotel. The people have still to go to Mountain Ash or Penrhiwceibr for social life, and so have the inhabitants of other new areas, like the Ynysboeth or Bryntirion housing estates. It does not help that quite a lot of damage is done frequently to public property by vandals in the form of smashing and destroying windows and telephone kiosks.

An industrial area is found at Ynysboeth, very near to the entrance to Abercynon, another mining town. Abercynon itself is divided by the river. Across the river is the zone of Glancynon, which is much more busy, as the new road from Traveller's Rest to Aberdare runs through it. The best houses in the town of Abercynon are over at Glancynon and overlooking the River Taff which joins the River Cynon near the Colliery.

Ynysybwl, which is on its own, belongs in most things to Pontypridd, but for administrative purposes it came within the Mountain Ash Urban District Council. It is another town which has depended on a colliery, and its colliery, Lady Windsor, is still in operation. The town itself is a mixture of good, solid working class houses, mixed with some new bungalows.

The hamlet of Llanwynno, which stands on the narrow road from Ynysybwl to Mountain Ash, consists of a church, an inn, and a few houses, and has not changed since the days of one of its notable sons, the incredible athlete of the eighteenth century, Guto Nyth Brân.

The villages and the towns of the Aberdare Valley grew without any careful planning, and virtually from nothing. There was no room to build as one would desire, for the ironworks were built or the mines were sunk in the limited floor of the Aberdare Valley. The lines of communication between Aberdare and Abercynon, roads, the canal and the railway, were also on the valley floor, and so the only available land for building houses was between the valley floor and the moorland edge. The extension of the settlements could only take place longitudinally along the valley side, and often controlled by the lines of the newly constructed road. Thus came into being the long lines of terraced houses, which have been satirised as 'salubrious dwellings for the industrious artisan', and others have been frightened by their lack of privacy (Francis C. Payne, 1943, p. 68).

Everything was bundled together — land, capital, organisation, labour and housing, and, to use Mumford's phrase, we have the " non plan ". Many of the villages in the Aberdare Valley took their names from local farmsteads like Blaengwawr, and others were decided at public meetings, with the result that Abercynon was adopted instead of the original names, Aberdare Junction and Navigation.

The houses in the valley have been built of stone and they are structurally sound, but monotonous, drab and depressing. Characteristically, these houses had a front parlour directly onto the street, a middle room, and a kitchen, with three bedrooms, but no bathroom (Carter, 1965, p. 313). There was an outside lavatory. By the end of the nineteenth century the fashionable bay window was to be found on many of these houses, together with a small entrance porch, stained glass doors and a small front garden. The early Council houses, built after the Housing of the Working Classes Act of 1890, are often indistinguishable from these terraces. In the inter-war years, semi-detached houses were built, as at Glenboi, between Mountain Ash and Abercwmboi, prosperous and termed by the locals as 'over-draft avenue'. In the post-war years we have seen the building of extensive housing estates, beginning with the prefabricated houses of the immediate post-war years, as at Ynysboeth, and continuing through to the toll point blocks at Hirwaun in the early 1960s. At the outbreak of the Second World War in 1939, the Aberdare Urban District Council owned, or had built, its estates at Trefelin, Tre Ifor, Trenant, Trewaun, Treheol and Abernant, some 576 dwellings. After the end of the war the need for houses became acute. Between 1945 and 1956, over thirteen hundred dwelling houses of various types were built in the Aberdare Valley alone. Over half of this total has been built at Penywaun, which is a neighbourhood in itself, having its own schools, shops, welfare centre and other amenities.

Little is known of the impact of visual environment upon people in mining valleys, but recently emphasis has been placed upon this aspect, as shown in the Lower Swansea Valley Project. The Aberdare Valley is not without its beauty spots, and the Aberdare Park is one of the finest in South Wales. There are many other charming spots within the valley, besides the Aberdare Park, namely:

(1) Abernant Park (where the General Hospital is situated) and Abercynon Park.
(2) St. John's Parish Church (12th century) amid trees and flowering shrubs.
(3) Dumfries Park (better known as the Graig), on the hillside between Aberdare and Maerdy. From the top of the Graig one is able to view the whole valley and, on a clear day, the Beacons can be seen. The view at night is also a delight.
(4) Croes Bychan and Cwm Ynys Mantan, a pretty wooded glen, near Llwydcoed.
(5) The Mountain Ash 'Gorsedd' Stones which were placed there during the National Eisteddfod of Wales which was held at the town in 1946. They are situated on the road from Mountain Ash (near the General Hospital) to the village of Cefnpennar.

These areas are appreciated, but there are other areas which are not so pleasant, and this we found out in the questionnaire that was given to a cross-section of the Aberdare Valley population.

The replies given were revealing:

" I am quite happy living in Mountain Ash, since the opening of the factories; it has provided the people with work because the mining industry is on the decline " (Mountain Ash housewife).

" *Pobl agos atoch* " (i.e., friendly people). " Quite homely. Very kind people. English and Welsh places of worship " (Mountain Ash housewife).

" The people are friendly, but not more so than anywhere else. Personally I prefer the country " (Abercynon Civil Servant).

" Not very good for the younger generation. Not enough entertainment facilities " (Barclays Bank employee).

" Very dull and lifeless for young people. Disgusting the rate of unemployment. Beautiful countryside surroundings. If I was from

England and came to settle in Wales, I would not choose either Merthyr or Aberdare Valley for my home" (a Barclays Bank employee).

The following were the reactions of some of the young people from the Aberdare area:

"Dirty, socially pathetic."

"Very hospitable, closely-knit community; disappointing shopping area. Excellent park, not very many good residential areas."

"Alright."

The adults and the young people were very much alike in their attitude to the neighbourhood, as these answers demonstrate:

"Nice, homely" (Mountain Ash inhabitant).

"Satisfactory. Derelict buildings could be removed to make the area more attractive" (Barclays Bank employee).

"Very good, especially from Aberdare to Hirwaun. Easy access to County National Park; quick transport with Heads of the Valley Road" (a Tower No. 1 Colliery N.C.B. Hirwaun worker).

"I like it. Some improvement could be made for the younger ones; for example, a swimming pool" (Tower No. 4 Colliery N.C.B. Hirwaun worker).

"Hirwaun all my life. Being born here and lived all my life in this neighbourhood and have found things very pleasant" (Tower Colliery worker).

"I enjoy every minute in my own town, facilities for shopping excellent, everything necessary for a happy life within a stone's throw of my house" (Retired miner).

"Place that needs improved facilities for sport and entertainment" (Mountain Ash miner).

"It's all right. If you join in and have interests in the place where you live" (Penrhiwceibr miner).

"Pleasant, friendly" (Penrhiwceibr miner).

"Good, pleasant, junction of two valleys (referring to Abercynon), fairly open and not congested. Community good, although a little vandalism takes place" (Abercynon retired Co-operative Manager).

"Good. But people pay rates to the A.U.D.C. and the people of Aberdare have the benefit of the Aberdare Park. It's all the Aberdare Park, but nothing for the sub-districts" (C.W.S. Creamery, Trecynon, Aberdare, Laboratory Assistant).

"Fairly good, but there is a place for improvement" (Hirwaun inhabitant).

"Pleasant, small, friendly, accessibility to large towns" (a Godreaman schoolteacher).

It is obvious that the sense of belonging, and the characteristics of the South Wales valleys, friendliness especially, have a great deal of appeal to old and young in the Aberdare Valley.

In this first section, under the heading neighbourhood, it was found that 39 out of 72 worked in the same place as they lived, a 54.1% of the group, while 17 did not work in the same place, a 23.6%.

A percentage of those who worked at home were housewives and the other group miners. Only 2 did shiftwork, while 35 did not do shiftwork. The answers to the questions on the environment were also revealing. One was courageous enough to be different, and to criticise the surroundings; 52, an 80%, were quite content, with a few reservations, with the Aberdare Valley, and 9 out of 16 youths, a 56.25%, believed it was not very good, because there was no entertainment. Mention was made of the facilities to the capital city of Cardiff, the beauty of the mountains, and the Aberdare Park, which is a large, beautiful park on the outskirts of the town of Aberdare, on the road towards Hirwaun. Three paid compliment to the religious life, and another three to opera as one of the cultural features of which they were fond.

The features they did not like were two in the main. One was connected with the coal industry — the Phurnacite plant at Abercwmboi, and the menacing tips that can be seen from Hirwaun to Abercynon.

The front page of the *Aberdare Leader,* August 14, 1970, mentioned the experience of a number of Yorkshire miners at the Phurnacite plant. "No English miner would work there."

A by-product of this is naturally smoke and dust, which is disliked by another six. The other objections were to do with bingo — four objecting, only one complaining at the bad roads, one at the wandering sheep, which is a very common sight in the valleys of Monmouthshire and Glamorgan, three complaining at the infrequent bus service and three at the multi-storey flats which have been built at Hirwaun.

Questions on kinship showed that 57 persons had relatives living nearby, being made up of 32 parents, 15 siblings, 33 uncles or aunts, 38 cousins, 19 in-laws, 9 grandparents, 18 sons or daughters, 10 grandsons or grand-daughters, 3 brothers, and nephews and nieces. Nearly 79.15% — 57 out of 72 — had relatives living around them.

This makes interesting comparison with work done in Bethnal Green, a working class area in London, by Michael Young and Peter Wilmott. In 1956 they investigated family and relatives in Bethnal Green and interviewed 933 people, of whom 369 at least were married with at least one parent alive. Of the 369, exactly half of the men and 59% of the women had parents living in Bethnal Green while an additional 18% and 16% respectively had parents living in an adjacent borough, yielding a total of 68% and 75% respectively with parents living nearby. The same trend can be discerned in the Aberdare Valley, which, like Bethnal Green, is a predominantly working class area.

There were only ten who answered this question, a 13.9%, who did not have a relative nearby; and 2 (2.7%) declined to answer.

This can be compared with the study conducted in another working class community in 1966, called St. Ann's, and subsequently published by Nottingham University — the work of Ken Coates and Richard Silburn — which shows that there is a large number of people without close personal ties with other people in the district.

If you have friends nearby, where do you meet? The responses in St. Ann's, Nottingham, and the Aberdare Valley were as follows:

	St. Ann's Out of 176	%	Aberdare Valley Out of 72	%
At work	16	9	26	36.1
Neighbours	61	34.6	41	56.9
At pubs	21	11.9	3	4.1
Clubs	3	1.7	13	18
In Chapel	—	—	33	45.8
No. of people in all with friends nearby	96	54.5	65	90.2
No. of friends nearby	78	44.3	65	90.2
No answer	2	1.1	3	4.1

The comparisons on similar questions, except one, are revealing. Unfortunately, the chapel is not considered at all in the Nottingham study. The place of work is similar in both, as well as the neighbourhood element.

The inn or the pub seems, to those interviewed, to play less a part in the Aberdare Valley than in Nottingham, and the chapel to play a relatively important role in the Welsh industrial valley. There remains in St. Ann's a substantial number which is apparently without either relatives or friends in the district, while the number in the Aberdare Valley is only one.

We asked people in the Aberdare questionnaire how often they dropped in on their neighbours, and how often neighbours dropped in on them. 56 people (77.7%) said that they dropped in on their neighbours, and 57 people that the neighbours dropped in on them. This again can be compared with the St. Ann's study. 107 people said that they never called in on neighbours in Nottingham, while a smaller number said their neighbours never called in on them (86 or 48.8%). On the other hand, 43 people (24.5%) were in and out of their neighbours' houses once a week or more, while 57 people (32.3%) had their neighbours dropping in on them as frequently.

We also in the Aberdare Valley, as they did in St. Ann's, tried to assess the attitudes underlying this pattern of behaviour by asking two questions: Whether people thought it better to try to get on well with their neighbours or to keep themselves to themselves; and whether people thought that their fellow residents were "like them, or different". The results are set out in the following tables:

TABLE 1

Aberdare Valley Total 72	No.	%	St. Ann's Total 176	No.	%
Sociability:			Sociability:		
Try to get on well	63	87.5	Try to get on well	89	50.5
Keep to self	3	4.1	Keep to self	80	45.4
Don't know	1	1.3	Don't know	5	2.8
No answer	5	6.9	No answer	2	1.1
	72			176	

Table 2

Aberdare Valley	No.	%	St. Ann's	No.	%
Identification:			Identification:		
"People are like me"	39	54.1	"People are like me"	93	52.8
"People are different"	12	16.6	"People are different"	48	27.2
Don't know	13	18	Don't know	33	18.7
No answer	8	11.1	No answer	2	1.1
	72			176	

The difference between the two areas is revealing. In the Aberdare Valley it is a part of the way of life to try and get on well with neighbours and people living in the same neighbourhood. The answers given are extremely interesting, as many of the respondents look upon this habit in the terms of an insurance policy, in case need will arise at some particular time, as well as being the norm to follow in their particular community. Nearly 87.5% — 63 out of 72 — of the people interviewed believe this, while in St. Ann's only half of the people interviewed believe it. In St. Ann's only half of the people tried to get on well, and almost the same number kept to themselves, while in the Aberdare Valley only three of the people interviewed kept to themselves. The other table, that of identification, was more descriptive, amounting to recognition of a common social status. There were 93 out of 176 in St. Ann's and 39 out of 72 in the Aberdare Valley, a 54.1%. In the latter the feeling of belonging to the working class implied also an effort to integrate oneself into the life of the community, while in St. Ann's this was not so obvious.

In our questionnaire it was asked: If you were in trouble and need, who would help you? Living in the Aberdare Valley for six years one often heard it said that members who attended the working men's clubs and other social clubs would help someone in difficulty more than a chapel person, etc., and this was the reason why it was felt necessary to test this generalisation by including in the list the most well-known people (if not personally, but as a symbol) in a working class area, namely, the Co-operative manager and the Colliery manager. The Co-operative Movement is still, in the majority of the people's lives in the Aberdare Valley, an institution that they belong to as shoppers, or depend on it for special occasions (i.e., funerals). A discussion of the role of the Colliery managers appears in this book.

TABLE 3

Who would help you if you were in a jam?

	No.	%
Family/Relative	60	83.3
Chapel Member	24	33.3
Club Member	3	4.1
Colliery Manager	1	1.3
Co-operative Manager	2	2.7
Neighbour	36	50

It was expected that the number mentioning family and relatives would be large — 60 out of 72, 83.3% — but it was a surprise to find only 3, a 4.1%, feeling that a Club member would be a help in need, and only one, a 1.3%, the Colliery manager. Two institutions, the colliery and the Co-op. store, have meant a great deal to the working class in South Wales. But it does show that many of the popular generalisations are often misleading, though, on the other hand, many of the neighbours listed, which reached the number of 36, a 50%, could be Club members.

And if one looks at the degree of formal association and activity in the Aberdare Valley, it appears to be high. In reply to the question: "Are you a member of any organisation?" we got the following answers:

MEMBERSHIP OF ORGANISATIONS

	Aberdare		St. Ann's	
	Out of 72	%	Out of 176	%
Trade Union	26	36.1	42	23.8
Chapel	35	48.6		
Church	10	13.8	49	27.8
Political Party	12	16.7	7	3.9
Others	23	31.9	11	6.2
Total in organisations	106		109	
In no organisation	0		73	
No answer	0		12	

The Trade Union allegiance is significant in both Aberdare and St. Ann's, a 36.1% in Aberdare and a 23.8% in Nottingham. Many of these Trade Unionists would only belong to their Lodge and Union Branch, and would not necessarily belong to the Labour Party, which has been the political wing of the Trade Union and the Labour movement. It is probable that in Local and General Elections they would vote Labour. The growth of the "white-collared" unions is another factor which cannot be ignored. In the twenties it was not popular to belong to the Trade Union Movement, and, indeed, most of the Trade Unions lost members in that decade. Trade Unions were an expression of the anger and the impotence of working men in face of the gross exploitation practised upon them during the early industrial revolution. Alan Bullock puts it well in his study of Ernest Bevin :

" Trade Unionism has a long history in this country, and it is a history of struggle against a hostile environment right up to the Second World War. Born in a revolt, the Trade Unions grew up in opposition . . . Throughout the greater part of their history they had to meet not only the opposition of the employers — that they expected — but the settled suspicion and hostility of the State, the propertied classes and every established institution, from the courts and the police to the Church and Press " (Bullock, 1969, p. 20). In the 60s the Trade Unions have become respectable and, in some ways, very powerful. The economy is weaker, and it is possible for a series of industrial strikes to make a serious damage on the country's balance of payments.

It is not surprising to find a high proportion of Church and Chapel members among the replies, as the questionnaires were answered within the context of the Church and Chapel structure. Members included people from the main denominations, especially the Presbyterian Church of Wales, the Congregationalist Church, the Wesleyan Methodists and the Baptist denomination, while a small proportion belonged to the Pentecostal movement, such as Elim Four Square Church. The Aberdare Valley, like all the other valleys of South Wales, had its share of chapels and churches. Every village has its chapels, and some have more than one chapel of the same denomination.

No one can deny that this valley is adequately provided

with places of worship, and especially Nonconformist chapels, and its history of over a hundred years as a predominant mining valley makes it an ideal site for a study of the social and industrial reasons for the decline of Nonconformity.

The majority of the working people of the valley are engaged in either mining or one of the light industries situated at Ynysboeth and Rhigos. I will deal with this in detail in Chapter 4 on the development of industry, and the valley itself has grown in population through the sinking of the mines and the industrialisation of the area. Appendix 2 gives the population statistics for the Aberdare area.

We see that the sharp increase in population came between 1841 and 1851. The Census of Great Britain for the latter year remarks rather laconically, in relation to Aberdare, " the great increase of population is owing to the extension of the coal and iron trade." People flocked from West Wales to work in the new settlements, and many of the descendants of these people are still active in the Welsh life of the Aberdare Valley. They brought their religion and their language, and the victory of Nonconformity was the triumph of a new society — the establishment of order over chaos. Other immigrants came in the seventies and the eighties of the nineteenth century, from England and Ireland in particular, and this was the beginning of the bilingual problem, and the descendants of these people are often among the political and Trade Union leaders of the valley. The sharp fall in population occurs, as it can be seen in Appendix 1, after 1931. This was due to a large extent to the depression which led to a considerable migration to other parts of the country, and which also affected the vitality of community life throughout the Aberdare Valley.

The loss to the mining industry was not so severe as one often imagines in those years. In Appendix 8, we have the Department of Employment and Productivity figures for 1929, 1939, 1949, and we find that for the Mountain Ash area in 1929 there were 9,354 employed in mining and quarrying and 10,331 employed in the Aberdare area. The next important industry was the distributive trades with 499 in Mountain Ash and 1,161 in the Aberdare area. In 1939 there was a drop in the number of people employed in the mining industry. There were 6,769 in the Mountain Ash area, a loss of 2,595; while in the Aberdare area there were 7,854 employed, which meant a loss of 1,497 persons in the mining and quarrying industry. Construction had 1,004 employed, and the distributive trades 1,493, which showed a substantial increase in the Aberdare area, and the same is noticeable for the Mountain Ash area. In 1949 we find a slight increase in those employed in the mining industry for the Aberdare area with 9,300 employed in the industry. No figures were received for the Mountain Ash area, or for the following years, but it does show that the mining industry up to the nationalisation in 1949 was the major industry in the valley.

And it is my intention to look in detail at this mining valley in the nineteenth and twentieth centuries in relationship to the life and witness of Welsh Nonconformity.

3

THE INVESTIGATION IN THE LIGHT OF OTHER SURVEYS

THIS investigation is, to a large extent, a pioneer work, but this does not say that I have not depended heavily in some respects on other studies. Within the Welsh scene, the one that was most valuable was T. Brennan, E. W. Conney and H. Pollins's study of *Social Change in South-West Wales,* which was published in 1954. Brennan and his colleagues were concerned with the changes in the general pattern of " associational life ", that is, with changes in the extent of interest shown by the inhabitants of that area in trade unionism, religion, politics, social and recreational clubs, and organisations catering for hobbies. It showed how religion, and Nonconformity in particular, had been a major force in the life of the mining communities, and it was valuable also in emphasising that even in the 50s the chapels were much more important in the South-West Wales area than in many other industrial parts of the country. In the Aberdare Valley this was also the case, but to a lesser extent.

Brennan and his colleagues' study was not concerned only with documenting the extent of the decline in the church and chapel membership. One has the feeling sometimes in discussing Nonconformity with some professional sociologists that the only purpose of studies of this nature is to put together a large mass of statistics. This was not Brennan and his colleagues' attitude, nor is it mine. For the study on *Social Change in South-West Wales* set out to explain the decline in " terms of the nature of the churches' constitutions, the social composition of their leadership or the taking over of some of their functions by organised political groups, especially the Labour Party " (Brennan, el et, 1954, p. 138). What these sociologists show is that over time, leadership of religious organisations in South Wales has become shared between the middle and working classes, and that, in consequence, class conflicts of political issues, which otherwise might have disturbed religious unity, have been avoided in their organisations by the simple expedient of avoiding involvement in such issues.

Other sociologists have emphasised the same thing as Brennan and his colleagues. Bendix and Lipset have shown that control of the Church and its policies is generally in the hands of officials drawn from one class, usually the middle class.

It appears from the study of *Social Change in South-West Wales* that the South Wales chapels rejected the political issues at the expense of a loss of mass membership. The rank and file members of religious bodies have turned away from the Nonconformist chapels towards the purely secular Labour Party.

Thus, Brennan and his colleagues do not give an account for the decline in belief in the Christian apocalyptic, in Christian eschatology, in Christian dogma, and in religious ideology generally, although this may also have occurred. They explain it in terms of the failure of organised religion in this country to come to grips with the social realities of the lives of its membership. Participation in religious organisation, that is to say, is seen as one type only of participation in group life for the realisation of certain values, and the function of religion in this respect may, apparently, be performed equally well by a political party.

The value of Brennan's study is that the Aberdare Valley, like Swansea and the Swansea Valley (which is, to a large extent, what is meant by South-West Wales), are areas that have been loyal to the Labour Party since the end of the First World War. In the Aberdare Valley, a Labour Party Member of Parliament has been returned since Keir Hardie gained the seat at the beginning of the century (Aberdare was a part of the Merthyr constituency at that time), and the majority of 23,000 for Arthur Probert at the 1966 General Election was one of the highest in the country, though the majority was halved by the Plaid Cymru candidate in the 1970 General Election.

To a question asked to a cross-section of the Aberdare population: " Are you interested in the Labour Movement? " answers were received which revealed the allegiance to the Labour Party.

	Out of 72	%
Yes	33	45.8
No.	23	31.9
Don't know	4	5.5
No answer	12	16.6

And it should be noted that out of the 23 who said that they had no interest in the Labour Movement, 9 were young people; a few who had stated that they were members of *Plaid Cymru,* the Welsh Nationalist Party, and even of the non-violent language organisation, the Welsh Language Society *(Cymdeithas yr Iaith Gymraeg).*

The hold of the Labour Party is noted in the other political question asked : " What political party did you vote for in the last General Election? "

	No.	%
Labour Party	31	43
Communist Party	—	—
Plaid Cymru	11	15.2
Conservative	4	5.5
Liberal Party	2	2.7
No one (the under 21)	10	13.8
No answer	14	19.4

The Labour Party not only dominates the parliamentary scene in the Aberdare Valley, but also in the local elections, though in the last few years (1966-1972) there have been gains by other parties, like *Plaid Cymru,* and non-political organisations of the nature of the Ratepayers.

Plaid Cymru seems to inspire a number of those interviewed, a 15.2%, and has taken the place of the Liberal Party in the interests of the Nonconformists. This is one of the great changes in the political life of Wales in the twentieth century, the decline of the Liberal Party.

The " Lloyd George " appeal has largely disappeared, though the older generation look upon him with respect, as the one responsible for the introduction of many of the benefits of the Social Service. The Labour Party, even though this is being slightly undermined, still has its strength among the mining population. The miner and his family cannot forget the battle of the inter-war years. Every one of the members of the National Union of Mine-workers Lodge at Penrhiwceibr Colliery interviewed were Labour

THE INVESTIGATION IN THE LIGHT OF OTHER SURVEYS 53

Party members and many of the Left Wing, while the majority of the *Plaid Cymru* members were Chapel or Church members.

There are two reasons to account for this. Brennan and his colleagues have mentioned the first reason — that many of those who play a prominent part in the Labour Party have transferred their allegiance from the chapels to the political party which represents their interests.

The second reason is that in an anglicised area like the Aberdare Valley, the chapels which hold services in the Welsh language naturally attract or retain the loyalty of those who are Welsh enthusiasts, and often in a Labour stronghold these people would vote *Plaid Cymru*. The same process that has happened in the relationship between the Labour Party and the Chapel can also happen again in the relationship of the Welsh chapel to *Plaid Cymru*. This danger and fear has been expressed by many of the ministers, but this is not so explosive a danger, as the vast majority of the Welsh ministers of religion in the Aberdare Valley would support *Plaid Cymru* in a General Election.

The fact that no one voted for the Communist Party in my investigation is not typical of the Aberdare Valley. They have a comparatively good following. There is one long-standing Communist member on the Mountain Ash Urban District Council, and a Communist candidate was elected in 1972 for Abercynon. This was the first defeat for the Labour Party in 53 years in Abercynon, though the victorious Communist candidate had polled well in the 1966, 1967, 1968, 1969, 1970 and 1971 elections. She was an attractive candidate and well-known in the locality for her left-wing views. In the Blaengwawr Ward of Aberaman a Communist topped the poll for years in the local and the Glamorgan County Council elections. After his death the seat was captured by *Plaid Cymru*. The Conservatives do badly at all levels in the valley — though there is always a Conservative candidate at the General Elections.

There is no doubt that Brennan and his colleagues have made us think of an important factor for the decline of Welsh Nonconformity in their contention that the Labour Party has won the interests and participation of a large number of people whose background is that of the Nonconformist chapels. The people we interviewed knew their councillors very well. Out of 72 asked, 45 (62.5%) knew who their councillors were, and 26 (36.1%) had been in contact with them, while only 16 (22.2%) had never been in touch or had no idea who was their local representative. Eleven did not answer the question, and there is no doubt that apathy has made the constituents much more apathetic today than in the past.

Another study which has been of value is that of E. R. Wickham, *Church and People in an Industrial City,* published in 1957. This study has an immense significance, for it gives a pattern of comparison, in an historical and sociological manner. It makes the Church look at itself in its missionary task, and there are a number of basic conclusions that emerged in Wickham's research. Wickham listed them in this way:

From the emergence of the industrial towns in the eighteenth century, the working class, the labouring poor, the common people, as a class, substantially, as adults, have been outside the churches. The industrial working class culture pattern has evolved lacking a tradition of the practice of religion. This will not be borne out in my research, for as it will be shown the working class, the common people of the Aberdare Valley, were influenced by the chapels up to the Second World War. The latest book to appear to prove this is Will Paynter's *My Generation,* published in April 1972. Gwyn Thomas, in a review of the book, makes a point of emphasising Paynter's belief in the hold of the chapel over the miners of the Rhondda and Aberdare Valleys in the 20s.

" I was surprised to find from this book *(My Generation)* how close the links were between Will and the Chapels . . . But he tells a story of something that happened in his late teens when he had been involved in some hostile action against blacklegs. A preacher, wishful to heal any rift in the madly fissile society he served, and keen to root out any sign of godless defiance on the part of the plebs, rushed into Will's kitchen as the boy was preparing to get the pit dirt off his body. The preacher, goaded on by Will's mother, made hysterical by this distress, burst into tears and threw himself down on his knees and demanded that Will, after nine hours underground, should join him on the floor and beg forgiveness from God and the coal-owner who, between them, had provided his chapel.

Will picked him up and put him out of the house. He confesses that the incident still appals him because the hold of the Chapel on the collective imagination of the valleys was immense. Within the chapel society there was light and comfort and acceptability. Outside there was the dark and danger. People who opted for disbelief and stepped out of the tribe still feel a draught of loss" (Thomas, 1972, p. 712).

Gwyn Thomas's review has been looked upon in detail as it shows from the life of Will Paynter that in the twentieth century the chapels were still an important part of the industrial working class culture pattern of South Wales. Gwyn Thomas has himself opted out of the chapel culture, and is in some ways expressing his own feeling and Paynter's in the sentence: " People who opted for disbelief and stepped out of the tribe still feel a draught of loss."

Wickham's second point is that the increasing collapse of the churches from the beginning of the present century has been through the losses of the middle classes of society, the industrial and professional middle classes, the lower middle classes, the inhabitants of suburbia, tradesmen, black-coated workers, superior working people. And this is borne out by Brennan as well as Bendix and Lipset studies.

Wickham's third point is that there is an obvious sociological conditioning of both participation and non-participation in the life of the churches, of both " faith " and " unbelief ", that calls for theological appraisal. A consequence is that the missionary endeavour (in the widest sense to include both making men Christian and " Christianising " society) requires an impact on society, in its structural and functional aspect.

Wickham feels that the inadequate impact of the Church as a whole on the gradually emerging new society, and the ultimate erosion of the Churches, are intimately connected with a theological deficiency that narrowed the concern of the Church to " religion " and precluded the exercise of a prophetic role. His last conclusion is that the inherited shape and structure of the local church are not adequate to the proper discharge of a missionary task in a highly urbanised and industrialised society.

All these conclusions will be borne out in this research on the decline of the Free Churches in the Aberdare Valley, and the need for the Churches to come to grips with their role in urban society.

We depended to a large extent on the work done in the Midlands by two outsiders. There is the work of R. H. Thompson, a New Zealander, called *The Church's Understanding of Itself,* produced in 1957. The aim of the investigation was to try and make some contribution to a more adequate understanding of the " deeper underlying general causes which bring about the unresponsiveness of the contemporary mind to the Christian message " (Thompson, 1957, p. 14). Four parishes were selected for study, and the term ' congregation' was given to the limited group of committed churchgoers, while the term ' parish ' or ' parishioners ' referred to the geographical area of all those living within the bounds of the parish regardless of their religious affiliation.

R. H. Thompson used the interviewing procedure, and interviews were completed in 352 cases. The usual pattern of the interview consisted of an explanation of the project, the specific questions, and general discussion. The answers were recorded immediately, and Thompson devised a questionnaire. Questions 1, 10, 13, 15 and 16 were taken from a questionnaire drawn up by G. W. Allport, J. M. Gillespie and J. Young, and the rest of the questions (19 altogether) were devised by Thompson. I did not use his questionnaire (Thompson, 1957, pp. 99-105), but rather devised a new questionnaire, though I did adapt to my use some ideas and questions formulated by Ken Coates and Richard Silburn in their study on St. Ann's in Nottingham.

The second study carried out in the Midlands was done by Dr. K. A. Busia, who later became the Prime Minister of Ghana. The work was called *Urban Church in Britain,* and published in 1966. The study was of value as it was primarily in the sphere of religion, attention paid to the attitudes and opinions, patterns of behaviour, and, in particular, Chapter 6, The Church and the Young. I compared the Sunday School in the Aberdare Valley with the Sunday School in the urban environment of Brooktown (a fictitious name) in Birmingham. Busia's study has been another model used, and especially I have followed the use he made of interviews, sermons and observations to substantiate the ideas put forward for discussion and agreement. It is a most important study.

Those four researches were of particular importance from a religious standpoint, while from the mining angle I used the work of Dennis *et al.* on Ashton, a mining area in Yorkshire, and on the structure of the mining industry I borrowed from Trist *et al., Organizational Choice.*

The West Riding of Yorkshire, like the Aberdare Valley, is an area where " from the inception of the industrial revolution to the present time industry has been the keynote of life for the majority of its inhabitants." It was in the 1950s that two anthropologists and a sociologist were looking at a mining town in the West Riding which they called Ashton.

Ashton could well be compared to Abercynon in the Aberdare Valley, and this was in my mind in the use I made of the material provided by Dennis, Henriques and Slaughter in *Coal is Our Life,* published in 1957. Ashton, like Abercynon, grew as the coal industry expanded. The first colliery, Manton in Ashton, opened in 1868; Abercynon in 1889. The size of the towns and the character of the housing reflected the emergency of the collieries.

Coal is Our Life provided a mass of valuable material, and especially with regard to the work and leisure of the mining community, and with material that could be used to compare two mining areas. Not all Ashton miners, for example, work in Ashton; indeed, nearly 1,500 Ashton miners travel each day to work outside the town where they live. This journey to work is characteristic of mining areas. There are miners from the Aberdare area travelling every day to the Neath, Merthyr and Rhondda collieries. But they work side by side with others who, while not from the mining village from which they come, are, nevertheless, from villages and towns where housing conditions, life chances and styles of life are essentially similar. But though there is unity of experience and background, there are also factors which divide the miners through highly developed local customs. The colliers' skill, seniority and even knowledge of technical terms are often not transferable from pit to pit, let alone village to village, district to district, or coalfield to coalfield. This may be a factor binding miners to their home towns and their home collieries.

While all miners share a largely common history of strike, lock-out and unemployment, each pit or village has its own special variant of the general pattern. It matters a great deal with whom one shares an experience. That is why I immersed myself in Trist,

Higgin, Murray and Pollock's study, *Organizational Choice,* first published in 1963, and have noticed how the structure of the small team in the mining complex and the structural pattern of a Nonconformist Chapel were complementary before the mechanisation of conventional longwalls.

The Aberdare Valley figures largely in the history of longwall development in South Wales, since it was at Deep Duffryn Colliery, Mountain Ash, that the system was first introduced into the coalfield. The man who was responsible was John Nixon and, according to Charles Wilkins in *The South Wales Coal Trade,* published in 1888, the time was around 1858. This date is deduced from Wilkins's reference to the system " after thirty years experience of its work " (Wilkins, 1888, p. 98). The longwall introduced by John Nixon was simply the longwall version of pillar and stall, and it is referred to as the single-place working.

It was the simplest form of traditional mining, each work-place comprising a small separate coal face and was occupied by a team of three to four men. The coal was won by hand picks and removed from the face in tubs. Various patterns of laying out the faces for working a seam were to be found. These methods — bord and pillar, rib and stall, gateway and stepwise longwall — are similar except for layout, and can, so far as work organisation is concerned, be treated as one type, and referred to as single-place working (Trist *et al.,* 1963, p. 12).

The panel longwall system did not come about until first the coal cutter and then the conveyor came into general use. With the exhaustion of the thicker seams in the Aberdare Valley experiments were carried out with mechanical coal-cutters with a view to enabling the thinner seams to be profitably worked. In 1906, therefore, we read in the publication commemorating their fiftieth birthday, *The Powell Duffryn Steam Coal Co. Ltd., 1864-1914,* that coal-cutters were introduced by Powell Duffryn into their collieries in the Aberdare Valley.

Conveyors, we can be sure, were not long in following, and it was their advent which made the biggest impact on the efficient and economic working of collieries, since they enabled the cutting out of a number of stall roads to the coal face, so that lengths of 100-150 yards of face could be worked between two roads. In

South Wales, in 1910, there were 50 conveyors (and 107 coal-cutters) in use, and a number of them were in use in the Aberdare Valley. In 1918 there were 214 conveyors at coal faces in South Wales and 156 coal-cutters in use, and in 1924 there were 671 conveyors at coal faces and 409 coal-cutters in use in the South Wales coalfield.

It was the early 20s that saw in the Aberdare Valley and South Wales a period of intensive development of the use of face conveyors, in particular in South Wales. This period also was very troubled, particularly in labour relations. There were extensive strikes in 1920 and 1921, and the coalfield was on stop for as long as six months in the great strike of 1926. These strikes were the consequence of the stresses which had affected the coal export trade and were, at the same time, the cause of further stresses. The Versailles Treaty which brought the war to an end was, in itself, a body-blow to the Welsh trade by providing for reparations in coal supplies from Germany to Italy and France, the most valued customers for South Wales coals. The growth of economic nationalism meant the erection of artificial barriers to the free trade under which the coal trade had flourished. Moreover, the Admiralty decided to abandon coal for the Royal Navy and turned to oil, and this example was followed by the Merchant Navy. The return to the Gold Standard in 1924 had its repercussions in making the coal of the Aberdare Valley costly for sale abroad.

Collieries began to close in the Aberdare Valley. Cwmpennar Middle Pit closed in 1920, and Bwlch, while Duffryn Merthyr had closed in 1916. In 1923 Abercwmboi closed, and in 1925 Wimber, where a coal-cutter had been introduced in 1916, the first in the mechanisation of mining in the Aberdare Valley. Lletyshenkin Upper and Cefnpennar were closed in 1927, and in 1930 three Valley collieries closed, namely, Blaengwawr Level, Llwynhelig and George Pit. A state of crisis was reached the following year with the Wall Street crash which had world-wide repercussions and which hit the coal trade so severely as to reduce South Wales to what became known as a depressed area with mass unemployment and depopulation. Another difficulty that beset the coal trade was the undercutting of prices by State-subsidised competition from Poland and Germany in the efforts by those countries to build up foreign credits. Fforchwen Colliery closed in 1934, and in 1935 Bwllfa No. 3 and Abernant No. 4, and Coronation and Gorllwyn in 1938. The position grew more stable, to be disrupted again by the war in September 1939, and in June 1940 came the European military collapse when Germany over-ran most of Europe, and Italy entered into war against Britain.

The coal export trade from South Wales virtually collapsed overnight. Collier vessels which were unloading in French ports had to settle their cargoes and make for home. Thousands of miners were drafted from the mines to the Forces and the war factories. Many collieries closed, and among them, in 1941, the Navigation.

The coal industry was in dire trouble during the war years. There were not the men nor the machines to do the job of production effectively. The long-standing depression in the coal trade meant that little investment of capital had been made in mechanisation and development work in the mines. Manpower was down in South Wales to 100,000 as compared with the peak of 270,000 in 1923.

As the war was nearing its close the National Government appointed a committee of seven mining engineers to make a report on the condition of the coal mining industry in Britain. Their report — known popularly as the Reid Report — will be dealt with in detail in Chapter 4, and said that nothing less than the complete reorganisation and development of the industry on a national basis was needed to save the industry. When the Labour Government came into power, one of its first acts was to effect the nationalisation of the industry under a National Coal Board. That Board was appointed in 1946 to operate as from 1st January 1947 and was vested with the responsibility for reconstituting an industry which, in South Wales particularly, had suffered grievous set-backs for more than thirty years.

From 1947 to 1957 the over-riding edict of the National Coal Board from the Government was to produce all the coal that could possibly be produced. But this did not stop the closing of three more collieries in the Aberdare Valley: Cwmneol Colliery in 1948, Cwmcynon in 1949, and Merfa Colliery in 1952. Measures were taken in this period which were to revolutionise mining methods.

In 1950 there was only one power-loader in the coalfield for cutting the seams and loading the coal into conveyors mechanically. Mining engineers were afraid that the seams of South Wales were so disturbed and faulted that it would be impossible to install machines. In 1967 there were 196 mechanised faces producing three-fourths of the saleable output of the coalfield.

Between 1957 and 1967 there was a transformation in the appearance of most mines. Five more valley collieries closed. In 1959 Tirherbert and in 1963 Aberaman, while Forchamman Colliery closed in 1964 and Abergorki in 1965, and in 1966 Albion, Cilfynydd, was closed.

But the collieries that were left were highly mechanised, like the Abercynon Colliery, which had been sunk in 1889, and Deep Duffryn, Mountain Ash, which was only sunk in 1950. £200,000 was spent at the Deep Duffryn in reorganisation, improving coal handling arrangements. Six hundred men produce 240,000 tons from five feet/Gellideg. Ninety-seven per cent of the output is power-loaded.

Lady Windsor, Ynysybwl, sunk in 1885, has 900 men producing 300,000 tons, while the surface and underground reorganisation has cost nearly £5 million.

Penrikyber Colliery in Penrhiwceibr is one of the oldest in the valley, sunk in 1872, and has 880 men producing about 300,000 tons from *Seven Feet* and *Five Feet*/Gellideg. Virtually 100 per cent of the output is power-loaded, and £1 million has been spent modernising and reorganising the main pit bottom.

The miner in the Aberdare Valley, like in Ashton, is required to present himself, summer and winter, spring and autumn, on at least five days a week at the pit, like the ones I have mentioned above, and to put his ability to work. Today the employer is a public Corporation, the National Coal Board, and it is unlikely that he will come across the people that are in charge of the corporation. The product of the miner's labours is coal. Once he has produced it, the miner has no further control over its ultimate disposal.

He is tied to the wage packet, and to the fundamental insecurity that goes with it. Wages are calculated by the shift and paid weekly. Accident or sickness can disrupt the process, and cyclical unemployment arising out of a " general decline in demand for goods on an international scale " (Dennis *et al.*, 1957, p. 19) was experienced in Ashton as in the Aberdare Valley from 1929 to 1933.

The chance of real social mobility for the Ashton miner is very small, as it is for most wage-earners in Britain. Lack of training, leisure, and income cut them off, now and forever, from " the ideals of behaviour, the good things of life, in short, the cultural ends of the society in which they live " (Dennis *et al.*, 1957, p. 31).

Dennis *et al.* put forward the following characteristics which were derived from the domination of the coal-mining industry on the society looked at :

(1) Class relationships seem to be intensified in mining areas. The actual job sets miners apart from other manual workers.

(2) Miners tend to live in relatively isolated villages inhabited mainly by other miners, and not in towns with mixed industries. It is this which gives the solidarity to the miners which is lacking often in factories, and often the bargaining between the miner and the deputy is carried out on the coal face.

Mining tends to bring all the members of the family into its web. There is no escape for the wife if the miner is injured or loses a day's work, and the family is expected to be hostile to the family of the employer, which is continually kept alive. Even the male children end up in the colliery, as there is little else that they can do in a society which has been geared to the industry. For years the miner was also one of the best-paid workers in the community. It was also imperative on one to be a miner to enter fully into the social life of the community — in the frivolous form and in the sober fashion of the Labour Party. Brennan and his colleagues found the same thing in South Wales, where the protestant ethic was stronger than in the West Riding of Yorkshire.

The home is the only place that unites the family, and the wife is expected to give of her best in looking after it. It does not stop her from visiting other friends and neighbours for " gossip ", or going to a meeting of her own friends and acquaintances, but it was not looked upon favourably for her to visit the public house or the betting shop. Like the colliery, this was a man's domain, where he could boast and swear to his heart's content and discuss the intimacy of sexual relationship without referring to his own wife by name. It was a man's world — a bitter, tough, hard-hitting world of rugby league or rugby football, of greyhound racing, boxing, wrestling, and extracting coal from the bowels of the earth.

The wife is to look after the home — to be a treasurer of the finances and a comforter of the sick and the reconciler of the feudal tensions. There are, in the opinion of the authors, in most Ashton families few activities which " demand co-operation or encourage the growth of companionship between husband and wife " (Dennis et al., 1957, p. 183). During the greater part of the life-cycle the woman's place is in the home and with her kin. She sees her man at table and in bed. The rest of the time he is at work or in the club. She is excluded from the world of ideas because she is excluded from the actions of Ashton men.

" . . . the club, the pub, the bookie's office, the trade union, all the places where men go to talk together are closed to women . . . " with one significant exception in Ashton — the Labour Party, and also, as in the Aberdare Valley, the Chapels and the Churches.

The authors, unfortunately for our purpose, devote a little over a page to the Churches of Ashton, which have, they say, declined in importance since the 1920s. This is a serious defect for our purpose. In 1953 there were two Anglican Churches, one Anglican Mission, eight Nonconformist Churches and one Roman Catholic Church. The largest Methodist Church had eighty members, mostly women. Average Sunday morning attendance is said to be eight women, four men, and twelve children.

Sunday evening has a somewhat larger adult attendance, with twenty-two women and ten men. One of the Anglican churches and its mission recorded one hundred communicants each Sunday, but the authors say the tradespeople were over-represented for their numbers in the town.

I have tried to follow in the study Dennis, Henriques and Slaughter in showing the intimate inter-relation between the miner's work, his family and his leisure, and have gathered that there is an additional dimension to what can look at first sight to be the sociologically meaningless activities of drinking and betting. Whom the miners drink with, and whom they do not, " gives us a means of understanding the differentiation of social groups and categories which interact in the daily life of a segment of industrial Britain" (Frankenberg, 1966, p. 139).

A later study than *Coal is Our Life* is *Working Class Community*, published in 1968, and written by Brian Jackson, with field notes by Dennis Marsden. Dennis *et al.* were concerned with Featherstone, and Jackson draws all his evidence from Huddersfield in the West Riding of Yorkshire. "In its valley, Huddersfield now presents a star-shaped cluster of grimy Methodist chapels, warehouses, factories. You remember it partly because of the slender black chimneys of mill-owners competing in height as they competed in trade" (Jackson, 1972, p. 21).

This sociological study of a *Working Class Community* is important for our purpose in its sympathetic approach to the clubs, a much more sympathetic approach than the one given in *Coal is Our Life*. And clubs have taken over from the chapels the function of being social centres in the Aberdare Valley. Jackson shows how the clubs arose, not as competitors to Nonconformity, but as part and parcel of it. The Working Men's Clubs, which play such a prominent part in any working class area, and especially in the Aberdare Valley, were in the beginning a religious organisation. The organising spirit was Henry Solly, a Unitarian minister, and a famous spokesman for the temperance movement. It was an attack on the "intemperance, ignorance, improvidence and religious indifference of the working class, and aimed quite sharply to take working men out of the pub and into a club free of intoxicating drinks. The clubs were an answer to the cry, What are we to do with our reformed drunkards? But in time this was completely changed, as the first working-class president declared: "Each Club should be altogether free from all vexatious, infantile restrictions on the consumption of intoxicating drinks and all similar matters" (Jackson, 1972, p. 41).

But the clubs have taken over the respectability of Nonconformity. It has been a strange take-over, as if the concepts of the contemporary American sociologist Robert Merton have been mixed up, the concepts of *manifest* and *latent* functions. The former are the conscious, deliberate functions of social processes, the latter the unconscious and unintended ones. Thus the *manifest* function of Nonconformity was social activity and witness, the *latent* function was to attach status indices to such associations. The purpose of the chapels was to convert men and women into activists, the result was often to produce bigoted, respectable individuals. Nonconformist chapels in working class areas became centres of respectability, but Brian Jackson shows how that respectability has become part of the Working Men's Clubs image.

To join, a new member must be proposed and seconded by two members of the club. His name is then put up on the board in the club for two weeks so that any club member who objects can raise his objections at the next club committee meeting:

" They'll say, ' Oh, he's a trouble maker, we're not having him ' " (Jackson, 1972, p. 44).

Inside the club, as in a chapel, one must have a very substantial community of interest and attitude with the members. Once inside, the whole tendency is towards conservation of the more stable elements in local society.

They imposed Nonconformist patterns of behaviour on their members, and people are barred from the clubs if they are ' rowdy ' and ' awkward '. " As long as Ah don't put me feet on t'seat, Ah'm all right " (Jackson, 1972, p. 46); and again:

" They have their rules, and if someone behaves badly he is expelled " (Jackson, 1972, p. 57).

A middle class temperance crusade was transformed into a system of working class drinking clubs, which have become as much a part of the scene in the Aberdare Valley as have the Nonconformist chapels.

Jackson's study and that of *Coal is Our Life* are two of the most impressive sociological analyses of the working class. They both based their inquiries on Yorkshire, and they both give us interesting material for comparison and insight into our subject.

The seven books have been discussed in detail, as they were the most valuable and relevant for the study, and with the addition of other historical documents, newspapers, interviews and questionnaires, supplied me with the necessary background for the study on the social and industrial reasons for the decline of Welsh Nonconformity in the mining valley of Aberdare.

4

CHAPELS IN THE VALLEY

In the nineteenth century the Aberdare Valley became a mining valley and Nonconformist in religion. It was a transformation in every way, from an agricultural community into a mining community, and a valley which had a few Anglican churches into a settlement which had chapels of the Nonconformist denominations in every village and town.

When Howel Harris, one of the outstanding men of the eighteenth century Methodist revival, visited the village of Aberdare in 1759, there were only two places of worship in the locality — the Parish Church and the Unitarian Church of Hen-Dŷ-Cwrdd, Trecynon, which had been established eight years earlier.

It was not until the 1790s that development first began in Aberdare of the Nonconformist churches which were later to dominate the life of the community for over a hundred years. It is possible to reconstruct the rise of Nonconformity historically and sociologically in the early stages, and this is what I propose to do in this chapter.

In the year 1798, besides Hen-Dŷ-Cwrdd Unitarian Chapel, there were no Nonconformist causes in the valley. It came through visiting preachers, or religious revivalists. They preached in the open air. A Baptist minister from Ystradyfodwg in the Rhondda Valley ministered to the few people, four in number, who had been baptized at Aberdare in 1791 (Parry, 1964, p. 27). A shop-keeper from Aberdare persuaded the Monthly Meeting of the Calvinistic Methodists to send three preachers to Aberdare in 1799, and they held an open-air meeting (Hughes, 1856, p. 87).

Nonconformity, however, as a "structure" would not have survived on the itinerant preachers or the open-air meetings. The organisation had to have a more or less permanent social group.

A temporary social group, like a crowd, needs no ideological basis, but if a group is to endure, it must have certain common values and goals which bind the members together.

This is what happened. The home became the centre of the Nonconformist group. It can be argued that the idea of a home has permeated other organisations. The sociologist Brian Jackson was told by a club member in Huddersfield:

"Ah couldn't rest me legs across a chair in t'pub. Here it's like being at home" (Jackson, 1972, p. 46).

We can borrow examples of the way that Welsh Nonconformity grew from the hearth from other areas besides the Aberdare Valley. Trefor Owen, in his sociological study of Glanllyn and Llanuwchllyn in Merioneth, has described how Nonconformity adopted the important institution of the *noson weu* (knitting night).

It is an example of the work pattern of a small domesticated industry being conducive to the Nonconformist character. The industry was overwhelmingly domestic in character and mainly supplementary to agriculture; it was fitted into the framework of life on the farm. Work was combined with leisure, and the members of the household of all ages and of both sexes would spend the evenings, especially during the slack winter months, knitting busily in the farm kitchen; one could talk as one knitted, and one could also take a stocking to knit in a neighbour's home (Owen, 1960, p. 207).

The religious revivalists of the eighteenth century realised the potentialities for their purposes of this informal and homely type of meeting. The fullest possible use was made of the *noson weu* in converting the countryside, and the meetings often acquired a religious flavour.

The meetings were informal. Sometimes the party consisted of the family and servants, together with a chance visitor; on other occasions, invitations to attend had been given. One who attended has given us this insight:

"Topics such as these were discussed there: original sin, the influence of the Holy Ghost, regeneration, justification, the sacrifice of Christ, His mediation, His godhead and His manhood, the nature and organisation of the Christian Church, and the obligations of men towards God and towards each other. There was a free and independent spirit among them" (Owen, 1960, p. 210).

Ap Fychan adds this:

". . . The knitting meetings were often closed by a reading and a prayer by one of the brethren — this served as the family devotions of that household for that occasion" (Owen, 1960, p. 210).

Nonconformity in the Aberdare Valley had similar meetings, though not based on the *noson weu*. But they were based on a home, a hearth, and in a family. This is the evidence for the year 1799 :

" In the same year, a man called Evan Sion from Glynneath, came to work at Aberdare, and he lodged in Tŷ'r Hewl. About the same time, at least within the year, a Lewis Lawrence, a carpenter, a native of Llandovery and a Congregationalist, also moved to the locality. These friends used to hold prayer meetings, for a period, in the house of William Jenkins, the Shop . . . " (Hughes, 1856, p. 88).

The *cegin*, or living-room, in Llanuwchllyn and Aberdare, became the meeting-house and the fireside settle a pew. The practice of religious devotions was brought within the orbit of family life on the hearth; children learned to read the Bible and later to pray in the daily devotions of the household (*cadw dyletswydd*).

The *cegin* would not last long in an industrial valley as the centre for worship. It moved out, at Trecynon, to a *llaethdy* (the place where they kept the milk), and afterwards to a room (Hughes, 1856, pp. 88-89). But there were possibilities of tension and friction in these " house meetings ", and it was a misunderstanding between a few of the early pioneers that meant the building of a Congregationalist chapel and a Calvinistic Methodist chapel.

The nucleus for a very long time was the home, the *hearth*. The Sunday School, which often became the nucleus of a chapel, was always held at the beginning in houses (Hughes, 1856, p. 90). And all the Welsh Nonconformist denominations began in the same way.

Between 1810 and 1813 the Welsh Independents, or Congregationalists, had three meeting houses licensed, namely, the New

Chapel in 1810, Ebenezer in 1811, and "a building situated near Hirwaun common" in 1813 (Morgannwg, 1874, pp. 191-201). Industrial depression around 1818 badly affected the plans intended for Hirwaun. But with the return of relative prosperity and increase in population in the early 1820s, the number of Dissenting meeting houses grew apace. In Hirwaun, four Nonconformist chapels were established between 1823 and 1826 (Morgannwg, 1874, pp. 191-201). By 1840 there were fourteen meeting places, all but one established in the iron period, and representing a fairly even distribution of strength between the four Dissenting bodies.

According to Walter Savage Landor, " Every sect is a moral check on its neighbour. Competition is as wholesome in religion as in commerce." This certainly seemed to be borne out by the number of denominations successfully represented in the Aberdare Valley by the end of the nineteenth century. Comparing the number of chapels built by 1837, which was virtually the end of the iron-works and the beginning of the coal-mining era, with the number which were set up by 1897 (sixty years afterwards), when the coal industry was firmly established, is an indication of how the scaling of mines meant also the building of Nonconformist chapels. In 1837 the Baptist denomination had three chapels, but in 1897 there were twenty, seventeen of them being Welsh. The Unitarians had only one chapel in 1837, Hen-Dŷ-Cwrdd, but fifty years later an English church had been built in Aberdare and a Welsh church at Cwmbach. The Wesleyan Methodists had only one cause set up at Hirwaun in 1837, but by 1897 they had fourteen causes, six of them being English. Congregationalists showed the biggest increase in building: from two in 1837 to twenty-five (four of them being English causes) sixty years later; while the Calvinistic Methodists had two in 1837, there were sixteen churches of that denomination in the Aberdare Valley in 1897. Every other branch of the Christian Church seemed to be making headway in the new mining society. The Established Church, which had failed to adapt itself to the new society until the episcopate of Bishop Olivant of Llandaff (1850-83), had only two churches for the whole valley in 1837, but had twenty by 1897. The same trend can be detected in the growth of the unusual sects, some of which are not regarded as traditional members of Nonconformity, as, for example, the Christadelphians, who had no cause in 1837, but by 1897 had a hall in Aberdare. In 1837 there were no members of the Church of Jesus Christ of Latter Day Saints.

Mormon missionaries began to arrive in Wales from the United States in the early 1840s. In a remarkably short period of time they had succeeded in gaining many converts and two meeting places were established in Aberdare, one in 1848 and the other two years later. Presbyterians were unknown in the valley in the iron period, but by 1897 they occupied a church called St. David's under the ministry of the Rev. J. Robertson, M.A.

Primitive Methodists, a branch of the Methodist movement which was not Welsh in origin or outlook, had seven churches in 1897, whereas fifty years before they had no church in the valley. The Salvation Army, under General Booth, did not come into existence until 1865, but was represented by three halls in 1897. Jews also wandered into the valley and met regularly for worship every Saturday in Dean Street, Aberdare. There were no places of worship for the Roman Catholics in 1835, but three churches had grown up by 1897.

Looking in more detail at this, the pattern can be visualised: of immigrants coming to work in the iron and, later, the coal industry and meeting at houses, or rooms, this in time becoming a church or a chapel. The way in which new chapels were established during the nineteenth century was often by separation, by agreement or disagreement, of a body of members from an existing chapel.

The Congregationalists established a chapel at Hirwaun and Trecynon, which later spread further afield to nearby Penderyn, Penywaun, Cwmdare, Llwydcoed, Gadlys, Aberdare, Abernant, Aberaman, Cwmbach, and Cwmaman, until they had causes in the lower reaches of the valley at Mountain Ash and Abercynon. The Calvinistic Methodists started at Trecynon, and, in the same way as the Congregationalists, went further afield, to Llwydcoed, Aberdare, Cwmdare, Hirwaun, and then down the valley towards Abercynon.

The Wesleyan Methodists had a Welsh and an English cause in Hirwaun, but in the coal-mining period spread out to Rhigos, besides establishing themselves in Trecynon, Aberaman, Mountain Ash, Penrhiwceibr, Ynysboeth and Hirwaun.

Baptists had churches at Penderyn, Hirwaun and Aberdare in the iron era. But with the arrival of a flood of immigrants to the coal industry their influence extended and chapels were built at Cwmdare, Llwydcoed, Gadlys, Abernant, Aberdare, Ynyslwyd, Aberaman, Cwmaman, Cwmbach, Abercwmboi, Mountain Ash (English and Welsh) and Penywaun (English and Welsh). The Calvinistic Methodists were represented at Hirwaun and Trecynon in the iron-works era, but in 1897 had spread to Aberdare, Llwydcoed, Cwmbach, Cwmdare, Cwmaman, Mountain Ash and Abercynon. The same pattern can be discerned in the Anglican Church. At first they had only two parishes — Penderyn and St. John the Baptist Church, Aberdare — but by 1897 other churches had been formed for the new industrial mining society at Hirwaun, Trecynon (two), Cwmdare, Llwydcoed and Aberdare (three), Cwmbach, Aberaman, Cwmaman, Mountain Ash and Miskin, and three mission rooms at Cwmpennar, New Town and Capcoch, the modern Abercwmboi. The Anglican Church had not so many meeting places as the Nonconformists, and that is why I stated at the beginning of this chapter that the Aberdare Valley was transformed into a Nonconformist stronghold.

Nonconformity in the Aberdare Valley had become a force to be reckoned with, and at the beginning of the twentieth century this was given a new impetus by the religious revival of 1904-5, when the ranks of the Nonconformists were swelled by the enthusiasm and the conversions witnessed among the " gwerin ". However, Nonconformity never again was in a position of being possessed by the passion for building new chapels, and the twentieth century only witnessed the setting of few new causes. It is not without significance that some of the ones built at the beginning of the century, like Hebron Welsh Calvinistic chapel, Godreaman, closed in 1962, and the same fate happened to other chapels built in the same period, as, for example, Noddfa, Mountain Ash, Miskin, Ynysboeth, and some of the other chapels which were built in that era (the Welsh Congregational chapels at Godreaman and Hirwaun) are in a weak position numerically. Sociologically, all this is interesting, for it points to a change in the interests and work of Nonconformity, and it is not insignificant that the Nonconformist denominations have never been able to foster strong churches in the new estates of Perthcelyn and Penywaun which have sprung up since the 1939-45 war.

Trefor Owen asks us to consider the possibility that the actual building and rebuilding of branch chapels, in which the fervour of the nineteenth century found a material outlet, may well have a detrimental influence in that it took the religious activities further and further from the hearth, where it was at the very centre of the everyday life of the individual and the family, to the chapel where it ultimately declined to a peripheral weekly experience. Indeed, it can be argued that the process was quicker in the Aberdare Valley than in Llanuwchllyn, and that the Methodists, for example, only stayed eighteen months in Trecynon on the hearth before moving out to a room, though there were only five of them. The new housing estates needed the house-church in the twentieth century, but they were given a building which was redundant overnight. Nonconformity had forgotten its beginnings.

All the Welsh Nonconformist denominations have witnessed a substantial decline in membership figures since the 1926 General Strike. The two denominations which had most members in the Aberdare Valley were the Congregationalists and the Baptists.

It should be pointed out that there is a great deal of similarity between them. The Church government of both denominations demands initiative. They are autonomous as congregations, and independent in their power to exercise their own standards. Their independence would strongly attract people who felt the shackles of authoritarianism in the mining industry, as they had felt authoritarianism in the person of the squire in the country districts, from where so many of them had come, repulsive to their dignity. Another sociological factor and asset was the way they could set up a ' gathered congregation ' whenever they wanted, and often we find two or three chapels of the same denomination in a village or town. Every individual church was held to be a complete unit in itself, consisting of a congregation of true believers, bound together in a covenant relationship — the concept of covenant was fundamental to Congregationalism. All authority was vested in the congregation itself, expressed through the agency of the church meeting, and none was given absolutely to any of its officers, ministers included. Their total freedom from outside control earned them the name of 'Independents'; the later variation of Congregationalist expressed the idea that every member of the fellowship participated in its administration. These features of classic Congregationalism are not altogether suited, as John D. Gay puts it, to an age of economic efficiency and ecumenical dialogue and have been modified in recent years (Gay, 1971, p. 134).

Gay, however, gives us information on the strength of Congregationalism in England today, and in particular in the counties of Surrey and Sussex. Why should Congregationalism have blossomed in these two counties and declined in one of its Welsh strongholds, the Aberdare Valley? John D. Gay gives the answer, that many of the Congregational churches in the south-east have adopted a new image. They have become community churches with the implicit role of achieving the social integration of the local inhabitants (Gay, 1971, p. 141).

In the Aberdare Valley the role is still that of a gathered congregation and not of a community church. There is no interest in trying to fulfil that role, a role which lends itself to the Congregational Churches. They have the essential autonomy which enables them to adapt to and be moulded by their new environment without too much fear of outside interference. One reason why the Congregationalist Churches in the Aberdare Valley are unable to accept the role that Congregationalism in the south-east of England has adopted is obvious: it is a declining church. They only managed to survive economically by drastic revisions, i.e., moving to worship from the Gothic cathedrals to the schoolroom and the vestry. And as we will see in the next few paragraphs, the Welsh Congregational Churches in the Aberdare Valley have gone progressively weaker, and some have disbanded, while others struggle to retain a nominal presence.

The decline in the Welsh Congregational Church in the Aberdare Valley has been a steady process, as can be gathered from the statistics provided for the Congregational Churches.

The Congregational churches, like all other churches, had a rich harvest in the Revival of 1904/5, reaching a membership of 9,454 in 1907. This figure was down to 7,550 in 1923, a loss of

1,904 members, and by 1954 was down to 4,455, a loss of 2,955 from 1923, a period of 31 years. The same story is repeated in the Sunday Schools of the churches, a decline from 1909, when there were 8,094 on the books, to 3,501 in 1947. It can be taken for granted that the decline since 1954 among the Congregational chapels and since 1947 among the Sunday Schools has shown a sharper drop than in the preceding twenty years.

Individual churches show the decline in a stark fashion. Siloa Congregational Church, Aberdare, had 661 members in 1899, while by 1907 it had gone up to 761, but by 1923 the decline had started, and the membership was 645. When the Rev. R. I. Parry was ordained in the church in 1933, Siloa numbered 501), but by 1954, a period of 21 years, there were 363 members, and by 1964 the membership had decreased to 191. Carmel, Penrhiwceibr, had 404 members in 1907, and twenty years later they had a loss of 124; by 1954 there were only 200 members. Ebenezer, Trecynon, had 564 members in 1907, and at the end of the Second World War they had 365 members. By 1954 they had 330 members; while Bethlehem, Abercwmboi, declined from 336 in 1904 to 143 in 1954. The story is the same for all the churches, and out of the 33 churches in 1954, they all showed a 'decline' since the 1910s and the 1920s.

The Welsh Baptist Churches have also, as the Congregationalists, declined substantially. The years 1880, 1926, 1946 and 1963 are years in which the growth and decline can be demonstrated.

The Baptists hold six principles in common :[1]

(1) The supreme authority of the Bible in all matters of faith and practice.
(2) Believer's Baptism. This is the most conspicuous conviction of Baptists.
(3) Churches composed of believers only.
(4) Equality of all Christians in the life of the Church.
(5) Independence of the local Church.
(6) Separation of Church and State.

---

[1] See Winthrop S. Hudson, *Baptist Concepts of the Church* (1959), and John D. Gay, *The Geography of Religion in England* (1971).

Statistics of the Welsh Congregational Churches of the Valley

(as printed in the Year Book, 1891-1954)

Year.	No. of Churches.	No. of Members.	No. of Members in Sunday Schools.
1891	20	3,884	3,946
1899	29	6,280	6,801
1900	29	6,148	6,655
1901	29	6,382	6,986
1907	33	9,454	8,611
1909	33	8,393	8,094
1910	34	7,936	
1911	34	7,794	7,506
1912	34	7,395	7,128
1913		7,352	7,046
1914		7,513	7,388
1915	35	6,315	6,943
1916		7,496	7,201
1917		7,331	7,160
1918		7,367	7,048
1919	35	7,179	6,843
1920		7,553	6,978
1921		7,414	6,947
1922		7,493	6,947
1923		7,550	6,797
1928		7,272	5,943
1929		7,132	6,033
1931		6,495	5,558
1933		6,068	5,010
1935	33	6,380	4,828
1936		6,426	4,864
1937		6,491	4,928
1938		5,619	3,786
1941	32	5,750	3,776
1945		5,736	3,731
1946		5,687	3,501
1947	30	4,871	
1948	29	4,903	
1949		4,610	
1954	33	4,455	

Statistics of the Welsh Baptist Churches
(as printed in the Baptist Handbooks, 1865-1963)

Year.	No. of Churches.	No. of Members.	No. of Sunday School Members.
1865	13	2,318	
1866	15	2,737	
1867	15	2,916	
1868	15	3,978	
1869	15	3,401	
1871	15	3,422	
1872	15	3,291	
1873	15	3,422	
1874	15	3,653	
1876	15	3,829	
1879	15	3,414	
1880	15	3,917	
1881			
1889		3,770	4,066
1925		3,539	
1926		4,443	3,675
1937		3,452	2,644
1939	20	3,229	
1940	20	3,157	
1941	21	3,147	2,179
1942	20	2,929	1,913
1943	20	2,677	1,582
1944	19	2,662	1,425
1946	20	2,834	1,684
1947	20	2,757	1,502
1948	20	2,676	1,395
1949	20	2,579	1,317
1950	20	2,493	1,258
1951	20	2,446	1,318
1952	20	2,506	1,366
1953	20	2,282	1,433
1954	20	2,297	1,320
1956	20	2,024	1,025
1958	20	1,782	931
1959	20	1,959	998
1960	20	1,906	937
1961	20	1,853	965
1963	20	893	

A formula can be made for the years 1880-1926 and 1926-1963. 1880 was one of the best years of the nineteenth century in the history of the Baptist denomination in the Aberdare Valley, while 1926 was the zenith in its whole history — 4,443 members, while 1946 was a good year for the 'post-war' period of decline, but 1963 had a dismal figure of 893, which shows that the real decline was witnessed between 1953 and 1963, with a drop from 2,282 members to 893 ten years later, a loss of 1,389 members, or 60%.

The Sunday School, which has proved itself as a handmaid to Nonconformist Churches, shows the same decline from 4,066 in 1889 to 965 in 1961, a loss of 3,101, or 76%.

The decline can be vividly grasped when we take a look at some of the statistics of the individual churches. Calfaria Baptist Church, Aberdare, where the Rev. Dr. Thomas Price ministered, had a thousand members in 1862; by 1871 it had 471 members, and by 1925 it was slightly down to 395, and thirty years afterwards the membership was 200 (1955). In 1961 the church had 183 members and 168 in 1963. Another example would be Seion, Cwmaman, built in 1861, and ten years afterwards had 76 members. By 1925 Seion had 398 members, but in 1955 the members had declined to 214, and by 1961 to 188, and 169 in 1963. A more substantial drop can be discerned in the statistics of the Baptist Church at Cwmbach. In 1925 there were 314 members, while in 1955 there were 140, and in 1960, 100 members. The Baptist Church at Abernant has been a more catastrophic 'drop' in the last forty years; a rapid decline from 398 in 1925 to 165 in 1955, 161 in 1961, and 137 in 1963.

The Welsh Baptist Church at Aberaman had 189 members in 1925, while in 1955 there were only 66 members, and in 1963 there was a further decline to 42 members. In less than forty years there had been a loss of 147 members. This decline is not confined to the Welsh church, but it is more apparent among the Welsh Baptists, as can be grasped by the graph on the next page, which shows how the membership of one particular church reached its climax in the 1904-5 Revival, and in less than fifty years had shown a drop of 400 members (Evans, 1965, p. 3).

The Presbyterian Church of Wales, or the Calvinistic Methodist Church, has also shown a decline in membership.

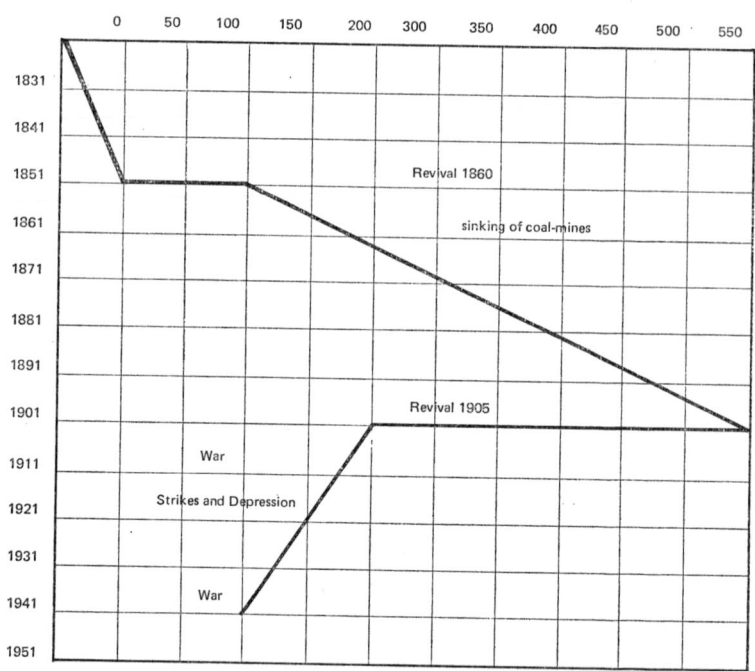

```
              0    50   100  150  200  300  350  400  450  500  550
        1831
        1841
        1851                         Revival 1860
        1861                              sinking of coal-mines
        1871
        1881
        1891
        1901                         Revival 1905
        1911           War
        1921       Strikes and Depression
        1931
        1941           War
        1951
```

The Presbyterian Church of Wales or the Calvinistic Methodist Church

STATISTICS OF THE MEMBERSHIP IN THE ABERDARE VALLEY

Year.	No. of Churches.	No. of Members.
1871	14	1,550
1900	18	2,909*
1922	20	5,874
1931	20	4,800
1939	20	3,381
1949	16	1,381
1960	15	1,238
1962	15	1,116
1965	14	1,042

* NOTE: Ynysybwl, Llanwynno, Pontneddfechan, were included in the lists for the Hirwaun District and the Aberdare District. In 1965 they were not members of those two Districts, but of the Pontypridd and Neath Valley District Meetings. Ynysybwl numbered 85 and Llanwyno 11 members in 1965.

Though it must be pointed out that the number of churches in 1965 is six less than in 1922, when the Calvinistic Methodists had 5,874 members, in comparison with 1,042 in 1965, the decline is much more revealing when we take the individual churches. Bethel, Hirwaun, had 500 as a congregation in 1931, while by 1965 it had become 143. Cwmdare Presbyterian Church had 305 in 1931, while in 1966 there were 71 members. But here their explanation about the 'gwrandawr' is relevant, for the statistics of the Calvinistic Methodists were swelled by these people in the Aberdare Valley. The presence of 'gwrandawr' is noted, for example, in the statistics of 1900, and undoubtedly was an important asset to the congregations of the Calvinistic Methodist Churches. A 'gwrandawr' would come to the services — he was a listener and not a member, and it is a phenomenon which has virtually disappeared in Welsh Nonconformity. The following churches had a large membership of these 'gwrandawyr': Libanus, Aberaman, had 152 members, but 355 adherents; and Tabernacle, Abercynon, 137 members and 218 adherents; Bethania, Aberdare, 243 members and 500 'gwrandawyr'; Soar, Cwmaman, had 264 members and 830 adherents; Ebenezer, Cwmbach, had 155 members and 410 'gwrandawyr'; Llanwyno 54 members and 100 adherents; Bethlehem, Aberdare, had 152 members and 310 adherents; Hermon, Penrhiwceibr, had 307 members and 570 'gwrandawyr'; Ynysybwl had 233 members and 430 adherents. The story is the same for the Hirwaun Dosbarth: Seion, Trecynon, had 209 members and 540 'gwrandawyr'; Carmel, Trecynon, had 125 members and 460 adherents, which meant that the Calvinistic Methodists had 1,000 'gwrandawyr' in the village of Trecynon besides 334 members, and more adherents than there were members throughout the fourteen chapels of the valley in 1970. Gobaith, Cwmdare, had 72 members and 160 adherents; while Bethel, Hirwaun, had 283 members and 520 'gwrandawyr'; Moriah, Llwydcoed, had 104 members and 235 adherents; and Jerusalem, Penderyn, 26 members and 48 adherents, while at Pontneddfechan there were 61 members and 200 adherents.

At Hermon, Penrhiwceibr, we realise that the adherent was a large part of the congregation. In 1931 there were 186 members, 61 adherents, and 52 children, making a congregation of 299. While there were 80 'gwrandawyr' in 1928-9, in 1932 there were only 20. The exodus during the Depression must have thinned the ranks of the ' gwrandawyr '. There was an increase the following two years to 25, but by 1950 there was only one.

In 1962 that one disappeared, and with him a unique class in the history of Welsh Nonconformity. The 'gwrandawyr' had followed the Nonconformist line in theology and politics and, on occasions, such as in 1851 and 1906, they gave Nonconformity a statistical importance it never possessed in reality in this industrial society. Rev. E. T. Davies has said : " It would be uncharitable to say that thousands went to chapel in those days because there was nowhere else to go, but such a statement is not devoid of all truth." Lest the figure should give the wrong impression, it is well to recall Dr. Thomas Jones's description of the immigrants who came to the industrial areas of Glamorgan and Gwent. " They came as Christians and as Pagans, thrifty and profligate, clean and dirty, and gradually sorted themselves in the surroundings according to tradition and habit " (Davies, 1963, p. 9).

The Wesleyan Methodists

The Welsh Wesleyan Methodists have never been strong in South Wales or in the Aberdare Valley, as it came after all the other denominations. The situation is rather complicated, insofar as the statistics are concerned, by the fact that there were two Districts, the Aberdare and Abercynon Districts, and included churches which are in other valleys. Treharris and Bedlinog are in the Taff Valley, and Cilfynydd and Ynysybwl would be in the Pontypridd area, and by the late 50s of the twentieth century two of the three churches which then belonged to the Abercynon District had ceased to exist. The churches at Cilfynydd and Treharris had closed. We have also only been able to find the statistics for the Abercynon and Aberdare Welsh Wesleyan Methodist Churches for the period between 1936 and 1960, but the trend is the same as all the other Welsh Nonconformist denominations. Abercynon District had 253 members in 1936, and only 100 members in 1960, which included the churches of Mountain Ash, Penrhiwceibr, Abercynon and Ynysybwl, having one Superintendent. The Welsh Wesleyan Methodists, who have the same hymnbook as the Calvinistic Methodist Church, have since closed the churches at Aberdare and Ynysybwl.

1. Aerial view of Aberdare.

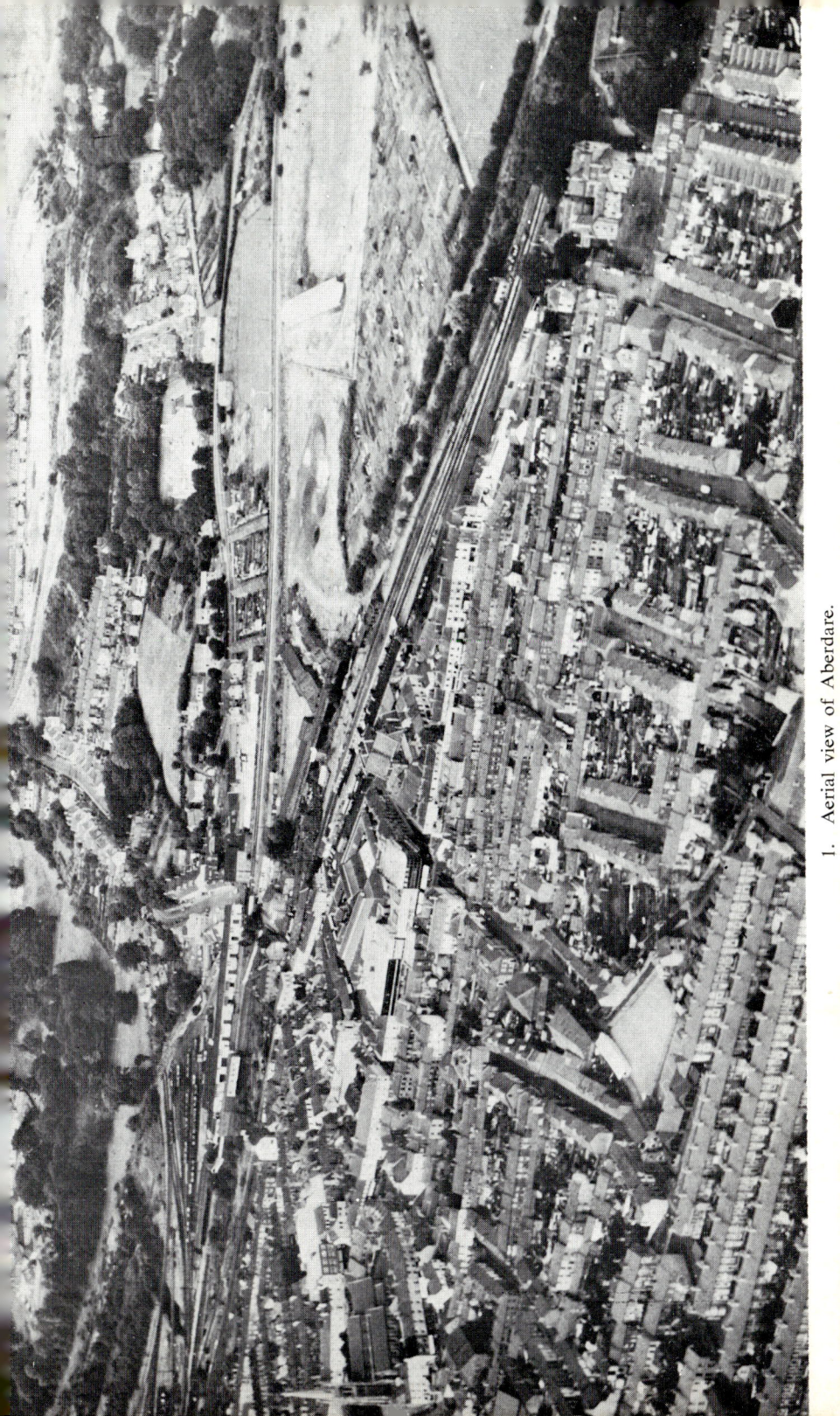

2. David Alfred Thomas (1856-1918), who represented the Merthyr Constituency as a Liberal. One of the "old brigade" and a friend of Nonconformity.

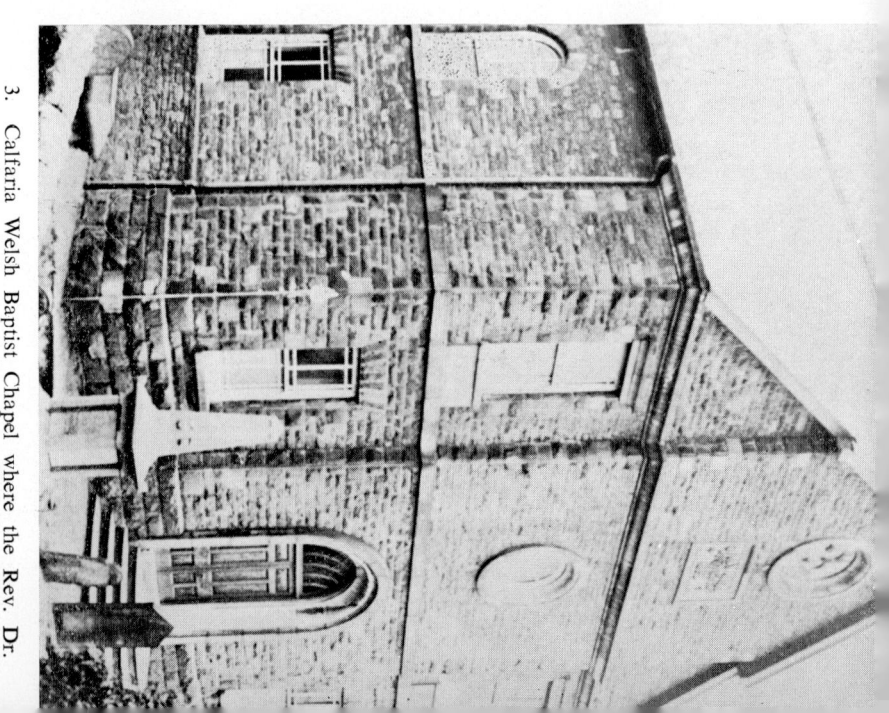

3. Calfaria Welsh Baptist Chapel where the Rev. Dr. Thomas Price reigned supreme for 43 years.

4. A view of the town of Mountain Ash from the resting place of so many of its inhabitants.

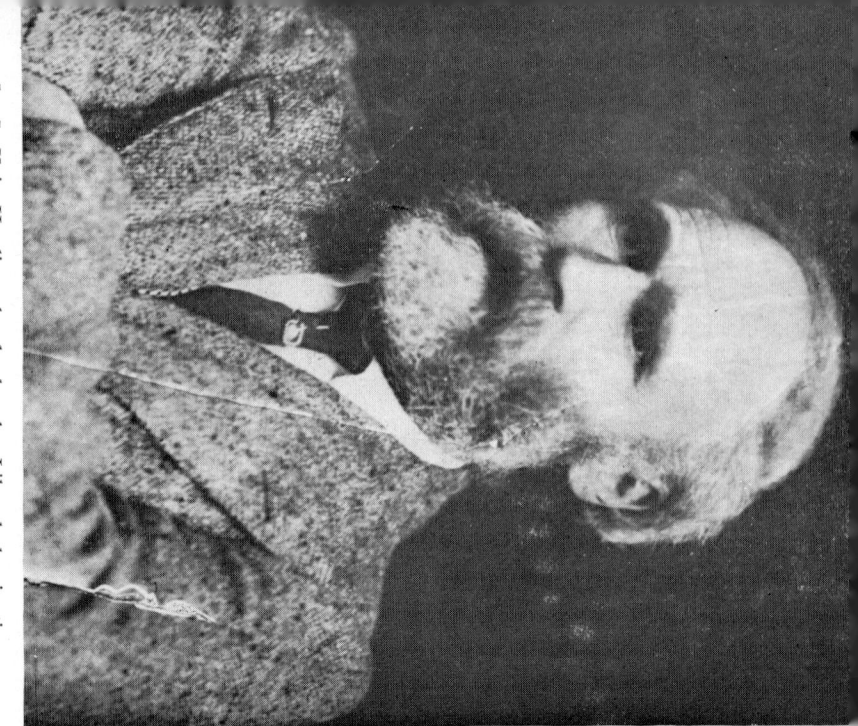

5. **J. Keir Hardie**, who broke the Liberal domination and began the ascendancy of the Labour Party in local and Parliamentary affairs.

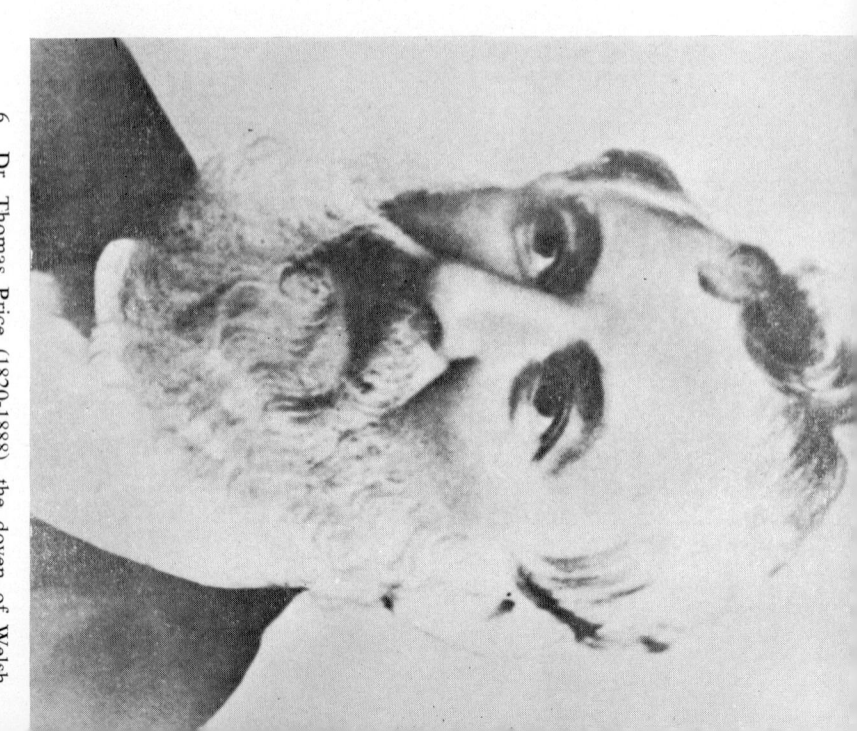

6. **Dr. Thomas Price** (1820-1888), the doyen of Welsh Baptist ministers and a charismatic figure.

7. Victoria Square, Aberdare, with the monument to the famous Welsh choral conductor, Griffith Rhys Jones (Caradog) (1834-97), dominating the town.

8. The new Co-operative store in the middle of the town of Aberdare. A typical Saturday afternoon scene.

9. Penrhiwceibr Workmen's Hall and Institute, built in 1888.

10. Bryn Seion Welsh Congregationalist Chapel, Cwmbach, near Aberdare. A monkey puzzle tree was a feature outside so many of the Welsh Chapels.

11. The Abercynon Welfare Hall, which is regarded as one of the largest in the Aberdare Valley.

12. A view of the town of Aberdare from Graig Mountain.

13. Hen-dŷ-Cwrdd Unitarian Chapel, Trecynon, Aberdare, and the oldest Nonconformist chapel in the Valley.

14. A view which includes the town of Mountain Ash, the village of Abercwmboi, and the golf course at Cwmpennar.

15. Hermon Presbyterian Church of Wales, Penrhiwceibr, where the author ministered from 1962 to 1968.

16. A view of Mountain Ash from the Perthcelyn Road, which leads to Llanwynn

17. Ynysboeth Industrial Estate in the lower Cynon Valley.

18. Penrhiwceibr Colliery.

19. Mountain Ash from Newtown Quarry.

20. The Aberaman Public Hall and Grand Social Club, which was erected by the contributions of the coal-miners.

21. An example of the modern, luxurious social clubs.

22. Hirwaun Trading Estate, which is situated at the upper end of the Cynon Valley.

The Decline in Membership of the Wesleyan Methodists

Year.	Town.	Total No. of Members.
1936	Aberdare	340
1936	Abercynon	253
		593
1937	Aberdare	335
1937	Abercynon	256
		591
1938	Aberdare	335
1938	Abercynon	247
		582
1939	Aberdare	324
1939	Abercynon	232
		556
1940	Aberdare	322
1940	Abercynon	211
		533
1941	Aberdare	310
1941	Abercynon	195
		505
1943	Aberdare	319
1943	Abercynon	269
		588
1946	Aberdare	319
1946	Abercynon (which included Cefn, Merthyr Vale)	189
		508
1947	Aberdare	301
1947	Abercynon	167
		468

The Decline in Membership of the Wesleyan Methodists
—Continued

Year.	Town.	Total No. of Members.
1949	Aberdare	243
1949	Abercynon	183
		426
1951	Aberdare	231
1951	Abercynon	148
		379
1952	Aberdare	222
1952	Abercynon	143
		365
1956	Aberdare	209
1956	Abercynon	124
		333
1959	Aberdare	188
1959	Abercynon	111*
		299
1960	Aberdare	198
1960	Abercynon	100
		298

With the context of the statistics, a decline can be seen, and especially a decline in the number of children belonging to the circuits. In 1936 there were 192 children in the two circuits, but in 1943 the total was down to 146, and by 1952 there were only 72, and by 1960 18 children in eight churches. This augurs badly for the future of the Wesleyan Churches in the valley, as the children are the future of the Church. The same decrease is not so critical

* In 1959 Abercynon also included Ynysybwl, Merthyr Vale and Bedlinog; only two of these are in the Aberdare Valley.

in the other denominations, though the Welsh Presbyterian Church at Penrhiwceibr had 110 children in 1927, but by 1965 there were only 16, and of those six were living away, but had been baptised at the church.

The loss in membership has happened, not to the extent generally believed, but there has been since the Second World War a gradual fall in membership. It is interesting to note that in some churches the membership is about the same in 1966 as it was in 1900. Tabernacle, Abercynon, is an example, with 137 members in 1900 and 133 members in 1966. The decline is more serious than the loss of members suggests. At the beginning of the century, up to 1930, as I have already mentioned, the Free Churches had as many, and even more, adherents as they had of members, but by 1966 they had disappeared from the Free Churches. The loss of adherents, therefore, is much larger than that of members, and points to the weakened habit of worship on the part of those who may not have been fully converted. It also points to the greatly diminished influence of Nonconformity on the public at large.

The decline in the strength of the Anglican Church is harder to measure, since there are no membership figures. The Anglican Church to a Nonconformist in Wales is not the Established Church since the disestablishment by the Welsh Church Act passed in Parliament in 1914 and which became effective in 1920. The six Welsh dioceses of the Church of England — Bangor, Llandaff, St. Asaph, St. Davids, Swansea and Brecon, and Monmouth — were elected into a new province, independent of the province of Canterbury. The Aberdare Valley is a part of Llandaff Diocese, and we have at our disposal some figures for the Aberdare Valley Anglican churches that demonstrate a decline.

In 1924, out of a population of 15,104 at Aberaman, which had three Anglican Churches, there were 500 electors, while in Abercynon, with two churches (one being a Mission Hall), there was a population of 14,979, but with 250 members. Abercwmboi had 127 electors. Aberdare had five churches: St. Mathew, Abernant; St. John the Baptist, St. Elvin, St. Mary the Virgin, and St. John the Evangelist, to serve a population of 22,413. The combined parochial electors of the five churches numbered 1,850. Trecynon, Llwydcoed, and Cwmdare had a population of 8,640, with three churches, having a combined parochial electorate of 307. Cwmaman had a population of 5,613 with an electorate of 338, while the church had 315 parochial electors. Hirwaun had a population of 4,220 with the 182 electors belonging to the Parish Church. Miskin had two churches and a Mission Hall, with a population of 5,986, having 417 parochial electors. Mountain Ash, with a population of 13,227, had three churches with a combined parochial electorate of 1,036. Penrhiwceibr had two churches with an electorate of 323 for a population of 10,836.

This can be compared with the figures we have at our disposal for 1930 (a gap of six years), to realise the slight ' decline ' which had happened. Aberaman had two churches with 459 electors, a decline of 41, while Abercwmboi had 132, an increase of 5. Aberdare had 1,830, the same as six years before. The Trecynon area had 350, an increase of 12; Cwmbach showed a decline from 315 to 117, a decrease of 198 electors; Miskin showed a decline of 33 to a figure of 386; Mountain Ash had a decrease of 36 to the round figure of 1,000 electors; Penrhiwceibr showed the same figure, 323. The decline is non-existent when we realise that the population of all these areas showed a decrease as the result, of the industrial depression of the 30s. Aberaman had 4,104 less inhabitants; Aberdare 2,413, while Abercynon had nearly 6,000 less inhabitants.

A study which is relevant to the chapter both as to the position of Nonconformity and the Anglican Church is the *Report of the Royal Commission on the Church of England and other Religious Bodies in Wales and Monmouthshire* in 1910. We find that Aberdare (which included the churches of Aberdare, Aberaman, St. Fagans, Hirwaun) had 2,741 Church communicants, while the Nonconformist membership in forty-nine Welsh and eighteen English chapels had 13,942 communicants and 10,744 adherents. An Anglican historian has analysed the figures of the study in the following way :

" Percentage of communicants to total number of communicants and members (i.e., Church and Chapel, excluding adherents) 16.4%. Percentage of members to total number of worshippers 83.5%. Percentage of communicants to population of 6.2%. Percentage of members to population 31.6%, the population being

44,104. Percentage of members and communicants to population 37.8%. Percentage of members and adherents to population 55.6%. Percentage of members, communicants and adherents to population 62.2% " (Davies, 1963, p. 178). This analysis re-states what has been put forward before in our examination.

(i) The class adherents.
(ii) The Revival helped the membership of the chapels.
(iii) The Welsh-speaking areas with 37.8% of members and communicants to the total population led English-speaking areas like Newport with its 16.3%.

Canon E. T. Davies rightly warns us in connection with the 'Report'. The study is incomplete. 1905 was an unsatisfactory year for reliable figures and, in any case, the changes in society which affected Church and Chapel were already in motion before that year. They were checked somewhat by the Religious Revival of 1904-5, and they quickly accelerated in the years before and during the First World War, and became apparent in their results after 1919.

Our statistical survey would not be complete without a reference to the Roman Catholic Church, a Church which is powerful throughout the world and a Church which has been well served in the field of the sociology of religion by a number of talented sociologists. The Roman Catholic Church in the valley has only four churches, and the Mass (a service which is built around the Sacrament of the Lord's Supper) is well attended. The Church, as in other areas of England and Wales, derived its initial strength in the area as a result of Irish immigration in the Industrial Revolution of the nineteenth century. The Irish immigrants came to the area devoid of all provision for their worship. We find that in 1905 there were 429 members of the congregation over fifteen, and 310 under fifteen, at St. Joseph's Church, Aberdare; and at Our Lady's, Mountain Ash, there were 1,110 members of the congregation over fifteen and 352 under fifteen. This can be compared with the 1962-3 statistics. Aberdare had 487 Easter Communicants and 500 Mass attendances out of a population of 4,707, which shows a slight increase over the figure fifty-seven years before. Abercynon had 148 Easter Communicants and 130 Mass attendances out of a Catholic population of 707. Hirwaun had

232 Easter Communicants and 320 Mass attendances out of a Catholic population of 594. Mountain Ash had 475 Easter Duties and 480 Mass attendances out of a Catholic population of 918, which shows a decline from the 1905 figures. The total Easter Duties for the whole valley in 1962 was 1,341, Mass attendances being 1,480 and the Catholic population amounting to 2,503. This can be compared with the total for the four Welsh language Nonconformist denominations which is 6,682. Nonconformity, if we took the English causes into consideration, was still the main medium to express the religious conviction of the Aberdare Valley in 1962, as it had been for over 150 years. And this religious conviction is expressed through the " community of the congregation " which assembles to hear the preaching of the Word and the administration of the Sacraments (Lord's Supper, usually every month, and the Sacrament of Baptism whenever the need arises) on a Sunday, to discuss and instruct children, young people and adults in the Scriptures through the medium of the Sunday School, and to gather in the fellowship meetings on a week-night, usually the *Seiat* or the prayer meeting, and the Women's Guild or Sisterhood. All this happens within the Nonconformist Chapel, and by analysing the structure of these institutional activities we will be able to answer the question: What goes on in a Nonconformist chapel in the Aberdare Valley, and what it means to be a member of that organisation?

Nonconformity has always looked upon all these agencies as a means of educating its members. This is why the *Seiat* — the week-night meeting — and the Sunday School have always placed so much emphasis on discussion and reading. Historians always refer to the contributions of the Sunday Schools, and it was for many generations this movement in Wales which often provided education to the ordinary people; formal education (apart from the " Three Rs ") was mainly dependent on this system. Through their own Sunday Schools and associated activities, people attained not only an experience of religion, but also an introduction to a culture, and not for children primarily, but for adults.

It is widely known that Wales has witnessed many experiments in religious education, and that the Circulating Schools of Griffith Jones in the eighteenth century were aimed at giving a foundation in the Christian religion to the children. The Sunday School Movement, under the guidance of the remarkable Welsh divine Thomas Charles of Bala, took upon itself a distinctively Welsh character. In addition to classes for the very young being taught to read or sing the Biblical account of the Birth of Christ, there could also be found in them classes of adults discussing the fundamentals of the faith and the intricacies of theology on a Sunday afternoon. It offered a cheap and rapid means of education to the working class, who often had neither the opportunity nor the means to afford a day-school education (Jones, 1938, p. 518). It provided two other social advantages. The Sunday School, in its organisation, allowed the working and the middle classes to mix freely. A salf-taught miner often would be the teacher of a men's class which could include one or two Honours Graduates and a schoolmaster. The other contribution was that it became a training ground for democracy. It was easier for someone trained in a Welsh Sunday School to take his place in the Council Chamber and in the Miners' Lodge meeting than for someone who had not been trained in skills of debate and discussion.

The Sunday Schools in the Aberdare Valley have seen, like the Churches, a decline in numbers. The Presbyterian Church of Wales's Sunday Schools, for example, were in a flourishing state in 1903 compared with 1967, as can be seen from the following statistics:

Name of Sunday School	Year 1870	Year 1903	Year 1967
Bethania, Aberdare	452	302	18
Tabernacle, Abercynon	Not in existence	195	61
Libanus, Aberaman	156	214	8
Soar, Cwmaman	113	250	14
Ebenezer, Cwmbach	203	230	Ceased to exist
Hebron, Aberaman	Not in existence	86	Ceased to exist
Bethel, Hirwaun	410	Not known	48
Bethlehem, Mountain Ash	150	319	28
Carmel, Trecynon	260	Not known	23
Gobaith, Cwmdar	69	Not known	7
Bryn Seion, Trecynon	278	Not known	Ceased to exist
Moriah, Llwydcoed	260	Not known	22
Hermon, Penrhiwceibr	Not in existence	370	6

The decline has been more obvious in the Sunday School among the Presbyterians in the Aberdare Valley (and the same is true of the other Nonconformist denominations) than among the membership of the Churches. The picture is just about the same in other areas of Wales, in rural as well as urban areas. The small parish of Llanfihangel-yng-Ngwynfa in Montgomeryshire has witnessed the same decline as Seion, Trecynon, and Ebenezer, Cwmbach; " and even the Sunday Schools have been discontinued in at least three of the smaller chapels " (Rees, 1951, p. 120).

Trefor Owen's study of Church and Community in Glanllyn, Llanuwchllyn, in Merioneth, also indicates that the Sunday School institution in the heart of Nonconformity is supported by a mere section of the community. In the Methodist chapel (the Welsh Presbyterian Church) in Llanuwchllyn village the proportion of the congregation which attended Sunday School fell from 52 per cent to 41 per cent between 1938 and 1949; and the average annual attendance during the same period fell from 41 to 28. Trefor Owen looks at the community as a whole — churchgoers as well as chapel-goers — and says that over a half of the households have no direct contact with the Sunday school at all, and the adults in a number of the remaining families maintain only an indirect contact through their children, as the following table indicates :

REPRESENTATION OF FAMILIES AT SUNDAY SCHOOLS

None	57.0%
Children only	20.8%
Parents or independent adults only	12.2%
Parents and child(ren)	10.0%

Trefor Owen reminds us also that the persons who neglect the religious services do not escape the influence of the Chapel. Most of them, as children, will have been regular members of their Sunday School; and this is as far as we can ascertain true of the mining valleys of South Wales. A minister of the Methodist Central Hall in Tonypandy, Rev. R. Bird, conducted a questionnaire in the social clubs of the Rhondda Valley, as well as the pubs and bingo halls, and among the questions asked was this one : " Were you at any time a Sunday School scholar? " Answers showed 708 in the affirmative and 155 in the negative. Eighty per cent of those interviewed, and who attend the clubs and the bingo halls of the Rhondda, are people who have been at one time or another members of the Sunday School (Roberts, 1966, p. 163).

In view of this remarkable and drastic decline, it was important to see if there were people in the Aberdare Valley unwilling to send their children to Sunday Schools, and how they regarded the Sunday School in general, for the Welsh Chapels' Sunday Schools would never turn a child away because he was English-speaking, but would care for him — as many of them did — with a certain degree of success.

The question "Would you send your children to Sunday School?" evoked the following replies:

	No.	Per cent.
Yes	62	80.5
No	—	—
No answer	10	13.8

In our questionnaire, 28 answered. Of these, one was a Mountain Ash inhabitant who had no children, and another was an Aberdare Barclays Bank employee who regarded himself as an agnostic; the remaining 26 (93 per cent) of the respondents were very much in favour of the Sunday Schools. Answers were largely coloured by the personal experience of those who attended and remembered their own Sunday School days. It is of some interest here to get an idea of the views of the rising generation as revealed by five children between the ages of 8 and 12 years who were interviewed at Brookton Sunday School in Birmingham. Their impressions were:

"Sunday School helps me to live better because the teachers tell me over and over again what is right and what is wrong."

"I think Sunday School ought to keep with it, and be bright and cheery places that people would like to come to. Not dark and dismal old furniture."

"I think stories every week are boring. I would like to do quizzes and puzzles."

"I think we ought to have a shorter service, then we can have a longer story-time and do activities."

"These stories are boring, but I like singing the hymns. I think we ought to sing modern hymns; some we sing are very dull.

I would like to do something different with story-time, like visiting other Sunday Schools to learn how they worship, or visiting churches and looking at things of interest, as we do at school" (Busia, 1966, p. 65). Dr. Busia notes in relation to these opinions the following extract from a report reviewing the year's work of a Sunday School where the children were given opportunities of expression work :

"We were interested to find that the children remembered two courses well, where we had some drama; also where pictures had been used frequently. They enjoyed taking part in worship, and we arranged that the readings in the service each week should be taken in turns" (Busia, 1966, p. 175).

The children's reaction to their lessons, and attendance at Sunday School, may be compared with the answers received from people from all walks of life in the Aberdare Valley.

Many of the answers to our questionnaire testified to personal upbringing, and it seems to be a continuation of a personal and, always, a family tradition.

"Because I was brought up to attend Sunday School" (a Mountain Ash housewife who has lived in Mountain Ash for 37 years).

"Hoping that they would be taught as I was" (Mountain Ash housewife who had lived for 48 years in the town).

"Because I went myself and would not give them a chance to decide about religion" (18-year-old Abercynon youth attending Mountain Ash Comprehensive School).

All the answers are in the same category. The respondents emphasise that the Sunday School is a place for gaining religious knowledge, an opportunity for preparing the pupils for life, even suggesting that it helps in their social upbringing. This is the standpoint that is often mentioned by leaders of churches : that Sunday School is a place for learning moral standards, and it is often suggested that few Sunday School pupils land up in juvenile delinquent courts.

Dr. W. E. Sangster, President of the Methodist Conference in 1950, preached a sermon on "This Britain" to his congregation at Westminster Central Hall. It was found to be of such impact that arrangements were made for its issue in the form of a sixteen-page pamphlet; and it found its way into big type on the front page of many national newspapers in 1953. Dr. Sangster suggests that a revival of religion would do ten things for Britain. It would pay old debts, reduce sexual immorality, disinfect the theatre, cut the divorce rate, lessen the prison population, improve the quality and increase the output of work, restore to the nation a sense of high destiny, make us invincible in the war of ideas, reduce juvenile crime, give happiness and peace to people (Sangster of Westminster, 1960, pp. 79-90). Under the fifth heading of reducing juvenile crime, Dr. W. E. Sangster suggests, like so many of the respondents to our questionnaire, the important place of the Sunday Schools in the attitude of young people towards crime and violence.

" A new tide of religion in our national life is the answer to the problem. It is a thing almost unheard of for a young thug to come out of a seriously Christian home. It can happen — but it hardly ever does. Moreover, it is exceedingly rare for a juvenile criminal to be associated with Church or Sunday School at the time his crimes are committed. No one is safe in goodness unless he wants to be good. Then he will be good in the dark. But what makes people want to be good? Sound religion does it" (Sangster of Westminster, 1960, p. 84).

The majority of the respondents to our questionnaire in the Aberdare Valley echo the words of Dr. W. E. Sangster, that sound religion is to be found in Sunday Schools, and that is why they send them there, to be taught morality and Christian belief. The respondents to the questionnaire were concerned with the value of Sunday Schools as a training centre for life. A 17-year-old Barclays Bank employee at Aberdare maintained "that it is an experience which I think is necessary for young children. They deserve a chance to find out things." All this is connected with morality, for Scripture teaching embodies ethics and Christianity is a way of life. " In order that they may learn the difference between right and wrong " (a housewife who had lived for 18 years in the Aberdare area).

" To help them to keep on the right road through their life " (a miner who had lived for 50 years in the Mountain Ash area).

" So that they would grow up to be good and useful citizens " (a miner from Tower 4 Colliery, Hirwaun, who had lived in the area for 50 years).

Many believed in the Sunday School as a place for imparting religious knowledge :

" Because they would benefit from it by learning about Christ " (18-year-old Abercynon Civil Servant).

" Because it has something to offer " (Aberdare Barclays Bank employee who had lived there for one year).

" To have the basic religious instruction " was the identical answer received from a member of the Medical Centre at Tower No. 1 Colliery, N.C.B., Hirwaun, who had lived in the area for 53 years, and a factory worker who had resided at Hirwaun for 36 years, of the Rhigos Industrial Estate. Another miner, who had lived at Hirwaun " all his life," believes that children should be sent to the Sunday School " so they may have religious uplift "; and a Darranlas retired miner, who had lived in Mountain Ash for 65 years, says, " I wanted them to believe in God ". An Abercynon 57 years old retired (through ill-health) Co-operative Manager would send his children to Sunday School " for a knowledge of the Bible and Christian Belief which is a basis for happy living "; and a Hirwaun youth who had lived there for only three and a half years feels that children who go to Sunday School go to learn about the Christian Belief. An 18-year-old C.W.S. Creamery Laboratory Assistant would send her children to Sunday School to " learn about Christianity and the teaching of Jesus Christ ". Another answer from a person who had lived for 25 years in the Aberdare Valley was " I believe all children should attend, as for many it is the only time they hear of religion ". A Hirwaun teacher who had lived there for 23 years, and who taught at Godreaman, writes " that children who attend Sunday School will increase knowledge; atmosphere of worship, social life," and an Aberdare Valley housewife who has been living in the area for two years would send the children " in order that they would be brought up in the Christian faith ".

A Barclays Bank employee who had lived at Aberaman for 21 years is most dogmatic " because this is my belief," while a colleague who had lived 20 years in the Aberdare area refuses to comment because he (or she) is " an agnostic "; and another colleague who had lived 18 years in the Aberdare area gives the explanation, " Nowhere near enough space for me to explain ". Two Mountain

Ash inhabitants, one who had lived there for 72 years, give the reason " because I believe in it ", and another who had lived for 52 years refuses to give an answer because the question is not relevant as they have " no children ". A Barclays Bank employee who had lived in the valley for only one year believes that it is worth sending the children " because it has something to offer ". A Penrhiwceibr underground colliery worker who had resided in the area for 45 years says, " I think they should have every chance to make up their own minds when they are older "; and another miner who had lived in Mountain Ash for 47 years would send his children to Sunday School " so that they gather with their friends in some harmless social activity ".

To the question " What do you remember of Sunday School? " 21 answered, giving out of 72 a 29%. Replies were as follows :

" It is a place where I was taught about the Bible and the New Testament " (Resident in the Mountain Ash area for 37 years).

" Learn the lessons of the Bible " (a housewife who had lived in the Mountain Ash area for 48 years).

" Anniversaries and outings " (Barclays Bank employee who had lived in the valley for 18 years).

" Quarterly meetings and Sunday School trips to the seaside " (50 years in Hirwaun, a miner at Tower No. 4 Colliery).

" Quite pleasant and enjoyable " (Hirwaun miner).

" Birth of Christ, Parables, Sermon on the Mount, Crucifixion " (Darrenlas retired miner).

" Questions and answers " (Mountain Ash miner).

" Being taught the teachings of Christ " (Hirwaun youth).

" Fair amount of what I have been taught " (C.W.S. Creamery, Trecynon, Laboratory Assistant).

" Presence of many children " (Hirwaun schoolteacher).

There were four who still attend. An 18-year-old Abercynon youth, an Aberaman Barclays Bank employee who is a " Sunday School teacher ", an Abercynon retired Co-operative Department Manager, and a 25-year-old Hirwaun person. The other answers are difficult to compartmentalise. A Barclays Bank employee " thought that it did get boring " and another employee remembered the Sunday School as a place where " people (were) sitting near me and commenting on what others were wearing in the middle of a service ". Three other Barclays Bank, Aberdare, employees answered as follows :

"Quite a lot"; "that it eventually became boring"; "not altogether satisfactory". A Mountain Ash housewife just gave "no answer," and a Penrhiwceibr miner did not keep to one church or denomination, "in fact, I went to every church or chapel you can name ". Another person who had lived in the Aberdare Valley 18 years said the same thing. A member of the Medical Centre at No. 1 Tower Colliery, Hirwaun, said that "the other boys in the same class stopped going to school". A Tower Colliery miner stopped because "of apathy"; and a Penrhiwceibr miner on a matter of belief as "I don't believe there is such a thing as the world hereafter". A Barclays Bank employee at Aberdare stopped because of "domestic circumstances"; and another member of the staff, "I stopped because I didn't see how I was learning anything"; and another member of the staff of Barclays Bank stopped "because I started to work". A Mountain Ash inhabitant who had lived there for 50 years stopped: "I was 14 years of age, and as a family we moved from North Wales to South Wales". A Barclays Bank employee who had lived for one year in the valley stopped because of "other interests". A Mountain Ash housewife stopped: "I was 21 when I stopped going to Sunday School". Only two of the 16 who answered are still connected with the Sunday Schools. A C.W.S. Creamery Laboratory Assistant is "still going", and a Darranlas retired miner "never did actually stop. Sunday School at my church is combined with matins on Sunday morning".

Only 3 of the 16 who answered found any fault with the Sunday School system. It is well to compare this seeming lack of criticism for the teaching methods, approach and Sunday School syllabus with a report from a member of the Birmingham survey on the Sunday School of one of the churches :

"My impression of the Junior Department is that they are numerically strong, have plenty of space and manpower, but lack the modern approach. From the children I gathered that the pattern of worship consists of hymn, prayer, hymn, Bible reading, collection, prayer, hymn, story, hymn, and benediction, and that this is never varied. None of them could ever remember having assisted in the conducting of the opening service ... Groups are formed round the room for the story period ... The National Sunday School Union handbook is used as a guide to the lessons ... I saw no evidence of creative activities and the leader confessed that little is attempted ... There is no preparation class to help the teachers with these things ... Some children take the Sunday School Scripture examination each year. The teachers' exams. have never been attempted " (Busia, 1966, pp. 65-66).

My observation of Sunday Schools in Nonconformist Chapels in the Aberdare Valley would differ on many of the points referred to in the Birmingham report. The Junior Departments are not generally numerically strong; and where they are, they do not seem to welcome the modern approach. Film strips are seldom used. The flannelgraphs have not been generally adopted. With the pattern of worship there are, indeed, similarities, but in the Welsh Sunday Schools opportunity was always given to the children to take part in the opening service. At Glancynon Presbyterian Church of Wales Sunday School it was the custom to start the Sunday School with one of the children reading a hymn, scripture reading, and reading a short prayer, followed by the Lord's Prayer, under the care of the Superintendent. It is true to say that of the Sunday Schools that I know personally — 20 schools in the Aberdare Valley — little scope is given to creative activity; and the teachers have no one to help them in preparation work, or in informing them of the material that is available. The Sunday School examinations are more popular with the Presbyterian Church of Wales in the Aberdare Valley than anywhere else in the East Glamorgan Presbytery. An interesting point is made also in the account given of a Young People's Class of one of the Brookton churches. It is interesting both for what it does and the problem it underscores; and that this is not generally practised within the Nonconformist Churches. The general pattern in a Young People's Class in a Nonconformist Church is to read the selected Scripture passage for the lesson, and then to follow the commentary, or for the teacher to explain the commentaries' explanation of the lesson. Every year the Welsh Nonconformist denominations produce between them a commentary on the syllabus which has been decided upon for all the age-groups. The age groups are as follows: 0-5, 5-7, 7-11, 11-14, 14-17, 17-21, and 21+. The English Sunday Schools within Nonconformity usually follow the Scripture Union syllabus.

The class at one of the Brookton churches was started in 1953, and it is an integral part of the Sunday School. It has 20 members, boys and girls between the ages of 15 and 20. The leader is a bank clerk, "over 20 years old"; she is also an officer in the Girls' Life Brigade. She has two young assistants, aged about 20, both of whom are engineering apprentices. The aims of this Young People's Class are stated to be:

1. To help members to apply in everyday life the theory of Christianity learnt earlier in school.
2. To help them to express themselves to others.
3. To deepen their faith, and lead the uncommitted to dedicate their lives to Christ.

The class meets on Sunday afternoons, and there is no set pattern, and ideas are not planned more than three or four weeks ahead. An effort is made to fulfil the three aims through:

1. Discussion of topical questions. Topics recently discussed included: Capital punishment; the colour question; the Christian view of sex; the Church and work; the Christian and news (using the daily newspapers).
2. Talks given by the members of the class about their experiences, their hobbies, their holidays, or their work (about half the members work whole or part-time).
3a. Direct Bible study, led by members.
 b. Discussions on the Christian faith.
 c. Use of films and film strips.

This pattern is unusual and, to my knowledge, was not widely used in the Nonconformist Sunday Schools of the Aberdare Valley during the period I spent there, from 1962 to 1968.

The Sunday Schools in the Aberdare Valley numerically, as I have indicated, are continually declining. David Martin gives evidence that as far as Sunday Schools in England and Wales are in question a diminishing support is quite clear. Church of England Sunday Schools covered 303 per 1,000 of the population aged 3-14 in 1897, and in 1958 only 149, although, as David Martin maintains, it should be remembered that Parish Communions now partly absorb the functions of Sunday Schools. In 1910, Nonconformist schools covered some three million scholars in England and Wales, and in 1962 only between 800,000 and 900,000. Of those who "never went" to any Sunday School the percentage had dropped in 1957 from 76 among those over 30 to 61 among those under 30. In that year one person in two claimed to send children to Sunday School, but in 1964 only one child in seven attended Sunday School regularly, and if a Church service is included, one child in four. Still, there remains a great deal of support for the notion of Sunday School attendance, and this is presumably linked to support for religious education in schools, and the teaching of prayers to children. At least four persons in five seem to feel that religion should be passed on in these various ways to children.

The problem of teaching religion as a compulsory subject seems to arouse considerable controversy. The objects of such teaching can be assessed from a selection of intellectual and philosophical replies to questions put to some religious education teachers in Brookton schools:

To establish the fundamental grounds of the Christian faith; to give knowledge and understanding of the revelation of God.

To convey the historical faith of Christianity which is relevant to life today and its day-to-day experience. (R.E. Teacher in Grammar/Technical School for Girls.)

One does seek to work towards a personal faith in God. One's aim is to try to get children to understand that there is a definite purpose in life and is best understood in an understanding about God. (Religious Education Teacher in Boys' Grammar School.)

To confront children with Jesus Christ in every circumstance of life. (Headmistress of a Girls' Grammar School.)

To show the Christian faith as a living faith and relevant to the child's personal needs and problems. (R.E. Teachers in Secondary Modern School.) (Busia, 1966, p. 74.)

It is obviously important to bear in mind the relevance of Sunday School teaching to that of religious education in day-schools. I, therefore, asked in the questionnaire: "Do you agree with

Religious Education being compulsory in Day-Schools?" Results showed:

RELIGIOUS EDUCATION COMPULSORY

	No.	Per cent.
Yes	49	68
No	12	16.6
Don't know	2	2.7
No answer	9	12.5

Some were enthusiastically in favour of compulsory teaching, while others felt that the conscience of parents should be recognised, and that it was the work of the Sunday Schools to convey religious instruction. Religious education was, on the whole, looked upon as an essential part of training for a child to face life. The answers given to my sample selection were those given by a cross-section of an industrial valley in South Wales, some of whom were not convinced Christians:

"Because some parents have no time for religion, or have not been brought up in religious homes. Their children are lacking in religious instruction" (Mountain Ash housewife).

"The only place where some children learn about religion" (Mountain Ash housewife).

"It puts a lot of children off religion" (Abercynon Civil Servant).

"I think it is necessary" (Barclays Bank employee).

"Freedom of choice should be allowed to parents" (Abercynon youth).

"I think that youngsters should be taught" (Barclays Bank employee).

"Many children wouldn't have any religious education otherwise" (Barclays Bank employee).

"Because it is a very interesting subject and helps with history as well" (Barclays Bank employee).

"Schools should concentrate on academic education" (18-year-old youth).

These opinions can be placed side by side with Alisdair MacIntyre's remarks: "It is just not true that children in this country are indoctrinated in Christianity as a result of the 1944 Education Act. What they are indoctrinated in is confusion. This confusion is rooted in the fact that on one hand religious instruction is compulsory and yet, on the other, it is clear that the schools do not take it seriously in the way that they do basic literature or subjects such as history or chemistry" (Barton, 1966, p. 88).

An example is given by Dr. Busia of a senior pupil in the Birmingham area taking religious education at 'A' level, who, though he intended to become a specialist teacher in the subject, considered it, nevertheless, unnecessary to belong to a church. His job, as he saw it, was to know religious education as an academic subject. School scripture lessons were different from Sunday School lessons in that the former could be given by teachers who were not convinced Christians; on the other hand, Sunday School teachers, even if they were not trained, had religious faith. One of the teachers, according to Dr. Busia, puts it : " The teachers of religious education in schools left out the grace of God " (Busia, 1966, p. 74). They treated the agreed syllabus solely as an academic subject; and I came across a number of teachers who felt this way in the Aberdare Valley. There were some who felt, like a Barclays Bank clerk, that religious education in schools could assist the work of the churches. She says: " In brief — gives a background to church ", but a colleague of hers felt that " pupils should be allowed to refuse ".

" It's the only place where young people are compelled to attend. Most children do not attend Sunday Schools " (Hirwaun miner). " As it is the only place that some hear of it " (Hirwaun adult).

" Because it will make them better citizens " (Hirwaun miner).

" Sunday School should do this " (Hirwaun miner).

" What good is any education to you unless basically religious " (Darrenlas retired miner).

" At choice of parents " (Mountain Ash miner).

" Because it's all part of their education " (Penrhiwceibr miner); " gives a smattering of religious knowledge " (Hirwaun schoolteacher).

" Benefit to all " (Penrhiwceibr miner).

" Necessary for a basic knowledge for juniors " (Retired Co-operative Department Manager).

" Sound grounding for adulthood " (Hirwaun youth).

" Otherwise some children would never hear the gospel " (Abercynon housewife).

" So as the pupils know what the meaning of Church of Christ is all about " (C.W.S. Creamery, Trecynon, Laboratory Assistant). This opinion is borne out by the discussion referred to by Dr. Busia which took place in 1963 under the auspices of South and Mid Brookton Council of Churches, that the young needed Christ. " They needed to be born again. They needed to see the relevance of Christ for today. Without this experience, nothing the teachers tried to teach would ' get over ' to the young people " (Busia, 1966, p. 74).

The Sunday Schools in the Aberdare Valley cannot still be ignored, but their place today is not so important in people's lives as before the Second World War. Hilda Jennings, in her study of Brynmawr, a town not very far from the Aberdare Valley, mentions a census taken by the Sunday School Union which took place on a particular Sunday in 1882, when it was found that nearly three-fifths of the total population of all ages attended Sunday Schools (Jennings, 1934, p. 122). Her observation on the importance of the Sunday School cannot be underestimated :

" Probably more important and far-reaching in influence than any of the Day Schools were the Sunday Schools, which were open to all irrespective of age and creed, and which, throughout Wales, attracted adult workers in large numbers " (Jennings, 1934, p. 125).

The Sunday School constituted a major working class institution in the Aberdare Valley till around the Second World War, and a source of an indefinable and persuasive influence upon the people at large, as we have seen from the comments of those who answered our questionnaire. Many other agencies sprang from the Sunday School movement, an army of Sunday School teachers and district visitors, and, later, on, the adult classes, Bands of Hope, Libraries, Penny Banks, week-night classes.

All these activities have also declined. It is difficult to find Sunday School teachers who are willing to prepare for the class, and the district visitors have disappeared altogether. Adult classes are never held, and the work has been taken over by the education authority in the Adult Education Centres in Abercynon, Mountain

Ash and Aberdare, and many of the classes, such as Comparative Religion and Conversational Welsh, attract clientele that would in the hey-day of the Sunday School Movement be found in the Sunday School Adult Class.

The decline of the Sunday Schools is distressing, and can be attributed to a number of reasons. Many adolescents tend to leave Sunday Schools because one of their friends stopped going, or because they had started work. We asked the question " Why did you stop going to Sunday School? " and only 16 answered out of 72, a 22% response. The main reason was that of age, as children and young people are very conscious of this, and many children between the ages of 12 and 14 drop out of Sunday School and give up going to Church. Do the leaders of the Churches fail them? Is the quality of example sufficiently convincing?

Great mobility afforded by modern transport has undoubtedly had its effect. The motor car enables the worker to get out and about at the weekend, the only free time he has. Other distractions from the Sunday School have come with the development of the gramophone, radio, cinema and, more recently, addiction to television. All this has weakened the Sunday School, but its influence in the past must be taken into consideration, as E. R. Wickham points out :

" Wherever the Sunday Schools were at work, young people were being brought under a civilizing influence, and where so many young people were touched at some time or other, the influence upon them and their adult attitudes, though impossible to calculate, should not be ignored " (Wickham, 1962, p. 155).

What happened? The opinion of one sociologist of religion, who carried out extensive research in the Sheffield area, has relevance to the Aberdare Valley with regard to the failure of the Chapels and Churches to win the allegiance of their Sunday School members:

" In fact, the turnover in the schools was high, and proves the strong pull of the world, and the failure of the Churches to integrate their scholars into the adult congregations " (Wickham, 1962, p. 155).

The other characteristic religious institution in Nonconformity is the *Seiat,* a group meeting for devotional purposes at a fixed centre. All the Nonconformist Chapels have a similar meeting, the

Baptists and the Welsh Congregationalists call it *Y Gyfeillach* and not the *Seiat,* as do the Presbyterian Church of Wales and the Wesleyan Methodists. In the nineteenth and the early part of the twentieth centuries it became the place where adherents expressed their deepest spiritual experiences, where children could be christened, where others were expelled for unorthodox behaviour, drunkenness or having an illegitimate child. I remember in the village in which I was brought up in Cardiganshire regularly attending the *Seiat,* and being one of a dozen children reciting verses. David Jenkins mentions the same situation in Aberporth, which is in the same county: " Even as recently as some fifteen years ago, twenty to thirty children under fourteen years of age attended the weekly *seiat* at the Methodist Chapel and there had ideas held out and ideals held up to them which, if not necessarily lived up to, were yet impossible to forget. Today, only two or three children attend (Jenkins, 1960, p. 20). David Jenkins mentions the coming of the cinema as one reason why they do not attend. During my stay in the Aberdare Valley, and attending *seiadau* in the Presbyterian Churches (1962-1968), I never remember hearing a child say a verse, or even seeing a child in the *Seiat.*

The original purpose of the " societies ", according to William Williams of Pantycelyn, was to maintain the " warmth " and " life " which existed in their members, to unravel and present for all to see the wiles with which Satan hoped to trap the simple believer. In such " societies " each member could be the watch and ward of every other member's life and behaviour; it was necessary that people should form a " society " that each might observe and admonish the other. Members were to help to bear each other's burdens, and in the " societies " they could describe their spiritual states and experiences to one another; each member was to be the means by which each of the others was strengthened to withstand his temptations.

Each " society " was to have a questioner who questioned members, and the " society " is still, as a general rule, conducted by the minister. The questioner was to be frank with the people, reminding them of the moral standards, and strengthening them in the " faith ". Each " society " was to be sub-divided into " bands " of single men, married men, single women, married women, and each "band" being questioned apart. The other members heard the frank "confessions" and sympathised with the failings. Everyone was a sinner, and he had to prove it to his fellow members. But it was emphasised also that they were different from the worldly people outside: they were a community of believers.

The *Seiat* has changed its approach and method, and it is seldom heard today of a member giving his religious experience. The *Seiat* usually is conducted in two ways: The Minister or an Elder asking for a verse or a hymn and commenting on them, or, alternatively, inviting one of the members to read a paper on a specific topic. An example of this method can be seen from the Reports of Tabernacle Presbyterian Church of Wales, Abercynon, for 1967/68 and 1969/70.

1967   *Topic*

March 7 : Introduction to the Book of Jeremiah.
      21 : Meditation on the Cross and Resurrection.

April 5 : Call of Jeremiah (Chapter 1).
    19 : Unfaithfulness of Judea (Chapter 2).

May 2 : Call of God on Israel and Judah (Chapter 4).
    9 : Meditation on Whitsun.
   23 : " Praise the Lord."

June 6 : The Judgement of God on the Jews (Chapter 5).
    20 : The Sermon of the Temple (Chapters 7, 1-8; 8, 4-22).

July 4 : A Cry and Lamentation (Chapter 9).
   11 : God's Greatness over Idols (Chapter 10).

Sept. 19 : Condemning the Unfaithfulness of the People (Chapter 11).
    26 : The Problem of the Sinful (Chapter 16).

Oct. 3 : God and the Prophet (Chapter 16).
   17 : The Potter (18 : 1-10).
   31 : Captivity to Babylon (24 : 1-10, 25 : 1-19).

Nov. 14 : Burning the Book and Re-writing it (36 : 20-32).
   28 : Ebedmelech (38 : 1-13, 39 : 31-34).

Dec. 6 : The Last Years of Jeremiah (42 : 1-18, 43 : 1-7).
   20 : Meditation on Christmas.

1968

Jan. 23 : The Philistines and Moabites (47-51).

The Scripture Syllabus for the Adult Classes of the Sunday Schools in Wales for that year was the Book of Jeremiah, and this was the reason for having so many of the topics from the Old Testament. The pattern was followed in the same Church for *Seiat* in 1969-70, even though the Church was without a minister.

1969 *Topics for 1969/70*

March 25 : Introduction to the Book of Revelation.
April 1 : Hymn of Easter and Resurrection.
      29 : The Beginning and Greatness of Revelation (Chapter 1 : 1-11).
May   6 : Sermons of the Festival.
      20 : Message to the Churches of Ephesus and Smyrna (2 : 1-17).
June   3 : Message to the Churches of Sardis and Laodicea.
July 15 : Opening the Book (5 : 1-14).
      22 : Hymn 341.
Sept. 9 : The Saints sealed (7 : 9-17).
      30 : The Book of Praise of the Hebrew.
Oct. 14 : The Fall of Babylon (18 : 9-24).
Nov. 18 : Wedding of the Lamb (19 : 7-9).
Dec. 16 : The Carols of Christmas.

1970

Jan. 20 : A New Heaven and a New Earth (21 : 1-8).
Feb. 20 : The Heavenly Jerusalem (21 : 21-27).

The same pattern appears in both, though the number varies. There were 21 in the 1967/68 session, while the number was 15 in the second. This can be explained by the fact that five who took part in 1967/68 had left Abercynon; another two were semi-invalids; and another two had not been asked or had refused to undertake the work. It should be said also that there were two in the 1969/70 list who were not asked to take part in the 1967/68 session of week-night *seiadau*.

One of the most successful of the religious institutions of Nonconformity in the Aberdare Valley is the Sisterhood. These are equally made up of a good cross-section of the congregation, and include young mothers as well as older members. Sometimes members come to the Sisterhood who never come to a religious service, and may even not belong to the chapel. The members can be often difficult to manage, and the leader — usually called the President — has to be a good handler and a diplomat so as to win the allegiance of the dissident member as well as the more sophisticated ladies of the congregation.

There are two functions to the majority of Sisterhoods in existence in the Aberdare Valley — one is to have fellowship, the other is the more exacting task of raising money for the chapel funds. The efforts of the Sisterhood often determine the financial situation of a chapel at the end of the year, and it is often said in a *Seiat* by an elder that this particular or that particular chapel could never exist without the work of the Sisterhood in raising money, for the contributions from the members are not enough to safeguard the future of the church, and to be able to meet the essential commitments of heating the building and paying for the services of the visiting preachers, to pay the different contributions asked for by Presbyteries or the Assemblies, and to be able to give to the annual appeals from charitable organisations.

The Sisterhoods usually consist of up to 20 to 24 members. These include a president, a chairman, a treasurer and a secretary. Funds are collected by contributions at weekly meetings, an annual Sale of Work, 'Bring and Buy' (members only), and the sale of Christmas cards and gifts. The aim is to raise up to at least £100 each year for presentation to the church.

The Presbyterian Sisterhoods at Abercynon and Penrhiwceibr are mainly a working session and have a speaker only occasionally, but those at Mountain Ash and Aberdare, and the Congregationalists and the Baptists in Abercynon, have a speaker at every meeting.

After the introductory part, the president welcomes the speaker and introduces the subject. Then the speaker, usually a minister of a neighbouring church or a local personality, doctor, councillor or social worker, is invited to address the meeting for 20 to 25 minutes. After his address, the secretary is called upon to deliver the announcements for the following week, and one of the officials or one of the members is called upon to propose a vote of thanks to the speaker. The meeting is then left open for informal discussion, while a few of the ladies bring around cups of tea with biscuits. The president usually announces the last hymn, and the blessing is pronounced by the speaker or the president. At some of the Sisterhoods there is a slight modification of the pattern. The meeting is closed before the tea is served so as to allow anyone who cannot stay for tea to go home. The Sisterhood provides recreational activities as well as fellowship for its members.

The Sunday School, the *Seiat* and the Sisterhood are in the main religious institutions of Nonconformist chapels, but there are other important meetings or services held, namely, Baptisms, Weddings and Funerals.

Christening or Infant Baptism is practised within the denominations in the Aberdare Valley. The Anglican Church, the Wesleyan Methodists, the Congregationalists, the Presbyterians all practise this method of initiation into church life; the one exception being the Baptists, who believe in and practise adult baptism. There is quite a difference, for baptism in the Baptist Church is the way also of becoming a fully-fledged member of the congregation, while in the other Nonconformist churches the infant baptism is an opportunity for parents to make vows of faithfulness and for the church to adopt the child into its care. To become a member means confirmation, and a training of a few weeks or months is provided by the Vicar or Minister for the interested candidates. Baptism is regarded as one of the two sacraments (Communion being the other).

It is well to look at the teachings of a theologian like John Calvin on Baptism, and it is he, above all, who has inspired the Calvinistic Methodists in Wales, and influenced many of the other denominations as far as their original theological teaching is concerned. Like Luther, Calvin draws attention to the religious content of the sacrament of initiation. Baptism appears to Calvin first of all as the sign of the remission of sins (Wendel, 1965, pp. 310-328). Its second religious significance resides in the fact that it " shows us our mortification in Jesus Christ, and also our new life in Him ". The third benefit that baptism confers upon our faith is that " we are so united with Christ that He makes us sharers in all His goods ". Calvin, however, cannot adduce a single New Testament passage containing a clear allusion to infant baptism; he had to be content with indirect inferences and analogies drawn from circumcision and Christ's blessing of the children. The Baptists made direct allusions, on the other hand, to the Scriptures for their practice. It is of interest to note that in many of the English Baptist Churches in the Aberdare Valley they did hold a consecration service in view of the demand of the parents who belonged to those churches.

The practice in Presbyterian Churches is to have the Christening Service at the end of the morning or as part of the morning service. In special cases, the service is sometimes held at the end of a Sunday School, or during the week-night meeting. Examples are sometimes cited, especially in the past, in which the service was held at the home. The Anglican Churches in Abercynon and Penrhiwceibr in the years 1962-1968 always held their Infant Baptism Services in the afternoon, when the parents, god-parents and a few friends would attend. It is becoming more popular in Nonconformist Churches to have god-parents, and this is following the Anglican pattern.

It is argued that many of those who insist on having god-parents are often people who have loose attachment to the Church. The Presbyterians and other Nonconformist denominations who hold the baptism during the morning service have the congregation present as well.

With regard to marriages, weddings in churches are still held regularly in the Aberdare Valley, though it is heard of many getting married in the Registry Office at Pontypridd. In the Anglican Church, marriages have fallen from 698 per thousand in 1899 to 474 in 1962, compared with rises in Roman Catholic and civil ceremonies, which, in 1962, stood at 123 and 296 per thousand respectively. (Martin, 1967, p. 32.)

The real problem associated with marriages for religious denominations is that of mixed marriages. Trefor M. Owen describes how this problem was tackled in Glanllyn, Merioneth, and other parts of North Wales by investing the congregation, through its officers, with a certain amount of authority over the individual's choice of spouse (Owen, 1960, pp. 227-229). An instance is given of Robert William, Wern Ddu, who was pastor of Llanuwchllyn's Methodist Church during the middle of the nineteenth century: " He kept strictly to every rule and excommunicated people from the society for marrying persons from the world exactly as if they had broken one of the Ten Commandments." The procedure which came to be generally adopted, and which prevails in Merioneth and the Aberdare Valley, is that when two persons of different religious persuasion marry, the wife in most cases changes to her husband's denomination. Trefor Owen gives a table to show the extent:

CHANGE OF DENOMINATION ON MARRIAGE

Sample: 233 marriages between persons living in Glan-llyn.

Husband and wife of same denomination	113
Husband changed denomination	26
Wife changed denomination	80
Others	14
Total	233

This does not work in the same way in an industrial valley, though, generally speaking, it does happen.

A change has also occurred with regard to marriages inside the community of the chapel. Trefor Owen cites examples of this: Nearly half of the marriages are between members of the same religious connection. This does not happen often in the Aberdare Valley, at least among the Presbyterians, whom I had an opportunity of knowing.

"It was during a Carol Service at Tabernacle, and afterwards going around Abercynon singing, that I met my late husband" (a 56-year-old Abercynon widow). This aspect is less important today in rural Wales as well as the industrial mining areas when secular opportunities and entertainments for social intercourse at whist drives, plays and *nosweithiau llawen* have grown in importance.

Marriage involves the whole family, and it is expected also, if the bride is a member of the church, for a few of the faithful (those who have not been invited to the wedding) to turn up to support and to give their best wishes. The reception can be held in the chapel vestry or in the local hotel, and then the young couple go off to a honeymoon when the reception is over.[2]

With regard to funerals, there is a world of difference between the customs carried out in rural areas, such as in West Wales, and in urban areas like the Aberdare Valley. Most of the funerals in the Aberdare Valley — at the crematorium or the cemetery — are gentlemen only, while in the country both men and women attend. In the Aberdare Valley only the close family, a few friends, minister and one or two others go back for a meal to the house after the funeral; in Tregaron the large majority are expected, and invited publicly by the minister on behalf of the family, to partake of the meal provided for them in the chapel vestry. The social aspect of the funeral is emphasised by the sometimes lavish preparations made to feed the guests, both relations and friends. The "exiles" are often buried at Tregaron, as Emrys Jones puts it: "The death of one of these — perhaps a Londoner — is often mourned as a loss to this community, for he never ceased to be a member of it" (Jones, 1960, p. 95). The "exiles" very rarely come back to be buried in the Aberdare Valley, for it is often the case of Aberdare people, who were born in the country, going back to be buried there. It is noticeable also that after the funeral, in the home or the chapel vestry, the conversation is about everything rather than the one who has passed away. It is a kind of safety-valve, a relief from the sombreness of the occasion. Very few Nonconformists have services in chapels in the Aberdare Valley as they do in Cardiganshire, where a minister is expected to deliver an address and a tribute.

These two different procedures are identical in pattern. The service at the home in the Aberdare Valley is very much like the one in the Tregaron area. Therefore the Nonconformist and Anglican funerals do differ from a Catholic funeral, especially in the past more so than today. Joseph Keating, a Mountain Ash Irishman, has described a Wake that was held at the end of the

---

[1] For a description of a working class reception, see Michael Young and Peter Willmott, *Family and Kinship in East London*, 1962, pp. 62-63. "The thirty-two guests squeezed down at the cramped tables for the wedding breakfast of ham and tongue, salad and pickles, trifle and jelly, washed down with ale and Guinness."

last century in the town after his grandmother's death. The description is valuable as an example of the difference that used to exist between a Welsh and an Irish funeral in the Aberdare Valley. Keating says: "When an Irish Catholic died in *The Barracks* — either a natural death at home or a violent death in the mines — all who could attended the Wake. Our kitchen was crowded with men and women, young and old, till three o'clock in the morning. Two lighted candles were at my grandmother's head and another at her feet. On a table near her were saucers of red snuff and tobacco, and a dozen long and short clay pipes. We played Cock-in-the-Corner, Hunt the Button, and told or listened to tales of leprechauns, giants, and old hags — wonderful stories that had never been written or printed . . . The tales enthralled me. A few of the old people, on coming in, would kneel beside the corpse. As soon as their prayers were finished, they joined heartily in the game.

We talked of everything except the dead. Good humour, humanity and religion were mixed together, and the Wakes brought relief and consolation to sorrow" (Keating, 1916, pp. 59-60). The Wake was not practised among the Irish community in the 1960s, though it lingered in their desire for a drink after the funeral. Coming from a funeral one afternoon, two of the dead woman's brothers asked to be dropped at the Navigation Hotel, Abercynon, so that "they could have a few drinks". On hearing what happened, a few of the friends who were gathered at the home referred to them as "they're proper Irish".

In the Aberdare Valley the corpses are not always kept at the home, but are often kept at the funeral directors' chapels. A Presbyterian Chapel at Abercynon, which was closed in 1966, has been bought by a local undertaker for use as a funeral chapel. This is to be compared with the place given in Tregaron to the parlour. "The parlour is, in fact, something of a shrine, which comes into its own on these family occasions, but especially so when someone dies, for here the corpse rests before the funeral" (Jones, 1960, p. 95).

This can be compared with the use of the parlour in the West of Ireland (Arensberg, 1937, p. 29). Emrys Jones adds: "Thus important steps in the life cycle of the individuals of a family are commemorated here (parlour) — birth, marriage and death. It is at these points in the cycle that the kindred come together and family unity is reaffirmed " (Jones, 1960, p. 95).

It was natural, then, that I asked in my questionnaire the question: In the past six months, which of the following Chapel/ Church services have you attended?

1. Sunday morning	38	i.e.,	52.7%
2. Sunday evening	42		58.3%
3. Sunday afternoon	11		15.2%
4. Christening/Baptism	16		22.2%
5. Weddings	24		33.3%
6. Funerals	24		33.3%
7. Sisterhood	26		36.1%
8. *Seiat*	6		8.3%
9. Prayer Meeting	13		18.05%

The answers, except for the first two, are the usual pattern. It is important that we remember a number of factors in our percentage of Sunday morning and Sunday evening attendances. The main point is that the question gave a span of six months during which the people could have attended. It is not for us to know if there were any important meetings in that period, services which usually attract large congregations, such as Civic Sundays, St. John Ambulance Brigade Sunday, Television or Radio Service from a particular church, a Children's Service or a Sisterhood Service, Preaching Sunday or one of the Festivals. Many of the questionnaires were filled in at the beginning of a year, after Christmas and the New Year Services. Christmas Morning Service, Christmas Eve, and the service on New Year's Eve are usually popular services in the Aberdare Valley, and people returning from parties and dances often turn into the Anglican and Nonconformist Churches. It cannot be denied that a good number of the respondents were devout and sincere Christians, who would feel it their duty to attend services on a Sunday.

There are certain other points that can be made as to the high percentage of those attending Sunday morning and Sunday evening services. From experience of being a minister at two Nonconformist Churches in the Aberdare Valley, it was evident that a large number of people attended both morning and evening services. This was the pattern of Sunday observance, as so many famous people in Wales testify. A good example from the Aberdare Valley would be the Davies family of Blaengwawr in the nineteenth century. In the book written on the third son of Mr. David Davies of Blaengwawr, namely, Lewis Davies, who was born at Hirwaun in 1829, it is said of him :

" From childhood the Sunday School, the services at the Wesleyan Chapel at Hirwaun, the preachers who were regularly welcomed to his home, the choir and those who took any public part in the services, to him were of paramount importance " (Young, 1905, p. 34). It was the custom in those days to attend all the services, and this still remains with many of the older members of the Nonconformist Churches. The only service which is not so well attended by the older members is the Sunday School, as the figure 15.2% shows. The Nonconformist Sunday Schools in the Aberdare Valley tend in the last decade to become more like the English Sunday Schools — children attending and the adults staying at home. The answers given by people in the Aberdare Valley indicate that a number of people leave the Sunday School in adolescence. A miner from Hirwaun stopped because " the other boys in the same class stopped going to school," and a Mountain Ash housewife stopped going for there was no " Sunday School class ". This is often a problem in Nonconformist Chapels in the Aberdare Valley, of grouping a number of children of different ages in one class. A young Abercynon Civil Servant maintains that she stopped going from " lack of direction on the part of the teachers," and a Barclays Bank employee because it was " too boring ". One or two mentioned that leaving school does have a bearing upon Sunday School attendance, as a Barclays Bank employee puts it, " because I started work ". It is obvious that in my study the attendance of twice Sunday has affected the returns. Alwyn D. Rees has observed that the ideal pattern for a Nonconformist is attendance three times a Sunday, a pattern which was strictly followed at one time, and which the older people still remember, and a pattern that is recognised as the right one, although the " gap " between it and practice continues to widen. (Rees, 1951, p. 128.) Several people, when questioned at Llanfihangel by Alwyn D. Rees about week-night meetings at their chapels, said that, regrettably, there had been none for several years, *fel y mwyaf o gywilydd inni* (the more shame to us). (Rees, 1951, p. 120.) The constant use of the word 'decline' needs to be carefully used in this study of the religious practices with the assertion: At any rate, the important and massive fact remains that in spite of the incentive to spend time in an alternative manner one-quarter of the population is in church at least once a month. And even if one allows for some tendency to exaggerate attendance on the part of those interrogated, that exaggeration is in itself significant. This is the picture we receive from the returns of our questionnaire among a cross-section of the population of the Aberdare Valley.

But the picture does not go far enough for my purpose, for what is "the image" of Nonconformity in the Aberdare Valley to members of the Churches and to others outside? Does the community feel that Nonconformity is an organisation that is worth belonging to, dynamic, or rather is it the picture painted recently by two ministers: "The dominant concern of the small flock is how to keep the place going, how to raise money, how to get more in. The talk is about amalgamations and how to resist them, of union, of the perplexing way in which the neighbourhood could not now care less what happens to the Chapel" (Jones & Wesson, 1970, p. 9).

I asked the question:

Do you regard Nonconformity as unattractive?

Seventeen people wrote an answer out of 72 people, and these are formulated as follows:

A 48-year-old Mountain Ash housewife was very cautious and replied: "If presented properly it isn't — but the way it is presented to them is unattractive." This was the opinion of others:

"There are other entertainments which are more attractive" (an 18-year-old person).

"It does not give way to the modern man. It dwells too much on the old tradition of 50-70 years ago, which is not modern in any way."

These answers are vague, and also the expected ones. It is well to remember, as R. H. Thompson warns: "although any discussion of remedies for the ineffectiveness of the Church of England usually turns quickly to suggestions for brighter services, more cheering and singable hymns, more homely sermons, warmer and more comfortable churches and so on, very little attention can be paid to these factors in this study" (Thompson, 1957, p. 10). He goes on to say that they are not unimportant reasons, as, indeed, the people who answered my questionnaire obviously show. The majority of those who answered my question would not agree with R. H. Thompson's viewpoint; nor do I as the one who formulated the questionnaire. I would not for one moment think that it is a new standpoint, as the quotation in Thompson's study from C. F. G. Masterman's "The Problem of South London" in R. Mudie-Smith (Editor), *The Religious Life of London* (London : Hodder and Stoughton, 1904, p. 210) shows : " All this would be very relevant if we could recognise large populations with real desire after religious devotion on the one hand, and a Church with a living message which can satisfy their desire on the other. The whole problem would then exhibit itself as a consideration of the method by which the one can be most effectively brought into contact with the other. But the conditions are just the opposite. On the one hand we have masses for whom the spiritual world has no meaning, and from whose lives the very fundamental bedrock effects of religion seem to have vanished; on the other we have Churches whose faith has grown cold, and whose good news sounds far removed from anything approaching the passionate enthusiasm of other Christian centuries. Were this indeed present, the problem of machinery would soon be solved. Preachers would be speaking with a conviction itself eloquent; the services would take on themselves a character of infectious courage; the people would themselves build, as always in the past, edifices reflecting in the very stones the characteristics of their faith; religion would impetuously flood out from their limited spaces into the common ways of men. And until such a wind of the spirit can animate the dry bones of religious organisation with some violent life, all conscious modifications of machinery become but attempts at creating the soul by the body, the artificial galvanising from without of an organism from which the inner life has fled." The comment is rightly made that " religion has flourished in the past despite draughts, dull sermons, and Hymns Ancient and Modern "

(Thompson, 1957, p. 13). A Hirwaun youth comments that there are in Nonconformity " too many old ideas — new ideas must be introduced to revive the interest in Church life ". In later adolescence this is a battle song — " new ideas must be introduced " — and is often referred to as the " generation gap ". It is usual for adolescents, as we have seen in the comment, to accuse their elders of hypocrisy. The Nonconformist elders and leaders often do not help, and contribute to this concept. Personal examples could be quoted at length. A few will suffice — of Nonconformist elders arguing at length over the application to rent part of their premises to a youth organisation; complaints over the behaviour of the young, that they only expect to receive and not to give. Nonconformist chapels, if their " image " is to be recast, will have to develop a sense of identity with youth based upon affection, interest, sympathy and experience. At present, as these comments show, each side exaggerates the differences to justify its own attacks. More contact, as a miner from the Lower Colliery, Hirwaun, says, are needed : " The Church should go more to the youth of today ". A Barclays Bank employee believes that the question is right " to a limited extent; and that youth is not sufficiently encouraged ".

The role of youth in Nonconformity cannot be exaggerated, in view of the answers received. A C.W.S. Creamery, Trecynon, Aberdare, Laboratory Assistant says that Nonconformity is unattractive because " it does not give way to the modern man, and is not modern in any way ". The adolescent to this Laboratory Assistant is the most sensitive indicator of defects in the religious organisations that we are studying. A young teacher adds that the reason is " failure to keep with modern trends of living ", which is an example of indicating the existence of a particular problem in a vague way, and without knowing what should be done about it. Appropriate action is the province of experienced adults; and yet the adults who answered this questionnaire had no plan of action. It was defeatism, as a Darranlas, Mountain Ash, retired miner maintains : " In general all religions are slowly fading out, otherwise how do we find that chapels are being turned into garages and, on the credit side, Ambulance Halls? " This defeatism was found also among the young people : " Modern man is in too much of a hurry to stop and think about much to realise what is wrong and right in the world" (17-year-old Barclays Bank employee). Though another colleague — 21 years of age — asserts that "modern man is a nonconformist," and thus implying, as Christopher Driver does, that the Free Churches or Nonconformity have a splendid opportunity. Driver argues that people of radical temper grope after a Nonconformist ethic — which is Puritanism — and he believes that only the Free Churches can unloose it (Driver, 1962, pp. 67-68).

A young Civil Servant from Abercynon echoes Driver's use of John Robinson's words as he took leave of the Pilgrim Fathers at Leyden in 1620, " I beseech you, remember, 'tis an Article of your Church Covenant, that you be ready to receive whatever Truth shall be made known to you from the Written Word of God . . . " when she says that "its appeal (Nonconformity) to Man now is still the same as it was" (Driver, 1962, p. 68). Driver adds to Robinson's quotation, "Little though there may be left of the pilgrim mentality in the chapels today, the words are there and cannot be forgotten. They do not provide Dissent with a special objective of its own : the vision of a social order permeated with Christian values is no longer, if it ever was, ours alone. The routes to the objective are a different matter, and only Dissent is under quite this constitutional obligation to search out new routes, and when it is brought to a standstill — 'a period in religion' — to fan out and infiltrate new territories of human experience. Puritanism in all its aspects — ancient and modern, sacred and secular — leads straight on to what Tillich calls 'the courage to be'" (Driver, 1962, p. 68). If this is the case, then Nonconformity will have to listen to a Hirwaun miner that "not enough effort is being made to attract"; and deal with people like the Penrhiwceibr miner, who does not see anything radically unattractive in Nonconformity, but who believes that religion is something personal, and has not anything to say to him : " I don't say Nonconformity is unattractive. I don't believe in religion, but every man should please himself."

I asked also the question " Do you regard Nonconformist chapels as old-fashioned? "

Twenty people answered the question out of a possible 72, giving 27%. The answers may be divided into two categories. Firstly, the defenders of the Nonconformist Chapels. Nonconformist Chapels are often criticised on architecture grounds, that they are plain and without any beauty. T. Rowland Hughes, the Welsh novelist and poet, has defended them on the grounds that it was in these Bethels, Seions and Caersalems that the Welsh people have their past, the inspiration for the future:

> " O'r blychau hyn daeth
> ennaint ein doe a'n hechdoe ni;
> Os llwm, os trwsgwl eu trem,
> Caersalem, Seion, Soar a Bethlehem."

A young Aberdare Barclays Bank employee, for example, feels that the "point is greatly emphasised in the decline of the chapels"; and an 18-year-old Abercynon youth that "my experience is that they are as modern as any organisation". They are in the minority.

Secondly, we have the critics of the Nonconformist Chapels, and it can be said that the majority of the respondents to my questionnaire were unhappy with the present set-up of organised Nonconformity. There are three criticisms: (1) That they do not go out to the young people; (2) that they do not adopt the modern style; (3) the buildings are unsuitable.

Taking the first criticism, two miners from Hirwaun, both middle-aged, claim that Nonconformity "is not catering for youth" and "youth should be catered for far more". The second opinion is a more balanced one, as the following remarks demonstrate.

"Reluctance to inject new methods of teaching to the younger members" (18-year-old Hirwaun youth).

"The majority of chapels are not willing for change and will not move with the times. They are too narrow-minded" (a person who had lived 25 years in the Aberdare Valley).

"Trying to run affairs of today with yesterday's ideas" (a Godreaman schoolteacher who had lived at Hirwaun for 23 years).

"Because they hold mainly to the old tradition" (a Hirwaun miner who had lived there all his life).

"They don't move with the modern times" (an Abercynon old-age pensioner who had lived there for 72 years).

"Things are not like they used to be" (a young 17-year-old Barclays Bank, Aberdare, employee).

"But they may present an image of living in the past" (Mountain Ash housewife who had lived there for 52 years).

"Again they dwell on the old tradition of fifty years ago, when they want to develop a modern setting built for the modern times of today" (C.W.S. Creamery, Trecynon, Aberdare, Laboratory Assistant).

Then the third complaint, which is one that a minister or an elder of the church often hears voiced by his members or parishioners for the lack of appeal. Usually the chapels, with their hard seats, are compared with the facilities provided by the clubs and cinemas, and this feeling was expressed by four of the respondents to the questionnaire :

"They were all right when people needed to be uncomfortable to listen. Nowadays they need comfort to listen and argue objectively" (an 18-year-old).

"Empty galleries could be done away with and the seating downstairs improved (65-year-old retired Mountain Ash miner).

This comment is an interesting one, for the majority of the Nonconformist chapels in the Aberdare Valley have galleries, which, according to observation from 1962 to 1968, were seldom used. The times in which there was need for the gallery was in a final rehearsal for the Cymanfa Ganu (Singing Festival); for the Singing Festival itself; a Concert; if the Television Authorities decided to televise a service or a singing service; or at the induction of a new minister, which in the sixties did not happen often.

A Presbyterian elder from Abercynon regarded the present Nonconformist buildings as being "much too big and draughty for present needs"; while a young Aberdare bank clerk maintains "that things are not like they used to be," and a housewife who had lived in the valley for only two years feels that there are not enough facilities.

A Mountain Ash housewife feels that "some of them" are old-fashioned; and a young Civil Servant, Ministry of Agriculture, feels that "I personally do not like 'pop' religion — I prefer chapels as they are". Only one protest against the Nonconformist's attitude over the Sunday opening of public houses, a Mountain Ash miner: "Their attitude on Sunday opening of licensed premises" which he regards as old-fashioned. Emil Brunner's dictum is interesting in view of the above answer:

"The Free Churches are forced to play for popularity; in their criticism of social conditions they dare not go to the last ditch; their mouth is stopped by consideration for the members who support them" (Brunner, 1947, p. 550).

This questioning of organisation is not the only questioning that is happening within the Christian Church, as a preacher puts it in one of the Pusey House Sermons:

"The Church, the University, the educational system and well-nigh everything else is being questioned and questioning itself. Nothing is to be taken for granted. So much is this so that many people come by sheer exhaustion and bewilderment to the conclusion that there can never be any agreed or reasonably assured answer to any question of importance" (Jenkins, 1965, p. 1).

Religious beliefs and moral principles have become subject to this trend of doubt and distrust. The Principal of the Bala-Bangor Theological College, Bangor, went so far as to state in a newspaper article that "the Nonconformist Churches were becoming nothing but humanitarian clubs" (Jones, Oswestry, p. 5).

This is an extravagant statement, for the majority of the Nonconformist chapels do have classes for communicants, when the opportunity arises, and where they are taught about the Christian doctrine and the implications of the doctrine, which is Christian Ethics.

Against this background, I asked the question "Do you believe in the doctrine of the Christian Church as embodied in the Creeds?"

	No.	Per cent.
Yes	42	58.3
No	8	11.1
Don't know	7	9.7
No answer	15	20.8

The "orthodox" had 58.3 per cent, while the "radicals", if it is fair to divide them into opposing camps, had only 11 per cent. There were 20.8 per cent who did not, for unknown reasons, answer the question.

But in the next question there is a change, as the table demonstrates. "Do you regard the idea of All-powerful Almighty God as being outdated?"

	No.	Per cent.
Yes	29	40.2
No	28	38.8
Don't know	4	5.5
No answer	11	15.2

This question, as A. E. Taylor, sometime Professor of Moral Philosophy, Edinburgh University, puts it, means that God is supreme over everything, or supreme everywhere (E. D. Wright, 1963, p. 31). It is doubtful if many of the respondents looked upon it in that way, but rather that God was dictating His will, a kind of Dictatorial God, which they could not believe in the twentieth century.

The question "Do you regard the narratives of the four Gospels as being essential to Christian beliefs?" had the following result:

	No.	Per cent.
Yes	42	58.3
No	4	5.5
Don't know	9	12.5
No answer	17	23.6

To the question "Who was Jesus Christ?" the following result was received:

	No.	Per cent.
1. A Good Man	16	22.2
2. Impostor	0	
3. Blasphemer	0	
4. Social Reformer	10	13.8
5. Son of God	55	76.3
6. No answer	10	13.8

The result shows that the orthodox view that Jesus Christ is the Son of God had a 76.3% response, while the more radical Unitarian view that Jesus was a good man had a 22.2% response. It is interesting to note, in this context, a survey conducted by Gallup Poll in Spring 1963 and reported in *A Sociological Year Book of Religion in Britain*, Volume 1. The question was with regard to Belief in Christ, and 59% of the respondents believed that Christ was the Son of God; $17\frac{1}{2}$% believed that he was just a man;

8% thought it was just a story; and 16% did not know what to think. In this survey, the respondents were divided into their denominational camps, and it was found that the Church of England and the Nonconformists had almost identical responses, while the Roman Catholics were more strictly orthodox. Women were found to be more orthodox than men and less likely to return " don't know " answers (Martin, 1968, p. 154).

I asked also in the questionnaire a question which people either ignore or which is taken as a natural course of events: " Do you believe in Life after Death? "

	No.	Per cent.
Yes	44	61.1
No	8	11.1
Don't know	11	15.2
No answer	9	12.5

In the survey discussed by Bernice Martin there was the following result: 53% of the respondents believed there was a life after death; 22% did not believe this; 25% did not know what to believe. My survey had a different result from most surveys, for there were 61.1% who believed in life after death, and only 11.1% who did not, though if we took those of no firm opinion with the " No's " we would have 28 out of 72, a 38.8%, who were not sure on this question. In many surveys, including the one mentioned in the *Sociological Year Book,* we find belief in immortality on the one hand and disbelief or no firm opinion on the other roughly divided in the population: 53% to 47%.

In the questions on Ethics two specific ones were asked, one on Divorce, the other on Christian Ethics: " Do you agree that the Church should refuse to marry a divorced person? "

	No.	Per cent.
Yes	10	13.8
No	35	48.6
Don't know	8	11.1
No answer	19	26.3

This response of 48.6% who do not agree that the Church should refuse to marry a divorced person is in line with the normal Nonconformist attitude towards the problem. Those who did not answer, a 26.3%, is also high. It is risky to try and compare the special survey of Roman Catholics in May 1965 on divorce, where it was found that the irregular church-goers favoured easier divorce more than did the regular church-goers, men more than women, and the lower more than the upper social classes (Martin, 1968, p. 171).

Christian Ethics is the framework from which the Christian tries to adapt his faith to the events of life. Church-going is not popular, and I felt that it would be appropriate to ask the respondents if they regarded the so-called virtues of the Christian faith as being relevant to modern days. The answer was thus: " Do you regard any of the following virtues of the Christian Ethic as being relevant to modern days? "

	No. (out of 72)	%
Pacifism	15	20.8
Love	43	59.7
Freedom	39	54.1
Good works	38	52.7

Pacifism is still regarded as inapplicable to the modern nuclear age, only 20.8% feeling that it was relevant. This result ties up with the way many a well-known pacifist in the Aberdare Valley was dealt with in the twentieth century. Rev. T. E. Nicholas, who fought in the 1918 General Election on a " pacifist " ticket, received rough treatment in his campaign. At Abercwmboi he was pelted with tomatoes. The late Emrys Hughes, M.P. for South Ayrshire, had the same treatment in his native town of Abercynon during the First World War. Rev. D. R. Thomas, M.A., Aberystwyth, who was minister of Bethania Presbyterian Church of Wales, Aberdare, during the Second World War (1939-45), was often snubbed because of his strong pacifist line. After denouncing one of Winston Churchill's most patriotic speeches one Sunday night as being " war-mongers' call ", a member of the church informed him: " Mae'r bregeth yna wedi golygu na chewch chwi godiad yn eich cyflog " (That sermon has meant that you will not have a rise in your salary). His wife was often embarrassed while shopping in Aberdare, when someone (often members of Churches) would say: " Aren't we lucky that our boys are fighting so that we can have food to eat? "

Love and Freedom are often loose terms which can mean different things to different people. The difference between love in the New Testament is revealing. We have three Greek words: *eros* (romantic), *philia* (friendship), and *agape* (the love of God), and there is a world of difference between the three concepts. Freedom can often mean different things to different people. To some it is freedom in political terms, to others freedom of speech, and to worship, and to live according to certain standards which are tolerated by the State. Good works are more meaningful to people; for it is doing certain actions, and carrying them out from day to day. Sympathy, kindness come into this category, and the people of Aberdare have always, like all the mining valleys of South Wales, been especially noted for their "togetherness". Good works would mean helping out the unfortunate neighbours, friends or members of the same family, and it does not seem to be the monopoly of Nonconformist Chapels more than the Social Clubs. It is part of the social life of a mining valley, and though it is regarded as one of the principles of the Christian religion, by today it is the way of life of the majority of the community.

The "crisis of faith" so often mentioned in the religious press does not seem to bother the vast majority of the respondents to my questionnaire. It seems that they are much more concerned with the decline and the crisis of religious institutions, and the break-down of communication between Chapels and Society, than in the break-down in religious beliefs.

This brings us to the social and industrial reasons for the decline of Welsh Nonconformity in the Aberdare Valley, which will be dealt with in Chapter 5. For it is one of the main purposes of religious sociology to study causes, and in Chapter 5 we will analyse the causes. However, we must beware of hasty generalisations, as M. le Bras said in 1931:

"The first quality required for understanding a state of affairs in religion is flexibility of judgement. There is a great variety of causes; one cannot be too careful nor too sensitive in discriminating them. Much more care is needed to explain figures than to collect them" (Boulard, 1960, p. 130).

5

THE DEVELOPMENT OF INDUSTRY

THE Cynon Valley population increased some fifteen-fold from 1750 to 1850. The number of houses in Aberdare in 1801 was 218, occupied by 224 families. There were one thousand people employed in agriculture, while only 70 persons were in trade, manufactures or handicrafts; there were also 416 people not employed in agriculture or in a trade. The total was 1,486, being made up of 831 males and 655 females. The parish of Llanwynno, which would comprise the lower reaches of the valley, and today forming part of the Mountain Ash Urban District, had only 104 houses, with the population totalling only 426. " The Hundred of Miskin" by 1821 had 1,548 houses, with 676 families agricultural labourers and 551 employed in trade, manufactures or handicrafts, with 408 in other occupations. The population was 4,352. By 1831 there were 6,393 people in the valley; in a decade it had risen to 9,322, and by 1851 had reached 18,774. It was this period that witnessed the opening up of the seam coal industry. Rapid industrialisation developed and it was in this era that Welsh Nonconformity attained its greatest influence. This chapter is an attempt to trace in outline the course of the industrialisation, and to show how population changes and industrial changes went hand in hand, and also how immigration brought in other factors which, in time, became problems in themselves.

In 1780 the Hirwaun Iron Works, hitherto a small-scale undertaking, was leased to Anthony Bacon of Cyfarthfa, Merthyr. Bacon had initiative and skill, and decided to manufacture heavy cannon for the American War. There was one snag; he was the Member of Parliament for Aylesbury, and so he was forbidden by law in the engagement of armaments. He overcame the difficulty by producing them in the name of his partner, Francis Homfray, and it was under the name of Homfray that the finished products were taken over rough bridle-paths by mules and pack-horses from

Hirwaun to the port of Cardiff (Parry, 1967, p. 194). Bacon expanded the industry with skill and initiative, so that when he died in 1786 he was one of the richest men in Britain. As his two sons, Anthony and Thomas, were too young, the Court of Chancery placed the Hirwaun works under the management of Samuel Glover of Abercarn. In 1799 Anthony and Thomas Bacon came of age, but they had no interest in the industrial enterprise. Anthony, having sold his share to his brother for £3,000, bought the Mathew estate lower down in the Aberdare Valley, and he retired to "the rural seclusion" of Aberaman. In 1802 Thomas Bacon sold his interest in the Hirwaun furnace to a company which included Jeremiah Homfray of Llandaff House.

The works manager of the new Company was George Overton, who is chiefly noted for his establishment of the first Company Shop in the Aberdare Valley (at Hirwaun in 1805), and for his provision of two cottages there for the joint use of the rapidly increasing Nonconformists.

The manufacture of iron at Hirwaun (the only centre for the whole of the valley) continued through the difficult Napoleonic era. It was not so booming as in the 1780s, though there were new improvements in communication. The Aberdare Canal was constructed in 1811 when the Glamorgan Canal (Merthyr-Cardiff, 1794) was extended from Navigation, as Abercynon was then called, up the Aberdare Valley. When peace came in 1815, there was a decline in the demand for iron, and Hirwaun suffered a severe slump. William Crawshay the second, the "Iron King" of Cyfarthfa, Merthyr, had no difficulty in 1818 in buying outright the entire interest from Bacon at Hirwaun. This gave a new lease of life, which culminated in 1830 in the purchase from the Gurney works of the first railway locomotive steam engine to be seen in the Aberdare Valley. The inhabitants of the valley flocked to see the new wonder at work, and in that year 9,035 tons of iron were produced at Hirwaun, and 35,715 tons of coal were consumed in the process. Nearly 900 men were in employment, and two-thirds of them were directly connected with the iron works. Most of them lived within the parish of Aberdare (Parry, 1967, p. 195).

Meanwhile, new enterprises had begun to change the life of Aberdare itself. In 1800 Jeremiah Homfray and James Birch had secured a lease on land at Aberdare for the purpose of sinking mines and setting up iron works. Two years later they were joined by the Tappenden brothers of Kent, who provided £40,000 fresh capital for the enterprise. In 1804 the Tappendens undertook the construction of a tram-road which passed by and served yet another new iron works which had been opened in 1800 at Llwydcoed. In February of that year the brothers John and George Scale had leased some 200 acres of Fforest Llwydcoed for the purpose of manufacturing iron. The two new companies of Abernant and Llwydcoed had their problems, in particular the prohibitive toll and duties which were exacted by the Glamorganshire Canal Company and the distance from the sea. In 1804 the Tappendens constructed the new tram-road to connect the two new iron works at Aberdare with the Neath Canal. Tolls for its use were to be paid by the other members of the Llwydcoed and Abernant companies, and in time it caused friction. Homfray and Birch decided to finish the partnership, and in 1815 the Tappendens themselves closed the Abernant Works for some time (Parry, 1967, p. 196).

The man who had witnessed the misunderstanding of 1807 when the original partnership of the Abernant Colliery was dissolved was Richard Fothergill, a native of Kendal in Westmoreland. In 1815 he took over the iron works at Abernant, and he and his family were to play a prominent part in the social and political life of Aberdare in the nineteenth century. The year 1827 saw the setting up of another iron works and the introduction of another noted family of industrialists to the life of Aberdare. The new works was located at Gadlys, and the founder was Mathew Wayne, who had been at one time furnace manager of the Cyfarthfa works at Merthyr. His enterprise was a small works with one furnace, but in less than a year he was sending down the canal to Cardiff 450 tons of iron from the works at Gadlys.

It will be remembered that Anthony Bacon (the younger) had retired to his estate at Aberaman in 1800. He lived there in relative " seclusion " till his death in 1827, and the house was occupied for another ten years by his son and his brother Thomas. In 1837 the property was put up for sale and bought by Crawshay Bailey of Nant-y-glo, the last of the iron masters whose names are connected with the Aberdare Valley. The 1,500 acres which Crawshay

Bailey had leased were not in close proximity to the canal, and the new iron master did not develop the site (nor did he come to reside in the area) for some nine years after his purchase. Meanwhile, having secured the support of Sir J. J. Guest, M.P., of Dowlais, he initiated the movement for the construction of a railway from Aberdare to Abercynon, to link up with the new Merthyr-Cardiff line. The branch was opened with much local festivity and excitement in August 1846, and in 1851 the Valley of Neath Railway Company extended its line to " the High Level Station " at Aberdare.

With the coming of the Railway Age into the Aberdare Valley, it seemed that the iron industry had nothing to fear, but unending prosperity. Early in the second half of the nineteenth century, it received its death blow. The local supply of iron ore was quite inadequate to meet the ever-increasing demand caused by the discovery of steel, the Bessemer process in particular. The iron masters generally found it more profitable to import large quantities of ore from Spain, and to establish their works nearer the coast rather than face the additional freight charges for transport up the valleys. One by one the fires of the local furnaces were put out. In 1859 the Hirwaun works closed, never to re-open on any scale, and by 1875 there was not a single blast furnace left working (Parry, 1967, p. 197).

Had the Aberdare Valley relied solely on its iron industry, things would have been critical, but a new industry had been making strides, an industry which was to dominate the life of the community up to the present day. This was the coal industry. Mining had been carried out on a small scale for centuries, and there are records of attempts at using the mineral wealth of the region in the Survey of Miskin, 1638, when a Thomas Griffith " houldeth a coale mynes in Aberdare. There are coale mynes upon the Lords demeane Lands called ' Gwayn-y-Person and Tir-y-lloyn Bedw ' within the parish of Aberdare." In 1653 it was granted to John Thomas for twenty-one years at the annual rent of ten shillings, and there are similar records up to 1697. By 1757 we find " All mines of iron ore or coal upon Ty'n Wain Wrgan (Hirwaun) being leased by Lord Windsor to John Mayberry of Brecon for a rent of twenty-three pounds! "

In 1837 Thomas Wayne of Gadlys persuaded his less enterprising father to sink a coal pit at Abernant-y-Groes, Cwmbach, and to sell the produce in the open market. The year 1837, therefore, is an important milestone in the industrial development of the Aberdare Valley. It marks not only the arrival of the last of the great iron masters, Crawshay Bailey, but also the arrival of the first of the great coal owners — Thomas Wayne.

The venture proved immediately a huge success, and created a demand for the steam coal for domestic and industrial purposes. The demand increased still further with the transition from sail to steam, and the Admiralty was persuaded of the effectiveness of this change by John Nixon of Werfa Colliery, Aberdare. In 1841 the output of coal from the Aberdare Valley was 12,000 tons. It rose to 500,000 tons by 1852, and to over 2,000,000 tons by 1870. Among the colourful personalities who dominated the new industry were the following : William Thomas, Llety Shenkin, who started to drill for coal at the beginning of 1843, and by the end of March of that year coal was extracted; Samuel Thomas, Ysguborwen, who sank a pit in 1849, and in 1856 at Bwllfa; David Davies of Hirwaun, who began at Blaengwawr, and by October 1844 coal was sent away for the first time; David Davies, Maesyffynnon (chiefly associated with collieries at Ferndale in the Rhondda Fach); David Williams at Ynyscynon in 1843, and later at Deep Duffryn in Mountain Ash (better known by his bardic name, Alaw Goch); Mordecai Jones at Nantymelyn in 1866 (a staunch Methodist — although he owned a brewery at Brecon!). Another enthusiastic coal owner was Thomas Powell of the Gaer near Newport and the owner of Cwmdare; Upper, Lower and Middle Duffryn were all Powell pits. The boom took place from about 1840 to 1852 in the upper reaches of the valley.

Mountain Ash was the first town to obtain coal from deep cuttings in the lower reaches. Deep Duffryn pit was in production by 1855, while the middle and lower pits were sunk by Thomas Powell to produce coal after four years; these were later sold to Sir George Elliot. Nixon's Navigation Colliery was started in 1855, the first sods being cut in the middle of an oat field; coal was raised five years later.

Development of the coal industry proceeded apace down the

valley towards Abercynon (then known as the Basin, Navigation or Aberdare Colliery), pits being sunk at Penrhiwceibr and Cwmcynon in 1873 and, finally, at Abercynon in 1889, although engineers had wanted this last site for sinking three years earlier. The Lady Windsor Colliery, Ynysybwl, was sunk in 1884, and coal was brought to the surface within two years.

These names associated with the sinking of the coal mines invite comparison with the earlier pioneers of the iron industry. Bacon, Crawshay, Scale, Birch, Tappenden, Homfray were all of English extraction, whereas the leaders of the coal industry, as their surnames indicate, were rooted in the Welsh soil. This accounts for the prominent part which they took in the social and religious activities of the district.

Mr. D. Davies, Blaengwawr, was continually inspiring the people who built a Wesleyan chapel in Mountain Ash around 1861. Other notable examples are Samuel Thomas, Ysguborwen, and David Williams, " Alaw Goch ". When a conference was held in Neath to arrange for the celebration of the bi-centenary of the Act of Uniformity of 1661, £250 were given by Thomas Williams of Aberdare towards the expenses, on the understanding that others would follow. Congregations had no need to depend on their own resources for building their chapels unaided, for prominent Nonconformists came forward to assist them.

The Davies family of Llandinam, owners of the Ocean Collieries, helped generously in building Welsh Methodist Chapels in those areas where their pits were situated. D. A. Thomas, M.P. (later Lord Rhondda), the son of Samuel Thomas, who was reputedly agnostic in his religious views, gave much support to Nonconformity in his constituency, which included Aberdare. He laid many a foundation stone for a new chapel, as, for example, Soar Welsh Calvinistic Church, Cwmaman. These men entered and influenced the lives of their employees much more fully than the early iron masters had done, and this ensured a happier relationship between Capital and Labour. The period 1840 to 1870 represents the " Golden Age " in the relationship between Nonconformist and industry at Aberdare. Moreover, the ever-increasing demand for labour led to a vast immigration, and during this period most of the immigrants came from the Welsh counties of Carmarthen, Pembroke and Cardigan. We know from the Report of the Commission of Enquiry into the State of Education, called " Brad y Llyfrau Gleision ", how labourers from the parish of Llanybydder in Carmarthenshire came into the valley and elsewhere, tempted by the better financial rewards of the new coal mining industry than they had as farm servants. In 1851 Aberdare parish had 14,999 inhabitants, 8,403 males and 6,596 females, while the lower end of the valley, which would come into the parish of Llanwynno, had 3,253 inhabitants. Within ten years the population of the valley had more than doubled. Aberdare parish in 1861 had 32,299 people made up of 17,323 males and 14,976 females, and Llanwynno had 8,702 made up of 4,751 males and 3,951 females. The vast majority of these immigrants were Welsh-speaking, but between 1871 and 1881 there was a change. During the decade 1881-91 the immigration went on, with an increasing number of people coming from the English border counties of Gloucestershire and Herefordshire and the south-west English counties; of the next absorption into Glamorgan during these ten years of 76,200, 63 per cent. came from the non-border counties, and this percentage was to be increased during 1901-11. It is important to realise that after 1881 the nature of these migrations to industrial areas, such as the Aberdare Valley in Glamorgan, was overwhelmingly English. The English migrants substantially outnumbered the Welsh migrants.

The immigrants came in to the new Eldorado. Merthyr had experienced it 40 years before, now it was the turn of Aberdare and the Rhondda Valleys. The population grew, the English immigrants being in the majority. Naturally, the Welsh chapels were suspicious of these English people, who brought with them English ideas and customs. Dr. Thomas Rees, a leading figure in Congregationalism, maintained that it was these English migrants who were the agitators in the industrial unrests. The consequence of this migration was a decline in the number of those who spoke Welsh. This showed itself in the Aberdare Valley, not in a net decrease in the number of Welsh-speaking people, but in a decrease in proportion to the increase in population.

An analysis of the census figures follows :

In the 1901 census the population of Aberdare Rural District was 39,932, with 23,067 Welsh speaking. Of these, 5,382 could only speak Welsh, while there were 11,307 who were English only. This meant that 59% of the population could speak Welsh. In the Mountain Ash Rural District, the population was 28,321, with 11,606 Welsh speaking. There were 1,937 monoglot Welsh and 14,726 English monoglots. By the 1911 census the population of Aberdare Rural District was 46,040, made up of 15,988 English only and 3,068 Welsh only, a drop of 2,314 Welsh monoglots since 1901, and 26,984 Welsh speaking, which meant that 59% of the population spoke the language. The age-group is a key to the understanding.

1911 Census

Age-group	Population M	Population F	English only M	English only F	Welsh only M	Welsh only F	Both English and Welsh M	Both English and Welsh F
Over 3 & under 5	1,182	1,195	517	510	108	115	424	447
,, 5 ,, 10	1,910	1,887	1,203	1,167	157	140	1,458	1,476
,, 10 ,, 15	2,574	2,622	943	966	97	97	1,483	1,497
,, 15 ,, 25	4,798	4,415	1,713	1,443	192	181	2,829	2,723
,, 25 ,, 45	8,498	7,135	3,038	2,305	417	325	4,982	4,441
,, 45 ,, 65	3,743	3,195	1,617	744	408	427	2,296	2,001
,, 65	710	970	199	221	136	268	368	474
	23,415	21,419	9,230	7,346	1,515	1,533	13,840	13,039

There were 102 Male Head of Families returned as speaking English only, and 113 Female, while there were only 29 Male Welsh and 30 Female Head of Families who were monoglot Welsh. There were 171 Male and 171 Female Head of Families who could speak the two languages. In the Mountain Ash area there was a population of 38,475, made up of 20,780 male and 17,695 female. Of these, 12,119 males spoke English only and 9,878 females. The monoglot Welsh were as follows : 635 male and 526 female. Then both Welsh and English : 7,438 male and 6,692 female.

	Welsh Only		Welsh and English	
	M.	F.	M.	F.
3-5	18	30	214	241
5-10	33	38	720	730
10-15	36	31	664	740
15-25	81	45	1,467	1,346
25-45	230	149	2,812	2,299
45-65	192	166	1,392	1,100
65 and over	45	67	169	236
			7,438	6,692

Head of Family returned as speaking were: Welsh only, Male 21, Female 19; both Welsh and English, Male 152, Female 116, while English only amounted to 248 Males and 245 Females. The Welsh language was quite flourishing in the returns looked upon above, and there was not the language problem that has become such an acute one in the present time. It was after the First World War, 1914-18, that the effect of the decline was felt in the Aberdare Valley. The Congregationalist Association of North Glamorgan, consisting of churches of that denomination in the Merthyr-Aberdare district, increased the number of churches from 50 to 56 from 1901 to 1910, but its membership went up only from 12,193 to 13,287 in the same period, and had it not been for an increase of 4,067 in the membership of these churches as a result of the religious revivals of 1904-5, the figures would have shown a substantial drop in membership during the first decade of the present century. In the 1921 census there was a drop of 20% in the Welsh Only column to 45%, and from 57.3% to 52.9% in both English and Welsh. In Mountain Ash the Welsh Only was 26% and both English and Welsh from 37.6% in 1911 to 29.8% in 1921.

The position was slowly getting worse, though in the Introduction to the 1931 census it was stated the "monoglot Welsh" is most frequent in Aberdare, Llwchwr, Rhondda, and Rural Districts of Neath and Pontardawe. These areas are also those in which bilingual abilities are generally commonest, as the following table indicates. Language spoken: proportion per 1,000 of the population aged three years and upwards, returned as able to speak Welsh only and both English and Welsh.

	Welsh Only			Both English and Welsh		
	1911	1921	1931	1911	1921	1931
Aberdare U.D.	65	45	15	575	529	547
Mountain Ash U.D.	30	26	8	376	298	293

It is as we analyse the 1961 census that the decline is obvious. The form of the Welsh language questions for the 1961 census reads:

(a) If able to speak Welsh only, write " Welsh ".

(b) If able to speak English and Welsh, write " Both ".

(c) For all children under age three and for persons unable to speak Welsh, insert a dash.

By 1961 there were 12,511 who could speak both Welsh and English — were bilingual — in comparison with 26,984 in 1911, 50 years before. We are able to look at each town and at each age-group to realise that the decline in the language means a similar decline in Welsh Nonconformity. The Welsh chapels are confined in their missionary activities to the Welsh population, which leaves them in a most difficult and heart-searching situation. Out of a population of 18,273 males in Aberdare Urban District, there are 99 monoglot Welsh, and out of 19,262 females there are 119 monoglot, while there are 5,780 bilingual males and 6,731 females. Aberaman has a population of 4,596 males and 4,827 females in 1961, while there are 25 male and 41 female monoglot Welsh, and 1,103 males and 1,295 females who are bilingual. In Blaengwawr there is a population of nearly seven thousand: 3,374 male with 17 who are able to speak Welsh only and 947 who are bilingual. There are 3,497 females, with 14 monoglot Welsh and 1,089 bilingual. In Gadlys there are 2,484 male population, with 18 who speak only Welsh and 1,037 who are bilingual. There are 2,700 females, with 15 monoglot Welsh and 1,222 bilingual. In Llwydcoed there are 5,410 males, with 25 monoglots and 1,894 bilingual, while there are 5,506 females, with 34 monoglots and 2,158 bilingual. In the town of Aberdare we have 4,141 population, with 29 monoglots and 1,765 who are bilingual.

In the Mountain Ash area we have a population of 13,894 males, with 72 of them monoglot and 1,815 bilingual. With regard to the female population, there are 14,269, with 59 monoglots and 2,181 who are bilingual. Abercynon has a population of 4,320, with 9 monoglots and 682 bilingual. Bryncynon has a population of 2,837, with 18 monoglots and 369 bilingual. Darranlas has a population of 2,329, with 15 monoglots and 672 bilinguals. Miskin has 11 male monoglots and 187 bilingual out of a population of 1,999, and 6 monoglot and 240 bilingual out of a total female population of 2,071. In Penrhiwceibr there are 2,808 male inhabitants, with 27 monoglot and 326 bilingual, and out of 2,780 females there are 18 monoglots and 371 bilinguals. This can be further divided into age-groups:

ABERDARE

Age	Bilingual	Male	Female
3 and over	12,511	5,780	6,731
3-4	69	38	31
5-9	244	123	121
10-14	440	172	268
15-24	837	363	474
25-44	2,630	1,278	1,352
45-64	5,370	2,586	2,784
65 and over	2,921	1,220	1,701

There are 218 who speak Welsh only, made up of 99 males and 119 females. There are two between 3 and 4, 3 between 5 and 9, 5 between 10 and 14, 23 between 15 and 24, 24 between 25 and 44, 109 between 45 and 64, and 52 who are 65 and over. In the Mountain Ash area there are 131 monoglots, 72 male and 59 female, and 3,996 bilingual, made up of 1,815 male and 2,181 female. The table is as follows:

	Speak Welsh Only			Both English and Welsh		
	Per.	M.	F.	Per.	M.	F.
3-4	3	1	2	23	9	14
5-9	5	2	3	88	36	52
10-14	8	4	4	171	80	91
15-24	12	9	3	299	148	151
25-44	28	16	12	742	368	374
45-65	49	26	23	1,572	738	834
65 and over	26	14	12	1,101	436	665

M.=Male.   F.=Female.   Per.=Persons.

The conclusion can be gathered for Welsh chapels that depend for their existence on people who are either Welsh-speaking or who can follow a Welsh service, the future is bleak. It is true that the Welsh schools are a tremendous help in the work of ensuring a continuity in the different chapels that belong to the Nonconformist denominations. But the Aberdare Valley has only one such school, at Ynyslwyd, near the town. It has over 275 children between the ages of 5 and 11. Some children in the lower end of the valley, from Mountain Ash, Ynysybwl and Abercynon, attend the Welsh Primary School at Pontshonnorton, near Pontypridd. But this is a small drop in the anglicisation of the valley. One Presbyterian Church in Penrhiwceibr has only three children between 5 and 11 attending its Sunday School. The class has to be in English. The most faithful of the three goes to a Welsh Primary School, and when it happens that he is there on his own, the class is conducted in the Welsh language.

Let me put another illustration. Abercynon has, according to the 1961 census, 682 bilingual inhabitants. To cater for their spiritual needs there are four chapels with a membership between them of 240. The biggest church has 130 members, and is one of the largest in the town, the other one has 60 members, the third 40, and the fourth a membership of 20. It is true that there are 440 Welsh-speaking people somewhere outside the churches, which, divided, gives each church a missionary total of 110 each. The future is not our concern, but the causes for the decline of yesterday and today. The language must be regarded as a possible cause. As a minister of a Presbyterian Church in Abercynon wrote in the

Chapel Report for 1935 : " If the members are not going to teach their children the language there will be no Welsh Church " (Bell, 1935, p. 1). The language problem has not helped Nonconformity in its missionary endeavours, or to resist the decline.

This period also saw a decline in the coal industry as well as technological developments in mining. This story is mainly provided by the Reid Committee (the Technical Advisory Committee on Coal Mining) appointed in September 1944, which reported in March 1945. The Committee's terms of reference were :

" To examine the present technique of coal production from face to wagon, and to advise what technical changes are necessary in order to bring the industry to a state of full technical efficiency."

The following account of technical development in the mining industry is based upon the report of the Reid Committee and of the account given by retired miners and miners still working at the coal face in the Aberdare Valley. The collieries still in operation are Fforchaman, at the top of the Aman Valley, Bwllfa Colliery, which is now part of the Maerdy project, situated at the top of the Dare Valley. Tower Colliery at Hirwaun and Treherbert Colliery at Hirwaun, which between them employ 1,600 men, have been on the danger list in recent years. In addition, a large number of the miners of Aberdare are employed at the Rhigos Drifts and collieries working in the lower end of the Valley — at Deep Duffryn, Mountain Ash, Penrhiwceibr, Abercynon and Ynysybwl.

Before the First World War, the different coalfields of the country tended to work in isolation, with local customs, traditions and methods of mining tending to prevent a widespread development of new techniques and machinery through the industry as a whole. The initiative of the individual mining engineer played a big part in what development there was in a particular mining company, and the papers read to the Institution of Mining Engineers helped to break down the insularity.

Even before the war, the Longwall advancing method of mining was gradually replacing the Room and Pillar system, especially in the newer mines and the more difficult seams where a quick return on capital was sought or where the more slowly developed Room and Pillar method was less applicable to underground conditions. Before the labour shortage of the First World War gave an impetus to the installation of machinery, mines were becoming larger and their equipment more elaborate and expensive.

The miners resented the introduction of new methods of mining, and the isolation of the pit was reflected in the isolation of the mining community, usually a self-contained unit. Everything depended upon mining, and the collier took pride in his craft. One of his delights was to accept his son into the industry, and to train him to use the tools of his trade. The introduction of machinery could also mean unemployment, and it took years before machinery was accepted.

As early as 1905 the Report of the Royal Commission on Coal Supplies and Resources had stated: "There seems to be no doubt that coal-cutting machines are now firmly established." But the new techniques did not spread rapidly, probably for the reasons mentioned above; between 1908 and 1913 the percentage of total output mechanically cut rose from 5 to 8 per cent; by 1927 it had risen to 23%, and had reached 61% by 1939. By 1954 85% of total deep-mined output was mechanically dug, mechanical cutting having become by this date general practice.

It was at the end of the First World War also that face conveyors made their appearance. While, in 1909, the number of cutters was 1,700, the number of face conveyors was only 180. By 1939 there were 7,750 cutters and 5,859 conveyors. Other forms of underground transport were introduced, with electricity gradually replacing steam and compressed air as the motive power of haulage engines, but the traditional endless rope, main and tail, and main hop haulages were still able to cope with the outputs of the day.

As the Reid Committee stated in their Report, the 1926 General Strike marked the end of an era in the mining industry. Competition from Continental countries was to prove more intense, and in the ensuing period the reorganisation of the German and Polish mines was to take their output *per* man shift to a higher level than in Britain by the outbreak of the Second World War. The post-General Strike conditions (which included, for the miner, longer hours and lower wages) stimulated some further introduction of machinery and technique. This was not, however, a very spectacular increase. The number of coal-cutters in use increased by only 9 per cent. between 1927 and 1939, although the total tonnage cut rose, due to improvement in machine design and increases in the machines' power, from 58.5 million tons to 142.2 million tons. The introduction of more and more conveyors during this period, when the change-over from Hand to Longwall to mechanised Longwall was proceeding rapidly, also played an important role in the achievement of this higher production. Only 28 million tons of coal were face conveyed in 1928 as compared with 134 million tons in 1939. By this year, 58 per cent of the total output of coal was conveyed along the working face, and although the use of conveyors was not as widespread as the use of cutters, during the post-1926 to 1939 period the use of conveyors was spreading to new mines, where the use of cutters was spreading mainly within the mines already using them. The use of pneumatic picks, a feature of mining development on the Continent during this period, did not spread very far in Britain.

During this period, too, the tonnage handled *per* haulage worker increased, and the number of men required on haulage decreased due mainly to an increasing use of belt conveyors on the gate roads, the replacement of hand drawing and horse haulage by conveyors or rope haulage, and the concentration of workings, allowing each road the possibility of dealing with larger tonnages.

The Reid Committee traces in detail the changes in the " tools " used to win the coal and the changes in the system of organisation underground for the purpose of achieving production. The main pattern of change involved a transition from hand getting, through the use of pneumatic picks (more used in the United States of America than in Britain) to mechanical cutting and mechanical loading and simultaneous mechanical cutting and loading.

It meant a revolutionary change in the small team unit which had previously been responsible for everything, from the selection of its members in the " team " to the cutting and the loading of the coal. A fairly typical breakdown of the labour force employed in a colliery under the new system would be :

2 Borers, 2 Cutters, 4 Gammers, 2 Breakers and 2 Builders on the first (cutting) shift; 8 Rippers on the second shift; 20 Fillers, each in his own length of 9 yards along the face, on the third shift.

Possibilities of building up a team spirit which existed before are limited under this system, with the result that there exists a great deal of difference between the rippers and the fillers in the team cohesion. This meant the introduction of problems in the technological development of the mining industry. The Reid Committee, in its detailed analysis, discussed some of them. It pointed out that by the time of the General Strike (1926), the effects of machine mining on the miner were already apparent. The Reid Committee states on page 6 of its Report:

"It is often very difficult to follow technical history while it is in the making, and this is perhaps especially true of another feature of machine mining. Before the system of Longwall mining with face conveyors became common, the coal had been gotten by small, self-reliant teams of men, able and accustomed to perform all the operations required in their working places for keeping themselves secure and for getting the coal. With the introduction of machine mining, larger teams were a necessary corollary. Where payment remained on a piecework basis, the wage was often pooled over these larger groups of men, so that the personal efforts of the individual made less and less difference to the total earnings of the pool.

"When conveyer faces were first started, and the co-operation of the miners was secured, there was a novelty about the project which caused interest and keenness, both among the officials and the men. As more and more faces were mechanised, interest and keenness waned. What was new became routine, and hence arose the phenomenon, frequently remarked upon by mining engineers, that the first mechanised face was often the best face they ever had. It gradually came home to the miner that, though he was spared on these faces the severe physical toil of hand-getting, he was still involved in considerable effort with little scope for the exercise of the skill he had acquired through the old system.

"Although the adverse effect of this change in the individual status of the miner was, and largely has been, confined to the coal-getter, it is he who has always been recognised as representing the miner's calling. Any lowering of his status, therefore, tends to react unfavourably on the workers throughout the mine. Unfortunately, it was not appreciated that machine mining was resulting in an impairment of his status, and that the effect of this upon his outlook and behaviour would be likely to reduce the advantages in productivity expected."

Mechanical loading was another development which was commented on. At the time when they reported, the Reid Committee were aware of the disappointing results so far obtained from mechanisation. But they were of the opinion that " development in mining technique must be directed . . . to a reduction in, and ultimately to the practical elimination of, hand-loading. The mechanical loader is a notable step forward along this route, and it also brings with it the important advantage that it is operated by a small team of skilled men. Wherever these machines have been installed they have been almost universally welcomed by the men, and it has been found that the spirit and regularity of attendance of teams operating loading machines are much better than prevail in large groups of men filling out the coal on Longwall faces. The interest in the work and the scope which it provides for skill and initiative have certainly a bearing upon this phenomenon, and the indirect benefits obtained, while difficult to measure, are nonetheless real " (p. 51). Since, for power loading to be effective, the coal must first be cut, the disadvantages of the 'rigid cycle of operations' noted above in connection with mechanical cutting and hand filling on Longwall faces, and the impossibility of including more than one coal-filling shift in each period of 24 hours, still existed.

The Reid Committee commented on other issues which would have to disappear with the small team unit of the pre-mechanical era, and the emergence of the small team of skilled men. " It is impossible to contemplate, for example, that the 'cavilling' system, under which the mine workers draw lots every three months for the places in which they are to work, can be allowed to continue. Again, the so-called 'Seniority Rule' by which the senior men are first employed on, or promoted to, any new or better-paid jobs, is incompatible with the necessity for selecting keen, young and adaptable men to work in the teams required for operating the most modern machinery " (p. 117).

Since nationalisation, the reconstruction and reorganisation of the coal industry which the N.C.B. has undertaken involves an extension where applicable of the Longwall retreating system of mining. Thus nationalisation has both intensified the development of tools, which was apparent by the end of the Second World War, and brought about some reorganisation underground as a result of employing alternative systems of mining. The effect of these various developments which have been summarised here is to permit technical developments to proceed alongside noncommittant organisational developments which, in their long-run effect, will permit a smaller group and, therefore, more effective organisation of manpower underground. The Room and Pillar system associated with hand-got methods is generally considered to have permitted the organisation of self-reliant small teams which exhibited a team spirit and cohesion which was gradually broken down as the Longwall Advancing system replaced Room and Pillar and, simultaneously, as machinery, at first single powered hand-tools and later more complex machines capable of replacing human muscle power, replaced the effort and energy required of the collier. The collier in the old system was regarded as a skilled craftsman, having a craft pride, albeit of a different sort from the craft pride of the engineer or the carpenter, and, to a degree, willing to allow his sons to follow in his occupation. The first forty-five years of this century saw this craft pride reduced with the development of Longwall systems and machinery. If the latest developments of machinery, capable of operation by *small* teams, will permit the re-creation of team spirit in face operations, certainly the skill required of the 'collier' will be of a different order from the skill previously required. Not the skill associated with human strength and human control over natural conditions, but the skill of the machine operator and, dependent upon type and thoroughness of training, associated or not with a knowledge of the working of the machine.

Where training of the boy by the father or the collier who might not be a relative might have been sufficient in a period characterised by human strength and human judgement pitted against natural conditions, in a period characterised by complex machinery the training demanded for the operator and the maintenance craftsman is more complex and formalised. The Reid Committee pointed to the shortcomings in the system of training employed in the mining industry up to the Second World War, and pointed out that those modifications which had been made in the provision for training during the twentieth century had been modifications introduced in response to changes in accident rates. Legislation had played some part in inducing such changes in the training provision as had been made. The Reid Committee viewing the industry as one owned privately, pointed to some of the difficulties in the way of making effective formal provision for training, but the nationalisation of the industry removed some of these difficulties and enabled training to be undertaken on a wider scale, effectively co-ordinated and planned for the whole of the industry.

The training of supervision and management, which also possessed certain shortcomings before the war, according to the Reid Committee, could also be undertaken on a different scale. The annual reports of the National Coal Board show the degree to which the Board has taken advantage of the opportunity afforded by the reorganisation of the industry to introduce more effective training schemes and to introduce into these training schemes some greater attention to principles of management derived from experience in other industries. Similarly, the requirements of the more mechanised industry of greater attention to planning, co-ordination and control could now be introduced, and standardised for the whole industry.

This period also saw the beginning of the third phase of the industrial revolution in the Aberdare Valley — the turning from heavy to light industries. The first phase was dominated by the ironworks, the second phase by the coal industry, and the third phase by the establishment of two industrial estates, one at the top of the Valley, the Hirwaun Industrial Estate at Rhigos, and the other industrial estate at the lower reaches of the Valley, namely, the Ynysboeth Industrial Estate. From a Valley of colliery workers, Aberdare has become (to a large extent) a Valley of factory workers. It was the Second World War which transformed the industrial habits of the Valley, and as 1837 was a milestone in the industrial history of the Valley, so 1937 was also a milestone in the third phase of the industrialisation; for in that year the Aberdare Cables Ltd. built a factory at Trecynon. It has since been several times extended and electric power cable manufactured by the Company is sent all over Great Britain and exported to all parts of the world. On the same extensive premises at Trecynon an associated company, Aberdare Engineering Ltd., has a separate large and well-equipped mechanical engineering factory; it specialises in soot blower equipment for power stations, and heavy fabricated steel products. Over six hundred people, nearly all men, are employed in the two works.

The pattern is the familiar one; throughout the Aberdare Valley light industry, and one outcome is the vast increase in the employment of women in the new industries. This is evident in so many of the factories, and one of the biggest of these factories is at Ynysboeth, where the majority of the working population are women. Most of the firms have by now been well-established. Among the firms established at the Hirwaun Trading Estate are Thorn Electrical Industries Ltd. (electric lamps, etc.); Dunlop Rubber Company Ltd. (latex products); Cambrian Castings Ltd. (non-ferrous castings); Welbow Manufacturing Company Ltd. (precision tools); Murphy Radio Ltd. (Radio and TV sets); Concrete Utilities Ltd. (concrete lighting standards); Cynanamed Products Ltd. (medicinal products); Purma Cameras Ltd. (photographic equipment); Sobell Industries Ltd. (Radio and TV sets); Fisco Ltd. (stationery requisites); Harry Smith (Moore Abbott) Ltd. (small instrument parts, etc.). There is an Ordnance factory at Robertstown, and the C.W.S. have a creamery in Trecynon, and Hoover Ltd. produce parts for their washing machines at the same town.

To the variety of products produced may be added: electric meters, machine tools, hand-woven materials, abrasives, flexible tubing, scientific instruments, gloves, carpets, i.e., at Ynysboeth, drain rodding equipment, clothing at Penrhiwceibr and Miskin, besides the small printing works at Aberdare and Mountain Ash. For a hundred years the Aberdare Valley relied on the mining industry, and although coal-mining is still an important and vital industry, the establishment of the many and varied industries has meant diversification of the industrial base within the valley. This naturally presents new factors to a sociologist, and an entirely different industrial pattern to that of the mining industry. Added to this we must mention the existence of the same type of industrial set-up in other areas that border on the Valley, such as the Treforest Industrial Estate, which is one of the largest in the whole of South Wales, and smaller estates at Pentrebach, Merthyr and Ystrad Mynach, besides the opportunities offered by engineering and other industrial firms at Pontypridd and Caerphilly.

This has introduced a factor which is important, namely, the dispersal of a part of the population to occupations outside the Aberdare Valley and the attraction of these people into a totally different kind of industrial situation. It has meant an outflow of labour as well as an inflow from other areas to the industrial estates at Ynysboeth and Rhigos.

We depend on the census figures on this aspect of the situation which were published in 1968.[3] The total working population of the Aberdare Valley in 1966 was 2,159. This was made up of 793 males in the Aberdare Urban District, 681 males in the Mountain Ash Urban District, and 382 females in the Aberdare area and 303 in the lower area of the valley. Of the 2,159 employed, 1,526 are employed in the Aberdare Valley. It is possible for 558 males in the Aberdare district, 454 males in the Mountain Ash district, 296 females in the Aberdare district and 218 females in the Mountain Ash district to find employment in the area that they live in. There are 633 people who have to commute to work, made up of 235 males from the Aberdare area, 227 from the Mountain Ash area, 86 females from the Aberdare Urban District, and 85 from the Mountain Ash District.

We even know to what areas these people commute. The 321 from the Aberdare Urban District travel to two counties: Breconshire, Monmouthshire, as well as their own county of Glamorgan. 17 males and 6 females work in the Vaynor and Penderyn area; 39 males and 8 females in the Merthyr Tydfil Borough; 5 males and 1 female in the Caerphilly Urban District; 93 males and 27 females in the Mountain Ash Urban District; and 41 males work in the Rhondda Valley and 21 females. We know that 12 males and 4 females work in the Neath area from the Aberdare Valley, and 7 males in the Pontypridd Urban District. 1 male and 7

[3] Sample Census 1966. England and Wales. Workplace and Transport Tables. Part 1. (London: Her Majesty's Stationery Office, 1968) pp. 268-270.

females travel by the Heads of the Valleys road to the Rhymney Urban District.

The same is true of the Mountain Ash area, with 227 males and 85 females having to commute to their work. 99 males and 44 females travel to the Aberdare area, which is the biggest number. The others travel to the following areas, as the table illustrates:

Area	Males	Females
Merthyr Tydfil C.B.	14	16
Caerphilly U.D.	14	3
Gelligaer U.D.	3	8
Pontypridd U.D.	31	6
Rhondda M.B.	46	3
Llantrisant and Llantwit Fardre	7	1
Bedwellty U.D.	2	3

But the flow is not one-way. There are a number of people who have to travel to the Aberdare Valley from other areas. Indeed, more people commute to the Aberdare Valley than leave the valley to their work-place. It is reckoned that in 1966, 862 men and women travelled from the surrounding valleys to work mainly in the Rhigos and Ynysboeth Estate. This explains why 278 males and 127 females from the Neath Rural District area travelled to the Aberdare Valley; and why 113 men and 78 females came from the Pontypridd area to the Mountain Ash district. 23 men and 8 females travelled from Cardiff to the Aberdare Urban District, and 49 men and 20 females to the Mountain Ash area from the capital city of the Principality. There were 6 males and 2 females who travelled from the Caerphilly area to the Aberdare Urban District, and 25 males and 1 female who travelled to the Caerphilly area. There were 6 males who came to the Aberdare area from the Gelligaer Urban District, and 24 males and 9 females who travelled from Pontypridd daily to the Aberdare area. We find that 15 males and 2 females travelled from the Rhondda daily to the Aberdare district, and another 6 males and 2 females to the Mountain Ash district.

Added to this outflow and inflow of labour daily and weekly, we have a number of people who have moved out of the valley altogether to live on the new housing estates at Rhydfelen and around Pontypridd, so that they can be nearer their employment, and save the traffic jams that daily are witnessed on Cilfynydd common, on the approach to Abercynon and the lower reaches of the Aberdare Valley. Some of them still keep a certain amount of loose attachment behind, and even those who commute often move their interests to the new places of employment as regards social activities. Their friends are their fellow-workers who live in the Neath area or the Pontypridd area, and their interest in the Mountain Ash or the Aberdare Valley where they live and sleep is often minimal. This has meant the introduction of an entirely new factor into the well-being of the traditional structures in the Aberdare Valley that depend upon allegiance to its meetings, and the loyalty of its members in attendance and participation. Indeed, these are some of the results of the third phase of the industrial revolution and other industrial and social reasons for the weakening of Welsh Nonconformity which will be dealt with in more detail in **Chapter 6.**

6

INDUSTRY AND RELIGION

I INTEND in this chapter to look at all the manifestations of links or non-links between industry and chapels in the Aberdare Valley.

1. *The relationship of the Management of the Mining Industry and Nonconformity.*

The biographer of Lewis Davis, an Aberdare Valley-born colliery owner, maintained: " The Englishmen who came to reside in Wales, with few exceptions, were bigoted Churchmen, or, if they were not originally so, they soon went over to the Church " (Young, 1905, p. 16). We have already shown how David Davies, Blaengwawr, and Alaw Goch and other colliery owners were devout Nonconformists and helped in the building of the new chapels that were built by the immigrants, mostly from Welsh Wales. It can be safely said that the personnel of the collieries — owner, chief overseer, and, later on, the manager, in many cases did their utmost for the Nonconformist Chapels, and sometimes would combine with the workers in making this provision. A good example to substantiate our contention that the owners/workers would combine in the building or setting up of a Nonconformist Chapel or Church would be Ebenezer Presbyterian Church of Wales, Cwmbach.

It was in 1837 that a pit was sunk and opened on the Abernant-y-Groes estate by Thomas Wayne & Company. When the Calvinistic Methodists decided to start a Sunday School cause at Cwmbach, it began in the house of Dafydd Sims, chief overseer in the Hen-Lety-Siencyn pit. His home became too small for the Sunday School and it was decided to build a chapel; this was done in 1851. One of its leaders in this period was David Evans, from

Dowlais, who became chief director in the mining company of David Davies in the Rhondda and Aberdare Valleys; he moved to Bodringallt and became one of the respected leaders of the Rhondda Valley. Another prominent member was David Evans, who became under-manager to the other David Evans.

The association of the owners and workers with the chapels is noted by various writers. The Rev. E. E. Evans, in the history of the centenary of the Bethlehem Welsh Calvinistic Church (1954), states: " The beginning of Presbyterianism in the Cynon Valley is connected with the beginning of the coal industry at Duffryn, Mountain Ash ". Dr. Hugh Jones, the historian of the Wesleyan Movement in Wales, makes the same point as regards the building of the Wesleyan Chapel at Mountain Ash in 1861. It was the sinking of the mines at Penrhiwceibr ten years later, according to the late Rev. David Jones, that gave impetus to the building at Hermon of the Calvinistic Methodist Church in 1883. Again, in 1889, it was the sinking of the mine at Abercynon that brought the immigrants, many of them from Dowlais, who were responsible for starting Tabernacle Welsh Calvinistic Methodist Church in 1892.

As these hard-working, intelligent men advanced in the pits, so did their influence grow in the chapels, and the height of personal success to many was symbolised, not only by the seat of authority in the local colliery, but also by a seat in the big pew of the chapel. Thus arose an influential figure in industrial Nonconformity — the Colliery-Manager Chapel-Deacon or Elder. So close was the connection between pit and chapel through the figure of the Deacon or Elder-Manager that in some areas, like Penrhiwceibr, the colliery became associated with the Calvinistic Methodist Church. A good, staunch Calvinistic Methodist would get a job because the manager was an Elder in the local Calvinistic Methodist Church.

There grew in the mining areas a certain resentment of the colliery owner or manager, especially the colliery manager. The colliery manager, after nationalisation, has not the same authority. The miners often give as one of their reasons for the Nonconformist Churches' apparent ' decline ' the reaction to the set-up that existed in the days of the private ownership of the mines, when so many of the colliery managers were elders in the Nonconformist Churches. In the questionnaire I asked the question: " Do you consider that the colliery manager-elder set-up in the early part of the twentieth century was a good thing for Nonconformity?" I had the following response:

Yes	16 (out of 72)	22.2%
No	30 (,,)	41.6%
Don't know	20 (,,)	27.7%
No answer	6 (,,)	8.3%

The respondents were given an opportunity of giving the reason for their choice, and 14 gave the following answers, which are mostly critical of the set-up that existed in mining villages in the Aberdare Valley:

"He set a good example to others" (Mountain Ash housewife).

"Yes, if a Christian" (Mountain Ash housewife).

"Before my time" (18-year-old Abercynon Civil Servant).

"People were afraid of these men" (Barclays Bank employee).

"They set themselves up as above ordinary men" (18-year-old Abercynon Comprehensive School student).

"It began the rift between employer and employee" (18-year-old Aberdare youth).

"Many of the old miners were reluctant to go to chapel to come in contact with officials on Sunday as well as in work" (Attendant at N.C.B. Tower No. 1 Colliery, Medical Centre, Hirwaun).

"Because of the power with which the colliery manager dominated the workmen" (Hirwaun miner).

Many a miner still feels this way; and even under nationalisation the colliery-manager is not always popular with the men. "You should hear him swearing underground," was what I heard often about some of the colliery managers, and a strike was held in 1966 at Mountain Ash Dyffryn Colliery when a fireman swore at a young trainee miner.

"Because people thought that they owed something to attend" (Hirwaun miner).

"It was open to abuse in the sense that favours and subcontractors could be given to loadies by managers" (Darranlas retired miner).

"Too much association with colliery management" (Mountain Ash miner).

"Wrong image" (Penrhiwceibr miner).

"Often Christian principles were forgotten in the mad rush for coal, with dire consequences" (Abercynon retired Co-operative Department Manager).

"It may have increased congregations by miners following their manager, but was the belief true?" (Hirwaun youth).

This resentment against the management is still present in mining areas. Dr. F. Zweig maintained, in 1948, after the nationalisation of the industry, that the "miner still believes that both the public and the management are against him, and he has the 'nobody-likes-me' feeling" (Zweig, 1948, p. 17). These remarks and similar ones are found through Dr. Zweig's study of the miner in *Men in the Pits*. "He doesn't keep his promises" is the worst accusation that can be levelled by the colliers against the manager, and also the accusation that the managers are "A pack of ex-owners sabotaging the work of the Government" (Zweig, 1948, p. 123).

The pit officials whose job it is to see the work is done are seen as enemies, at least during working hours. The very fact that in Ashton, as in the Aberdare Valley, officials belong to the same clubs as the ordinary workers may itself be indicative of this hostility. Thus one of the three under-managers in Ashton, who belonged to and frequently visited two of the Ashton clubs, said to the authors:

"When I'm out for a drink, a chap is liable to get a bit drunk and come over to me and start being nasty. If I'm in a pub there isn't much I can do about it. In the club, all I have to do is to call a committee man, tell him what is going on, and I can be sure of redress" (Dennis *et al.*, 1957, p. 142).

These negative attitudes of the miners explain to some extent the historical background, and the links that were made in the nineteenth century between chapels and colliery management and workers. It explains some of the bitterness that was witnessed between the labour leaders of the twentieth century; the leaders that rebelled against the chapel structure in which they were brought up as they identified the class struggle in terms of Chapel/Colliery Owner/Management. Many examples could be cited, the most outstanding one being A. J. Cook (1885-1931), who became, in 1924, General Secretary of the Miners' Federation. Born in the West Country, he came, at an early age, to work in the collieries of the Rhondda. He came under the influence of the 1904-5 Religious Revival at Porth, and during the First World War he was " stoned out of his native village because he dared assert that Christ would not countenance killing under any guise " (McAllister, 1935, p. 44). Cook became disillusioned with Nonconformity and made a clean break with the chapels. But he still could not forget his background : " He was an earnest Christian and he believed that his Lord would not tolerate the poverty and degradation of his comrades in the pits " (McAllister, 1935, p. 172). Cook brought the same " zealous, frenzied religious enthusiasm to his public speaking as he had done to his revival work in Wales " (McAllister, 1935, p. 173).

Cook and so many of the leaders of the mining industry in South Wales were emotional and enthusiastic, as McAllister put it, " frenzied, religious enthusiasm ". This brings us to the second link between mining culture and the Nonconformist culture.

2. *The 'Emotionalism' of the Chapels and the 'Emotionalism' of the Mining Culture.*

Professor Michael Fogarty has shown in *Personality and Group Relations in Industry* how emotion plays a part in the industrial scene. This is true also in the history of Welsh Nonconformity, which really was born in the Methodist Revival with " enthusiasm " and *hwyl*. This was the new element introduced into Nonconformity — emotionalism. Welsh historians are at pains to tell us of how the Dissenters, with their emphasis on " rationalism ", gave way to the brand new " enthusiasm " of the Revivalists. The Methodist Revival was concerned, more than anything else, with the mystic doctrine of salvation by personal experience. The Methodists taught that the only way to be " saved " was to experience an awareness of having sinned, to repent and to experience directly forgiveness from God. Observance of the sacraments of the Church were not enough. They would not ensure salvation, said the Methodists, nor was the true salvation attainable by the performance of good works and living a pious life alone. This is Welsh Nonconformity, and tended to make religion an emotional experience.

The reason why "emotionalism" is our concern is that it became part and parcel of the religious outlook and vocabulary of Welsh Nonconformity. The success of the meeting is judged by the emotional powers of the preacher, and the gusto and crescendo of the hymn-singing. Singing festivals — *Cymanfa Ganu* — is a remnant of this way of thinking — and still remains with the Welsh Nonconformists an integral part of their religious calendar. This "emotionalism" we are discussing as something integral to Nonconformity has made it almost inevitable that large-scale revivals are looked upon as the success-point of the story. Welsh Nonconformity was to achieve, it can be argued, its position of supremacy in Wales through a series of revivals in which intense individual experience played an important part.[1] People suddenly became conscious of the sinful lives which they had been leading, and this realisation of sin was followed by scenes of penitence. Indeed, it could be said that such scenes are no more witnessed within the Welsh Nonconformist denominations in the Aberdare Valley, but rather at the newer Pentecostal sects.

Revivals broke out in East Glamorgan and Monmouthshire at regular intervals in the nineteenth century. They were usually confined to a place, or an area, or to a visit of a "charismatic" preacher. General Booth, it is said, had such an impact on his visit to the Rhondda Valley. The two main Revivals, however, were in 1859 and 1904-5, which had an impact all over Wales.

The 1859 Revival was instrumental in the setting up of Nonconformist Chapels in the valley. Mention has been made of this, and it appears also that the 1859 Revival swelled the numbers of the different Churches, giving them a new lease of life for at least thirty years, but by the end of the century this was changed. The Rev. Rhys Morgan, a minister in the rural village of Llanddewi Brefi in Cardiganshire, could write in *Y Drysorfa* (the Calvinistic Methodist Journal) in 1893 that a decline had set in. He traced it to the rationalist thought, and the work of Darwin, Huxley,

---

[1] The Rev. Edward Parry noted 14 revivals in various parts of Wales between 1790 and 1892, and the Rev. Gomer M. Roberts noted 16 between 1785 and 1904. See E. Parry, *Llawlyfr a Hanes y Diwygiadau Crefyddol yng Nghymru* (Corwen, 1898); G. M. Roberts, "Y Cyffroadau Mawr", *Y Goleuad* (Caernarvon), 22 Oct. 1952 and 24 June 1953.

Spencer and others. It is true to say that Wales did see the foundation of a Welsh University, Welsh Intermediate Education Act, and the general Education Act of 1871 by the last third of the century. The Welsh working class were beginning to read the works of some of the Socialist thinkers, and a new Welsh newspaper made its appearance in Aberdare, *Tarian y Gweithiwr*, the organ of the I.L.P. in South Wales. This newspaper was unhampered by the nineteenth century traditions of Welsh newspapers, which had kept *Y Faner* and other papers tied to Nonconformist thought and attitude. An anonymous writer says, in 1910, in *Y Geninen*: " The ideas of Darwin, Wallace, Spencer, Huxley, Taylor, Machennan and Max Muller had been penetrating into Wales for some years (before the Revival) and a crisis was facing Nonconformity." This was the situation at the beginning of the twentieth century.

Y Geninen for 1906 paints the picture : " Everybody who had taken a little trouble to observe the condition of the country must agree that there was a heart-rending sight to be seen before the commencement of the present revival. Most people seemed to have given themselves up to the Devil. Agnosticism had raised its ugly head very high. There was a terrible apathy inside the chapels and the churches. The workers had fallen into a state of frightful callousness, and the whole country had descended into a pit of corruption, lust and drunkenness, worldliness and worthless things had possessed the minds of all people."

Nonconformity was facing a crisis at the beginning of the twentieth century, such a crisis as it had not faced for forty years. Its supremacy in the life of the people was being challenged, emotionalism was being thrown out for learning within the " Nonconformist culture ". " Origin of Species " was taking over from the " Origin of Sin " and the heathen forces were tempting the Welsh people to follow suit. It can be argued, then, as C. R. Williams and others have done, that the 1904 Revival was a reaction to a new set of circumstances which was drawing the people of Wales from their old allegiance.[2] (Williams, 1952, pp. 242-259).

[2] Many of the features that were part of the background of the revival of 1904 were specific to the period, the advent of the New Theology which emphasised the immanence of God as against His transcendence,

It is often believed that Evan Roberts was the instigator of the Revival of 1904-5. This is not correct. A feeling of despair had overtaken many of the Welsh ministers within Nonconformity for a decade before the Revival. In 1891, Dr. John Pugh (1846-1907), a Calvinistic Methodist minister, began an evangelical campaign in a tent in Cardiff, and from this grew the Forward Movement, a home missionary movement which established Churches at Abercynon, Penrhiwceibr and Mountain Ash in the Aberdare Valley. In 1893 the Rev. John Evans (1840-97), of Eglwys-bach, a Wesleyan minister, was " given freedom from the ordinary plan of his Church " to found a mission in Pontypridd. Conventions had been held at Llandrindod and other centres, and inter-denominational prayer meetings were started in Carmarthen and in South Cardiganshire, under the guidance of an uncle and a nephew, Rev. Joseph Jenkins (1859-1929) and Rev. John Thickens (1865-1952). And it was at one of these Conventions in South Cardiganshire that a young former miner and blacksmith from the background of deep piety in the Welsh Calvinistic Methodist Chapel at the village of Loughor in Glamorgan, who was preparing himself for the ministry at a denominational preparatory school, was caught up in the wave of intense religious emotion which the Revival of 1904-5 released.

The Welsh Revival was a remarkable example of popular religion; it came from the people, the ordinary folk of the mining valleys and the villages of the countryside; their emotions and their religious aspirations shaped it, and they consciously repudiated professional ministerial guidance or other attempts to guide and control it along lines traditional to revivals of the past.

The leadership passed into the hands of the young people.

" The leadership passed into a young man's hands, to the hands of one considered less suitable than themselves, but ' my thoughts are not your thoughts '," explained one of the young ministers at the time of the Revival, Rev. Eliseus Howells.

The Revival reversed the roles of different members of the congregations : the young people commonly took over the meetings

fear of the consequences of Balfour's Education Act of 1902, the working of the reformed system of local government, the extended State Educational provision, the coming of new forms of leisure-time entertainment.

and women became extremely prominent. Before the Revival began, the work of managing a chapel's affairs and of conducting its meetings was in the hands of the minister and diaconate. Though women were the most numerous attenders at prayer meetings, at meetings of the religious society, the public work of reading, praying, contributing testimonies of one's experience, and addressing the meetings on relevant topics was exclusively the work of the men present. Apart from Sunday School work and "young people's" activities, the contribution of the women was virtually limited to reciting a few verses when asked to do so. Women who did become prominent were extremely few.

At the end of a *Seiat* at Libanus, Aberaman, the young people insisted on having their own prayer meeting. "It was the most terrible meeting" that the minister, Rev. J. Harries Jones, had been present at. "There was praying, and failing to pray, crying and tears," an unordered spontaneity.[3] The young people at Trecynon visited every public house in the area, and preached outside to the willing listeners.[4]

The miners held prayer meetings in the Aberdare Valley, and children played "revival meetings".[5]

A Cymanfa Ganu for children at Abercynon, according to one eye-witness, went on for hours. People would get up in the middle of a meeting and pray. Others would follow suit, and meetings went on for hours. Some, according to older residents of the valley, went on for hours, and even, on occasions, throughout the night. The emphasis lay on the personal testimony, on their emotional experience.

A foreign observer, J. Rogues de Fursac, said that "The revival was a unifying movement. It did not create a new sect. It did not raise barriers of hate between people. On the contrary, it re-united people with bonds of charity — Methodists, Baptists, Congrega-

---

[3] For an account of the revival in Aberaman and Trecynon see J. Harries, "Y Diwygiad yn Aberaman", *Y Diwygiad a'r Diwygwyr* (ed. T. Francis) (Dolgellau 1906), pp. 196-198.

[4] The quotation is on page 198. J. Morgan, "Y Diwygiad yn Trecynon", op. cit., pp 182-186.

[5] ibid., pp 158-162. "Y mae y glofeydd o'n cwmpas i gyd yn gydgyfarfod" (All the collieries around us are holding meetings) (p. 158). For an account of the Revival in the South Wales valleys see H. Elvet Lewis, *With Christ among the Miners* (London, 1906).

tionalists and Wesleyans have ceased to condemn one another, and, in their different chapels, worship the same God . . . Evan Roberts preaches a Christianity so wide that it embraces all Christendom . . . This is an isolated case of mysticism, not likely to occur again, not even in Wales. The Welsh people are already coming out of their cultural isolation, and it is this cultural isolationism which has provided the fundamental conditions necessary for a popular mystical movement of this kind. Already the Welsh middle and upper classes are becoming enlightened and this enlightenment will soon soak down to the lower classes " (de Fursac, 1907, pp. 183-8).

This mystical element was an impressive part of the religious phenomena associated with the 1904-5 Revival. The impression given is of a kinder attitude towards each other. J. Rogues de Fursac met a Dowlais collier during the later months of the revival and asked him what he thought of it. The answer given was as follows: "We spoke (says the visitor of himself and the young convert) of the influence exercised by the Revival on the economic struggle which existed in Wales as in other countries. The young man felt that the Revival was rather favourable to advanced ideas. It may be true, he said, that at the beginning the matters of Heaven were tending to make people forget the things on this earth, but it is also true that now the economic and social questions are regaining their proper place. We believe, he said, that God has said to Man that he shall earn his bread by the sweat of his brow, but we also know that God never said that the worker shall also provide bread for the shareholder who does nothing . . . Socialism has lost nothing by the Revival, and trade union membership has not suffered in any way. The young man said that the Revival was essentially popular and democratic . . . and it would probably lead to the workers relying more than ever on unity and a sense of brotherhood."

The tributes given by magistrates and other people as to the good effect of the Revival are many. Social life was improved. Morality became a powerful influence for good. Sir Marchant Williams, stipendiary magistrate for Merthyr and Aberdare, testified to a marked reduction in the numbers of persons brought before him charged with drunkenness, disorderly conduct and the use of bad language; the improvement he attributed to the effects of the Revival. A Presbyterian elder remembers the largest public house in Penrhiwceibr — The Lee Hotel — virtually empty during the Revival. Instances are cited of innkeepers giving up work and following the chapels, and hardened drunkards becoming elders and ministers.

The most lasting influence of the Revival was that it gave Nonconformist Chapels a new lease of life. A " breath of fresh air" swept through all the denominations, revitalising them. Chapels with their way of life were preserved for a longer period.

It is argued by its defenders that nearly 100,000 converts were made, and certainly membership figures for the denominations increased (Evans, 1969, p. 146). But within a few years of the Revival, complaints were heard from all quarters that chapel membership was declining once more. Many dissatisfied converts turned to Pentecostalism and other sectarian activity (Evans, 1969, pp. 192-7). Young people were not attending the *Seiat* and the Sunday School and the Prayer Meetings. In 1909, according to an observer, " The Aberdare Valley chapels are very poorly attended in the mornings, although it is a bit better in the evenings . . . The *Seiat* has become a formality and the anniversary preaching meetings are a farce . . . " And a newspaper report mentions the same decline :

" The great congregations of the Revival have disappeared. This Chapel in Penrhiwceibr enrolled 64 new members during the Revival and reached a total membership of 112, but now we have only 50 " (*Tarian y Gweithiwr,* November 19, 1908). It can be mentioned that the Revival gave a lease of life to Nonconformity, and, in spite of the loss of the converts of 1904-5, enough young people were won to ensure the production of yet another generation of Nonconformity sufficiently powerful to exercise an important influence on Welsh life. Had it not been for the Revival, the Chapels would have ceased to be as important in the life of the people in the 20's, and many would have been forced to close their doors before the 50's and 60's.

The Revival gave Nonconformity two new factors : (1) A new impetus and enthusiasm; (2) An awareness of the contemporary issues. The " enthusiasm " is discernible when we read the denominational weekly newspapers and the Welsh press. It was an enthusiasm on behalf of the Sabbath, morality, education, and of the welfare of the common folk. The two factors are really interlinked and inter-related to each other. A few Nonconformist leaders even pleaded the cause of Christian Socialists, and people of the calibre of the Rev. Tudwal Davies, Rev. Silyn Roberts, Dr. Clifford, Rev. T. E. Nicholas preached the need for a union of Christianity and the social gospel. All these young, active, politically progressive ministers had a great influence on the workers, and it can be argued that the Revival was the connecting link.

The 1904-5 Revival's influence sociologically was that it gave Nonconformity in Wales a new lease of life.[6] Through the Revival, Welsh Nonconformity showed that it was not yet dead and that it still merited respect. The influence of the Revival has largely disappeared; and every year sees the disappearance of people who had been partakers of the " emotional " spiritual uplift that Welsh Chapels had at the beginning of the twentieth century.

Nonconformist ministers and leaders in general subscribe to the above hypothesis that the Revival in the past revived the corpse of Nonconformity, so a Revival is the only hope for the future of the Chapels and Churches. It is a fair question to ask: Does enthusiasm and emotional *Hwyl* have the same effect on the miners as in the by-gone age? Would a Revival influence the people who are self-sufficient and feel that the Churches are largely irrelevant to their needs? For J. Rogues de Fursac, the French psychiatrist who observed the Revival, one simple test would suffice: put a French working man among the Welsh miners at a typical meeting and there would be no hope of converting him since, he argued,

---

[6] The sociological material on the Revival of 1904-5 is very little. The only attempt is C. R. Williams, " The Welsh Religious Revival, 1904-5 ", *The British Journal of Sociology,* iii (London, 1952), pp. 242 ff, which has been severely criticised for " no effective statistical research ", raising questions, and " providing vaguely grounded generalisations " by Professor Basil Hall in " The Welsh Revival of 1904-5 ", A Critique; *Popular Belief and Practice, Studies in Church History* (Editors: G. J. Cuming and Derek Baker), Volume 8 (Cambridge, 1972), pp. 291-301. Another interesting attempt at a sociological survey of the Revival is David Jenkins, *The Agricultural Community in South West Wales at the turn of the Twentieth Century* (Cardiff, 1971), Chapter IX, " The Religious Revival of 1904-5 ", pp. 219-244.

these conversions took place because of the " milieu " in which a Welshman grew up in an environment of Bible, of Sunday School and of hymns, utterly alien to that of the wholly secular " milieu " of a French working man (Hall, 1972, p. 297).

In an age of Secularisation and Urbanisation, has the comment of the French observer of the 1904 Revival that a similar event is not likely to happen more of a meaning than when it was written? We cannot sociologically give an answer, except to say that emotionalism is an integral part of any religion, and that God's Spirit moves in a mysterious way. The " Pentecost " experience is still experienced. An account appeared in the Baptist Welsh weekly paper, *Seren Cymru,* of a strange Sunday that took place in November 1966 at Noddfa Church, Trecynon.

Two young people were to be baptised, but before the end of the morning service three more had asked to be baptised. By the end of the afternoon service two or three other young people were asking to be baptised. Some of these young people, according to the minister, Rev. John Lewis, had refused to be baptised when invited months before the date. Mr. Lewis explained the behaviour of the young people in terms of the power of the " Holy Spirit ", which is, after all, the essence of any Revival, with some amount of the " emotionalism " that we have analysed, but the instance at Trecynon was an exception to the rule in the religious life of the Aberdare Valley in the 1960s.

The emotionalism of the Chapel today is confined more to its cultural activities than to its religious services, for leisure activities are regarded as an opportunity to relax, sometimes in an informal atmosphere, and at other times in a more formal setting of a lecture or a meeting. To the majority, culture is quite clearly demarcated from work, and belongs to one's leisure time activities. I asked the question: " Do you regard Welsh culture as a recreation? " The results were as follows:

	No.	%
Yes	38	52.7
No	11	15.2
Don't know	13	18
No answer	10	13.8

The majority of the respondents regarded the usual cultural activities, i.e., *Eisteddfod, Cymanfa Ganu, Noson Lawen,* Concerts, *Cyfarfodydd Diwylliadol* (Literary Societies), Poetry Readings as recreation and a part of the cultural setting.

This would be the attitude of the miners, though, basically, the cultural activities would be very different from the cultural activities of the Chapel. What I have defined as emotionalism, and *hwyl,* would be witnessed in a gathering of miners in a working men's club as it would be witnessed in a Chapel Vestry. Dennis, Henriques and Slaughter argue in their study of the mining town of Ashton in the Yorkshire coalfield that the " emotionalism " of the mining culture is vigorous and predominantly frivolous in the sense of " giving no thought for the morrow ". This would be my observation of much of the mining culture of the Aberdare Valley, and would agree with Dennis, Henriques and Slaughter that a miner uses his culture in a frivolous way due to the insecurity arising from the danger of being killed at work — a danger which is very real to a worker.

Insecurity of employment is always in the background, as they remember the thirties and the days of the depression. Dennis, Henriques and Slaughter mention that there is insecurity based on the fact that the miner cannot be sure that he will spend his life in a well-paid job; in his youth he may work as a day-wage man, and return to it in his fifties.

Most of these considerations apply to the Aberdare Valley; and it is still not uncommon to read of a miner being killed in a Valley pit. Aberdare Valley is near Senghennydd, where over 400 were killed in 1913, and Aberfan, where 146 children and adults were killed by the moving tip in 1966. Gresford, near Wrexham, is another Welsh disaster which is remembered, as the words of a miner's ballad maintain :

" You've heard of the Gresford disaster,
    The terrible price that was paid;
Two hundred and forty-two colliers were lost,
    And three of the rescue brigade.

Down there in the dark they are lying;
    They died for nine shillings a day;
They have worked out their shift, and now they must lie
    In the darkness until Judgement Day.

Farewell, our dear wives and our children,
Farewell, our dear comrades as well;
Don't send your sons down the dark, dreary pit,
They'll be damned like the sinners in hell."

Associated with death is severe injury, which may disable the miner from working for life. This can either make him save as much as he can, so that he has something kept over for the rainy season; or makes him decide not to bother, but to live from day to day and make the most of it. This attitude is present among the working class of Ashton as it is among the people of the Aberdare Valley, and tends towards emotional pleasure and enjoyment as a pursuit and a motto in life. These pleasures are mainly drinking, gambling and bingo. A Drinking Club was opened in Margaret Street, Abercynon, in the sixties, which immediately was overwhelmed with requests for membership.

It was a frequent sight on a Sunday to see them queueing outside for admittance at mid-day, coming home at 2.0 when the Nonconformists were on their way to their respective Sunday Schools, and going again about 7.30 in the evening as the congregations were coming out from their chapels. Bingo sessions were held between 12 and 2, and this would naturally attract the women, and on Sunday nights there was often a concert at which artists could earn for an evening's entertainment the sum of £25.

Dennis, Henriques and Slaughter regard the Working Men's Club as the cultural institution which appeals to more Ashton miners than any other institution. It would be true to say the same thing of Aberdare Valley miners and the majority of the industrial workers. The Working Men's Clubs in Ashton in the fifties were predominantly male institutions, with only one of six clubs admitting women. The club membership is half as large as the total male population.

The only difference between Ashton and Aberdare is the female's place in the institution. Women are admitted in the Valley and, indeed, go with their husbands in the evenings and especially Saturday and Sunday nights. This has meant that many of the clubs have changed in appearance from a dingy, purely drinking place to one of pleasant atmosphere more resembling a hall. But, as Charles Booth maintained at the beginning of the century, in his study *Life and Labour of the People of London*, 1903, Vol. 1, Part 1, at all the clubs the bar is ". . . the centre support . . . the pole of the tent ". The majority of the men spend most of their time at the bar having discussions, or perhaps looking at a television screen. Football is a subject that is always popular; in Ashton Rugby League is a popular topic, and in the Aberdare Valley Rugby Union. Many of the sporting organisations have their own licensed premises; Rugby Union or the Golf Clubs. The clubs in the Aberdare Valley are made up of all kinds of organisations : Labour Clubs, Working Men's Clubs, Conservative Clubs. Many of the miners and other industrial workers belong to more than one club, and this could explain the high proportion in Ashton and the Aberdare Valley who belong to them.

It is often said that the clubs welcome ministers to visit the premises. My experience has been less fortunate. I approached the Managing Director of the Pontyclun Breweries who, as Treasurer of a Presbyterian Church at Cilfynydd, welcomed my plans. It was, however, up to the individual clubs to accept me; he suggested two clubs, one in Penrhiwceibr and the other in Mountain Ash, who dealt with them as breweries. I tried in vain, but excuses were always given — the night I suggested was inconvenient, alterations were to be made to the premises, and so on. All this rather substantiates the contention that the only really welcome guest would be someone willing to sit round the table, or by the bar, drinking, exchanging stories, or talking rugby or sport. The discussion, according to Dennis, Henriques and Slaughter, is almost always about concrete cases, whether of incidents in work, or on the field of play. In Ashton and in the Aberdare Valley concerts are an integral part of the club's activities, and comedians and pop groups are paid to entertain the members at the weekend.

It is possible now to compare in detail the emotionalism of the culture of two mining areas : one being Ashton in Yorkshire and the other being Aberdare Valley in the South Wales coalfield. In both areas the " Miners' Lodge " or the Miners' Union (in the Aberdare Valley the South Wales Union of Mineworkers, and in Ashton the Yorkshire Area of the National Union of Mineworkers) are a force to be reckoned with in the political and social life of the community.

At Abercynon in 1965 the Miners' Lodge secured their representative as the official Labour candidate of the Ward in the Mountain Ash Urban District Council against the local Labour Party candidate. Members of the Miners' Lodge attended the selection meeting who never attended a Labour Party Ward meeting for the only reason of selecting their candidate. The Union binds him to his fellowmen—and the word solidarity has a real meaning for a miner.

At Ashton one of the most important organisations stemming from the colliery is the brass band, the Ashton Workmen's Band. The word "workmen" is not intended to indicate that it is the workmen who finance and manage it. There is a levy of one penny per week on the wage of all workmen at Ashton Colliery. There are no brass bands connected with any of the Aberdare Valley collieries, though there are bands connected with collieries in South Wales.

One other cultural activity closely connected with the collieries in Ashton and the Aberdare Valley deserves mention — the St. John Ambulance Brigade. It is viable as an association because it has a clearly defined and socially approved purpose directly relevant to the needs of the town or the area, namely, the administering of first-aid to the injured. Due to frequent accidents in collieries, the St. John Ambulance is a vital part of any colliery, and in the Aberdare Valley every colliery has full-time St. John Ambulance workers. Many of the ones who answered the questionnaire were St. John Ambulance Brigade members. A Rhigos industrial worker (Questionnaire No. 7) attended a St. John Ambulance every week. A Hirwaun miner, and a Darranlas retired miner, and a member of Hirwaun Tower No. 1 Colliery Medical Centre personnel belonged to the movement. The advantage of the St. John Ambulance Brigade is that it trains its members in some way, and they can never feel that their training is pointless and divorced from reality.

Another similarity in the "mining culture" of the two areas is the welfare provisions, for coalmining is one of the few industries in which the provision of leisure activities by employers is required by law. The Mining Industry Act of 1920 established a Miners' Welfare Fund. A Miners' Welfare Committee was constituted at the same time to administer the fund . . . " for purposes connected with the social well-being, recreation and conditions of living of workers in and about coalmines" (Mining Industry Act, 1920, Section 20(i)).

The Miners' Welfare Institutes in the Aberdare Valley, at Hirwaun, Cwmaman, Aberaman, Mountain Ash, Penrhiwceibr and Abercynon, are by far the biggest buildings in the valley, and in this respect resemble the Miners' Welfare Institute in Ashton.

The institute served Ashton in 1956 as a minor centre of cultural activities, as it did in the Aberdare Valley, in the following ways:

(1) The local Dramatic and Musical Society used it for a fortnight each year.
(2) Other organisations will put on occasional concerts.
(3) Each Sunday throughout the year a dance was held on the premises.
(4) It is used by the Boys' Club and Boxing Club.
(5) It is used for billiards.

The Mining Institutes in the Mountain Ash area housed also a library. The Mountain Ash Public Library was held in the Welfare Hall until 1969, so was Abercynon till 1968, when new premises were found and they moved from the Welfare Hall. A new innovation in the sixties has been the bingo sessions, and these are held regularly, as at Abercynon (twice a week), with approximately a thousand people attending some of the sessions.

On the remaining nights (4 to 5) "movies" are shown, and these are attended by an average of one to two hundred at each performance.

This means that it is very difficult to hold concerts in the Welfare Hall, as the Committee are unwilling to disturb the bingo nights as they are the money-spinners; and the organisations have to use local chapels for their concerts and their performance of *Messiah*.

The halls are used in Ashton and the Aberdare Valley by some organisations as their regular meeting place. St. John Ambulance meets in the Abercynon Hall, the local National Union of Mineworkers have their office there, and, as in Ashton, it is the centre, too, of the local Labour Party.

There are minor functions. In the Aberdare Valley Miners' Welfare Halls, sessions of whist drives are held regularly, and in Ashton a boys' club, catering for 15-18 age group, meets twice weekly. Its activities in practice are restricted to table-tennis, and to cricket and football.

There is a billiard-room in the Ashton Institute, as well as in most of the Aberdare Valley Institutes. Billiards and snooker constitute the only activity for which the institute is utilised continuously throughout the week. They are usually open from 10 a.m. to 9.30 p.m. In the 1930s this was a popular rendezvous for unemployed miners. Today, the billiard-rooms are frequented mostly by youths under 18, and, as in Ashton so in the Aberdare Valley, the Miners' Welfare Institute does not play a very important part in the leisure time of the miner.

After Nationalisation — the Coal Industry Nationalisation Act, 1946 — the welfare duties were given to the National Coal Board, and the other activities were taken over by the Miners' Welfare Commission. In 1948 the Miners' Welfare Commission and the Coal Board came together in a National Miners' Welfare Committee in order to co-ordinate their welfare functions. By 1951 it was decided to separate the functions again — without losing sight of the need for co-ordination — by forming a Coal Industry Social Welfare Organisation to deal with "social welfare". The Coal Industry Social Welfare Organisation is concerned with more aspects of leisure than merely the fostering of Miners' Welfare Institutes. Its field of activity covers:

(1) Outdoor schemes: to provide facilities for healthy recreation, with special but not exclusive reference to the need of youngsters.

(2) Indoor schemes: there were 700 Miners' Welfare Halls (in 1956).

(3) Holidays: The C.I.S.W.O. maintains Miners' Holiday Centres.

(4) Health: 20 convalescent homes are provided.

(5) Education: Investments allow scholarships and exhibitions *per* year for the income for "Workers in or about coalmines and their sons and daughters".

But the Welfare Halls are regarded as white elephants, and many of them have been converted in South Wales into luxurious drinking bars to try to appeal to the modern-day miner. This, it seems, is more of a success story financially than the traditional methods, though many of the older miners bewail it and feel that the idealism of the past is being trampled underfoot. It means that the halls are being converted, and it can cost anything between £4,000 and £40,000. The money comes, without interest, from the Breweries. During the last few years this has happened in the following South Wales valley villages: Wattstown, Maerdy, Lewis Merthyr, Porth, Blaen Rhondda and Fernhill, Rhisga, Glyn Neath, Cross Keys, Tredegar (where Aneurin Bevan used to study), Treharris, Bedlinog, Trehafod, Lewistown, Maesteg, Cwmbach, Aberdare and Nixon Welfare Hall, Mountain Ash. (Rees, 1966, pp. 55-56.)

The "emotionalism" of the mining culture takes other forms from my description and comparison with Ashton, as, for example, pigeon-racing, greyhound racing, but the majority of the miners express themselves emotionally in argument and singing in the working men's clubs. Their solidarity is expressed in this way, and their concern for others is as deep and sincerely felt as any other section of society.

I feel also that the mining industry and Nonconformity have structural similarities, and this brings us to Section 3.

3. *The Structural Similarities.*

The resemblance between the way in which work was organised down the pits and the structure on which chapel administration was based shows the complementarity between the industrial and religious systems.

When we examine the relationship of Nonconformity to the industrial background, the questions that arise are: Did the industrial organisation of the coalmine lend itself to the social structure of the Chapel? Did the system of hierarchy in the Chapels commend itself to the newly emerging industrial worker? Two things must be made clear: (1) The organisation of Nonconformity must have paved the way for the working-class leadership in industrial disputes. (2) The Dissent of religion, to quote George F.

Thomason, became the radicalism of politics, and a militant force in relation to industry. The Nonconformist Churches have a democratic form of government.

In the Baptist and Congregationalist Churches it is considered that each congregation is a Church in itself, not requiring any special class or hierarchy of peers, but only a brotherhood of true believers. The ordinary member has considerable power in the running of his church. The churches usually have a minister and also a management committee of deacons, who are elected by the members. The minister himself is "called" by the members of the congregation to serve among them; it is usual for the minister and deacons to gather together at some time every month in the church "meeting". Churches usually associate voluntarily in the local Congregational or Baptist meetings, which serve an area, and with the National Union which covers the whole Principality.

The Presbyterians or Calvinistic Methodists have one parity of ministers, none of whom enjoys a status of superiority, spiritual or ecclesiastical, over the others, all rank the same among God's people. A parity of ruling elders takes an equal share with the minister in management of church affairs. There is also free election of ministers to all charges. All communicants in the congregation have a right to elect any person duly qualified under regulations of the church to be their minister, subject to the "call" being sustained by the Presbytery. No pastor can be appointed against the wishes of the congregation. In a Wesleyan Methodist Church the members have fewer constitutional powers than their counterparts in a Congregationalist, Baptist or Presbyterian Church.

It has been agreed that this form of Nonconformist government, with its democracy and equal opportunities, paved the way for the participation in Trade Union affairs. An historian has pointed out how Presbyterianism, in the form of Unitarianism, played an important role in the awakening of radicalism in Merthyr in the 1830s : " Presbyterianism was the catholic name given to the new liberal theology which made such inroads into the old Dissent in the late 18th century. The rationalist, scientific Dissent which carried many of its professors into Unitarianism in the early 19th century, which, indeed, carried some of them into East Glamorgan which was one of their strongholds. It was these men who launched the political union" (Williams, 1966, p. 15). There is no doubt that the middle class and largely Unitarian radicals of Merthyr were the midwives of the working-class movement.

Many of the leaders of public life in Wales in the nineteenth and twentieth centuries, as they have testified themselvs, had their initial training in leadership at the Nonconformist Chapels. There are endless examples. While many of the major Welsh labour leaders, like Mabon in particular, and David Watts Morgan, remained faithful to the Chapel throughout their public careers, others, like A. J. Cook and Arthur Horner, the left-wing miners' leaders, did not, although their earliest public experience came through the evangelical Welsh Nonconformity. For some years, Arthur Horner, the future dedicated materialist Marxist miners' leader, was a noted Baptist preacher.

The democratic form of Church government within the Nonconformist Chapels made an obvious appeal to the emerging working-class of the industrial revolution. This is brought out in the Congregational Year Book for 1873. " The social position of the Congregationalists of Wales differs from that of our brethren in England. The bulk of our congregation is made up of working classes, only a comparatively small number of the upper middle class, and none of them validly belongs to us." This can be compared with the Anglican Church, which was a Church of the upper class Tories, and a " theocracy and not a democracy ". Nothing can be done in the Anglican Church without the Vicar's approval, and while he is expected to confer with the parochial church councillors and churchwardens, he need not do as they advise. He is instituted by the Bishop of his diocese and is responsible to his Bishop and not to the congregation.

This could well be one of the reasons why the Anglican Church never had such a grip on the emerging working class of the 19th century as the Chapels did; the Anglican organisation was too authoritarian. The parish church also was often inadequate, being built to serve a scattered population, and with the opening up of the valleys, was often set at some distance from the new aggregations of the community.

The Dissenting sects, on the other hand, followed the frontiers of settlement, and chapels were built when the need arose, contagious to the mines. Brennan, Cooney and Pollins maintain that as a result of a survey made in South-West Wales about 1950, the point seems clear that Trade Union leaders are produced by the democratic and working class Chapels. It is also evident that the industrial set-up in the coalmines could be a factor in the multiplication and vitality of the Nonconformist Chapels. For the mining industry provided the conditions in which the small community focused on its place of work, could continue to uphold in its social structure (both inside work and outside it) the particularistic philosophy which imbued the Chapel. Within this small community an intense neighbourliness could be kept, and the "particularism" of religion find expression.

Let us now take a look at the organisation of the coalmines following Trist, Higgin, Murray and Pollack's "organisational choice", so as to see the change within the organisation in the last hundred years, from the conventional longwall to the cutting longwall. Trist *et al.* maintain that the weaning methods with which we are concerned have one characteristic in common: all are cyclical systems in which a sequence of operations have to be carried out for each "web" of coal that is extracted. They are to be distinguished from the continuous methods in which operations are carried out simultaneously rather than successively, so that a steady flow of coal emerges from the face each shift. Another common factor underground is the absence of forced and consistent conditions in the physical environment.

The threat of instability from the environment makes the production task much more liable to disorganisation, but with this has come "responsible autonomy", built up from: (1) acceptance of responsibility for the future cycle of operations; (2) recognition of the inter-dependence of one man or a group for the other effective progress of the cycle; (3) self-regulation by the whole team and its constituent groups.

It could well be claimed that this "responsible autonomy" of the miner can be discerned in the role of the Nonconformist minister and elders in: (1) acceptance of responsibility for the well-being of the fellowship; (2) inter-dependence of members, not so much for safety, but for the success of the Church; (3) self-regulation in the " operational roles " performed for the furtherance of the Church.

Nonconformity has realised the efficiency of the " task groups " in the mining industry, and there is a similarity between the two organisations. This can be seen in : (1) " activity group " which is the Church within the Church, manifested in the smooth running of the work and its meetings like the *seiat* and the prayer meetings; (2) " identical role " same amount of work for the miners could mean in the Church the " parity of ministers and members "; (3) " reciprocal role " which allows a miner, like a minister, the right to carry out a main task alone. It would probably be pressing the organisational role too far to say whether the " work culture ", the managing system which covers everything supporting the productive operations and includes the deputy, overman and under-manager, has affected the organisation of Nonconformist meetings, circuits and synods.

In the " single place " tradition, as Trist *et al.* term it, similar psychological traits may be found. In the " single place tradition " the nature of the coal-face, which is only about six to eleven yards in length, imposes certain conditions on the miner. A " single-place " worker is a complete miner who supervises himself and is the person directly responsible for production.

The primary work group is the " marrow group " composed of men who share the same pay-note through working in the same place. The group select themselves, as they are choosing mates who are all expected to be of an equal standard in work performance.

A further example of complementarity of the pit and the church organisations can be seen in the seam-coaling, for a seam is a unit with sociological and technological reality. When accepted as a member, a man is said to have been granted " seam status ". Recognition of a person as a Church member can be made through one of three ways : (1) a letter of recommendation from another Church; (2) being made a member through the " communicants' " class, or (3) the congregation demonstrating its acceptance by a " show of hands ". A person who is not a member is either a *gwrandawr, dyn dieithr,* or *ymwelydd.*

A miner, in fact, joins a " seam " rather than a pit and,

similarly, a member joins a Chapel rather than a denomination, though both really follow. A man cannot be a member of a "seam" unless he is part of a specific coal mine, and a person cannot be accepted as a member of, say, a Presbyterian Church without at the same time being a Presbyterian. The miner cannot be moved from the "seam" if there is work there; neither can a Nonconformist member lose his membership if he attends regularly, lives morally, and pays his dues. Both the miner and the person have graduated to gain their membership.

"Single place" systems were adapted to the conditions of unmechanised working, which was the situation in the coalmines of the valley until the 1920s; work rules and organisation had remained the same for the last one hundred years. It was the face-conveyor that brought about the first major change. Its introduction allowed the development of the longwall as distinct from gateway and step-wise longwall, which were nothing more than groups of single places laid out in sections. Longwall system represents a break, more so in the case of cutting than in heaving longwalls. In contrast to the one all-round work role, there is a formal division of labour with special tasks carried out by a number of groups of varying size. The large task groups are identical role groups in which all members are supposed to do the same amount of the same task; relations in such groups tend to be troublesome when differences in capacity and willingness become apparent. The small task group — where each member worked independently, found relations more amicable, especially as such groups are self-selected.

Thus following E. L. Trist *et al.* we can suggest similarities as well as differences in the Chapel and Colliery organisational roles. It is possible to see reasons why a small team in a single tradition could maintain a "Chapel culture" intact and in isolation from others within a particular community setting. An ex-miner minister remarked recently that one good Chapel man in a "team" meant that the team would be kept discussing religion and Chapel all day. This organisation offered itself in the Revival of 1904-5, when prayer meetings were held underground at Cwmdare and Abercynon. When the "small team" lost its supporting base, it was more difficult for one person to influence the attitude of the larger, more disintegrated unit.

Another factor which must be noted is that the " small team " and the " marrow group " was conducive to the adoption of the *dynion dwad* (immigrants) from the rural areas into the different conditions and to the new " frontier townships " that they found themselves.

They brought with them the Chapel-culture, which was conducive to the " small team " set-up of the colliery. For the Chapel-culture itself derived its birth and strength from the hearth and the small group *cymortha* or the *noson wau* as T. Owen suggests in his study of Glanllyn, Merioneth. The focusing on the *Noson Wau,* as T. Owen suggests, and the small group combining for particular work purposes, as David Jenkins shows in his study of Aberporth, were restricted in a different form in the industrial valleys of South Wales, in the formation of the Chapels and the " small team " in the Colliery. This meant an emphasis on the " small community " of the Chapel rather than the " familism " mentioned by Trefor Owen in the rural areas. The industrial valley of Aberdare was populated by a large number of " rural dwellers " who spoke the language and worshipped in these new undignified Victorian chapels. The pattern was to gather a few men in a private house, and then some years later the construction of a building; this was how Carmel, Trecynon, Bethania, Abercynon, and many others came into being. The emphasis was often upon the " small community " who had come from the same locality. This was the deciding factor also in determining what denomination they would christen their chapel.

Furthermore, if they were driven to the chapels from the mines by their conditions, they then received from the pulpit a " Sermon of Life " which praised good, solid, hard work.

In the second phase of the industrial process in South Wales, we have what George F. Thomason calls " depression of individual type and form " and concentration of employment opportunities on a scale inappropriate to the community in which they are located. The " small team " with the coming of mechanisation was swept away, with the result that the old communal ties have been severed. The old pattern of father and son working in the same colliery has disappeared with the coming of light factory industries. The concentration of the main new employment in a limited number of locations, which feed upon an area of recruitment, has taken the place of the industry located in every township.

To sum up: The old pattern of the mining industry of the "small team" had, in common with the small independent chapels, (a) a strong degree of togetherness, (b) a sense of belonging. Both have been affected. The "small team" is uneconomical and unheard of in the new factories. The predominant characteristic of Nonconformity is that members belong essentially to a particular chapel, and this particularist element tends to be strongly streamed in the psychological response to membership. The Anglicans and the Roman Catholics have strong ties with a particular place of worship. But the organisational structure, as Harries and Rosser state, "which stresses that each church is a part of the whole rather than the whole federation of the parts", means that they are, in contrast to most Nonconformist faiths, "filling station religions", in Fogarty's phrase, in that their members can call in early at any church of the denomination on a Sunday and transfer their attendance easily from one parish to another with physical moves. The Chapel member is much more tied by sentiment, as well as by the fact of membership, to a particular building. The organisation pattern, which at one time gave to Nonconformity its great strength, is today (because of physical depression of its members) tied to the new trend of industrial set-up and location. This has crippled it and tended to deliver to its numerous chapels what may well be a deadly blow.

4. *The Advent of the English and Non-Border Population.*

The mining industry in time delivered another deadly blow to Welsh Nonconformity. In Chapter 4 it is seen how the early pioneers of mining were sympathetic to Welsh Nonconformity, and gave their support in the building of numerous chapels. But the development of the mining industry, and its need of more miners, meant an influx of English-speaking people from England and the border counties of Hereford, Gloucestershire and the West Country, to work in the mines of the Aberdare Valley. The Irish also came to work in the mines, and a son of one of these Irish immigrants has given us, in his autobiography, a description of mining life and conditions in Mountain Ash.

Joseph Keating described his experience of going to work on his first day, on his twelfth birthday, April 16, 1883, at the Navigation coal pit.

"Two of my brothers were in the pits already. All the boys in school looked forward with longing to the day when they would be allowed to begin work. Release from boredom of school might have influenced them; but my happiness was not so much in leaving school as in the idea of actually going to work underground. We saw the pit boys coming home in their black clothes, with black hands and faces, carrying their food boxes, drinking tins, and gauze-lamps. They adopted an air of superiority to mere schoolboys. We humbly bowed to this. They had experienced danger amidst thundering falls of roof, and had mysterious adventures in deep levels and headings, with blue balloons of gas threatening to explode around their lamps. They associated with big men and wonderful horses. They earned six shillings and ninepence every week. Never would one of them dream of giving up the pits. Life began to be worth living when once they had gone down" (Keating, 1916, pp. 37-38).

His mother was not so enthusiastic, but she realised that the money would be of great assistance to them as a family. But for the young Joseph Keating there was nothing like this adventure in mining:

"For me, the prospect of going to work in the mine contained more glittering romance than if its black mouth were the entrance to Ali Baba's cave of gold. The day before I was twelve I had to walk to Aberdare, four miles away, to get my baptismal and school certificates from Father O'Reilly, our parish priest, a saint and a gentleman, who later rose to be Vicar General of the Diocese." This eagerness was evident in the fact that he wrote after arriving home from Aberdare:

"My eagerness to go down the pit was so great that as soon as I came home I interviewed Dai Morgan, the overman of Navigation Colliery, on my own initiative, and showed him my qualifications: I should be twelve years of age on the following day and had entirely satisfied Parliament that my education was complete. He said: 'Right you are, Keat'n'" (Keating, 1916, p. 38).

The description of the actual preparing and going to the colliery is revealing:

"Next morning I was up at half past five. It was a grey, sunless morning, but I was thrilling with happiness, and I could scarcely sit peacefully at the table to take my breakfast of bread and butter and tea without milk. My mother put my food in a small tin box and filled a 'tin' jack with cold tea, and said: 'May the Lord bring you safe home!' as I left the house. I went to the pit-head in an ecstasy — the colliery was just behind our house — with a thousand men and boys, amidst iron trams, iron tracks, grease and machinery. I was given a long gauze-lamp, called a 'sprag', entered the pit cage, and, crushed in between about a dozen boys and men, was lowered into the darkness. The swift descent took my breath away and I gasped with fright and clung to my friends' dusty clothes" (Keating, 1916, p. 39).

These men, like Keating, brought in the main two new elements; one was the English language, and the other a new militancy in industrial relations.

I have already mentioned in Chapter 4 how the coming of the English and Irish immigrants seriously meant a decline in the Welsh-speaking population, and also a disruption in the life and witness of Welsh Nonconformity.

Nonconformity is not peculiarly Welsh. Indeed, it came from England, and it was an English importation, except for the Calvinistic Methodist or Presbyterian Church of Wales, which had a distinctively Welsh origin. But it is important to realise that even if Nonconformity is English in origin, it took on a Welsh dress and found its expression through the medium of the Welsh language. Consequently, with the decline of the language there follows suit a decline in Nonconformity, for the chapels depended on the Welsh-speaking migrants for their membership and their adherents.

This difference between Welsh language Nonconformity and English language Nonconformity has to be noted, for the decline of Welsh Nonconformity should have meant increase in the English "causes", but this generally is not the case. In Abercynon, the chapel with the largest membership is a Welsh one, with two other English causes with about the same number. The English Presbyterian Church in Abercynon closed in 1966 with 12 members, while the Welsh Presbyterian Church had 130 members, while in Penrhiwceibr the English "cause" has 20 members, the Welsh Presbyterians having 68 members, and at Mountain Ash the English "cause" in Duffryn Street closed in 1966, while Bethlehem Welsh Presbyterian Church had 120 members.

The chapels which have turned their services into English generally are not able to attract more listeners. A Welsh Congregationalist Chapel which turned its Sunday evening service to try and cater for their young people found that two of the most faithful young people came to the Welsh morning service and stayed away from the evening service. Another mother and a daughter, who could not speak the Welsh language, informed their minister that they did not want a completely English service, but rather a Welsh reading, prayer, hymn-singing and bilingual address so that they could follow. A Presbyterian minister, in 1956, tried an experiment in Penrhiwceibr. He was in charge of two churches in the same town — one Welsh and the other English. Perturbed by the language problem, he took along the young people who could not follow very well the Welsh service to the English church. They only went for a month, and they were back in the Welsh chapel. One comment made: "I prefer to go to Herman (the Welsh Church) and not understand one word, because of the Welsh singing, than go to Penuel (English Church) with its drab, colourless hymn-singing."

Nonconformists are divided on two issues: Is the language essential to Nonconformity, or are they separable?

This was asked of people in the Aberdare Valley in the questionnaire, namely: 22(a) Do you regard the Welsh language as essential to Welsh Nonconformity? 22(b) Is religion more important than language? They were invited to give reasons for their opinions. The results were as follows:

Table		No.	%
(a)	Yes	31	43
	No	24	33.3
	Don't know	7	9.7
	No answer	10	13.8
(b)	Yes	42	58.3
	No	12	16.6
	Don't know	8	11.1
	No answer	10	13.8

Table (a) has 31 people out of 72, a 43%, who agree with the pamphlet, written by three leading Congregationalists, that the " Language is essential to Welsh Nonconformity ". It is interesting to note that there were 11 out of 16 young people, a 68.75%, who did not agree with the supposition.

Table (b) has 42 people, a 58.3%, who maintain that religion is more important than the language, and they would agree with Principal Owen Prys, who said, in 1903, that religion and language are not bound together.

The respondents' reasons for their opinions are revealing, and are as follows:

" To me, religion is the same in any language " (Mountain Ash housewife).

" To those who have always been members in a Welsh Chapel " (Mountain Ash housewife).

This is a valid point, and it is the experience of so many who are not fluent in Welsh. Rev. Joseph Evans, President of the English Conference of the Presbyterian Church of Wales for 1906, referred in his valedictory address to the " persistent obstinacy of those in authority to make any change in the language of the ministry," and as a result the young were being lost many of them had been brought up to speak only English and so could not understand the Welsh service which they attended with their parents (Knox, 1969, p. 14). The problem still remains in the Aberdare Valley in 1975. In many families, only one parent spoke Welsh, and the language of the hearth was English, but out of traditional family loyalty the family attended Welsh services and children even learned to recite Welsh verses which they did not comprehend.

" A Belief knows no lingual *(sic)* barrier " (Barclays Bank employee).

" The two must go hand in hand as far as Welsh Nonconformity is concerned " (18-year-old Aberdare youth).

" Religion knows no barrier " (Barclays Bank employee).

" Being a Christian does not entail speaking a special language " (Medical Centre Tower No. 1 Colliery, N.C.B., Hirwaun).

" Because it is the language of our country " (Tower No. 4, Hirwaun, miner).

" People can belong to English-speaking Chapels " (Retired Mountain Ash miner).

" Religion should be universal " (Mountain Ash miner).

" Every Welshman should be able to speak his own language. I am sorry I can't " (Penrhiwceibr miner).

" The knowledge of Welsh is necessary to preserve the Welsh culture and way of life " (Abercynon retired Co-operative Manager).

" Church must change to the needs of the community " (Hirwaun youth).

" Most young people do not speak Welsh. So, if they want the younger people to come into the Church, then they must give way, and make room for it " (C.W.S. Creamery, Trecynon, Aberdare, Laboratory Assistant).

" Religion is the same in any language " (Hirwaun schoolteacher).

" Christ didn't speak Welsh on earth after all " (Abercynon housewife).

Only eight answers were given to the question: " Is religion more important than language? " The question, it can be argued, was an answer in itself, as the first reply suggests:

" Religion is more important than language " (Abercynon Civil Servant). This answer was from a person who would object to having an entirely English service in a Welsh Chapel, as she was a member of the militant Welsh Language Society, and an active worker with the Welsh Nationalist Movement.

" I don't believe a lot in religion " (Barclays Bank employee).

" Because it is known throughout the world " (Tower No. 4, Hirwaun, miner).

"I consider that it is better to have a grasp of religion than to speak ten languages" (Darranlas retired miner).

"Fundamentally, religion is important to all people, and language should not be a barrier" (Aberecynon retired Co-operative Manager).

"Religion is important, whatever the language" (Hirwaun youth).

"It is a part of everyday life. And it is life on its own" (C.W.S. Creamery, Trecynon, Aberdare, Laboratory Assistant).

"Religion is the same in any language" (Hirwaun schoolteacher).

Nonconformists in the Aberdare Valley are conscious of the dilemma facing them in the loss of elderly people, through death, who speak the language, and the young people who barely understand it, or who at the most have a smattering. Inside so many of the Nonconformist Chapels there is this "generation gap", and it is no exaggeration to say that, for the present, English has to be introduced into the services. The Young People's Services which were held at Tabernacle Presbyterian Church of Wales every month were bilingual, and the minister had to deliver the address in the English language.

This situation is being accepted by many of the Nonconformist leaders and ministers in the hope that the next generation will be Welsh-speaking. This optimism rests on the establishment of Welsh schools in the area. The only Welsh school in the valley is the Aberdare Welsh School, which was established in 1949. Already many of the Welsh Nonconformist Chapels have gained from this; a good example is Bethania Presbyterian Church of Wales, Aberdare.

There has been an entirely new attitude; and the Sunday School, which used to be conducted in English, is carried on in the Welsh language. The minister, Rev. E. Emrys Evans, maintained, in 1968, that he could address the children at a Sunday morning service entirely through the Welsh language.

The leaders of the Welsh Chapels in Abercynon, in view of successes such as the Aberdare one, and being aware of the crisis they are in, in 1967 tried to establish a Welsh nursery school at Abercynon to serve the lower end of the valley. A few children from Penrhiwceibr in 1967 travelled to Pantsionnorton, outside Pontypridd, to a Welsh school — but the number was extremely small.

At a St. David's Dinner of the "Undeb Cymru Fydd" (New Wales Union), held at the Welfare Hall, Abercynon, March 1967, an appeal was made for the establishment of a Welsh class in the town. It was felt that this was fundamental for the Welsh life of the town and for the future of the Welsh Nonconformist Chapels. The appeal was widely publicised in the local valley paper, *Aberdare Leader*.

Many of the local political leaders were interested, and especially the representative for the area on the Glamorgan County Council, a Council which has a very enlightened policy on bilingualism, the late Mr. D. J. Bond, J.P. On the Friday evening, 9th June 1967, a meeting was convened at Tabernacle Presbyterian Church of Wales to discuss the whole problem.

A good number attended, including two of the local Labour District Councillors, and the meeting was addressed by Mr. I. Morgan, Headmaster of the Aberdare Welsh Primary School, and County Councillor D. J. Bond, a non-Welsh speaker. Mr. Morgan dealt with parents' fears:

(1) Can my child learn Welsh?

(2) Would there be any English taught?

(3) Would a child be at a disadvantage if it came from an English-speaking home?

Councillor D. J. Bond spoke of the policy of Glamorgan County Council and stressed that the goal should be a Welsh School and not a Welsh class.

It was decided to elect officers and a committee, and I was elected Chairman; Mr. J. D. Maddox, J.P., a Welsh Congregationalist deacon and an outstanding local social worker, as Secretary; County Councillor D. J. Bond, J.P., as Treasurer. The Committee of twenty members was elected, thirteen of them being members of the Welsh Churches.

The next meeting was held on Monday, 10th July, at which two members from the Aberdare Welsh School Parents' Association, Mr. Rees and Mrs. Palmer, spoke in support of the venture, and it was decided to canvass every house to enrol pupils for the Welsh Class. This work was never done properly, though some of the Committee members did visit, and suggested the names of parents who had shown an interest.

But at the next meeting, on Tuesday, the 18th July, only four names had been received, and it was further decided to hold a meeting at Hermon Presbyterian Church of Wales Vestry, Penrhiwceibr, at the end of the month. This meeting was poorly attended, and addressed by Mr. Eric Evans, Welsh Language Organiser for Glamorgan.

The meeting on Friday, 1st September, was addressed by Mr. Timothy, Divisional Education Officer for the Aberdare Valley, and Mr. Eric Evans, and it was decided to start a Welsh Class, on the basis of the names submitted (12 being the minimum requirement), at the Navigation Primary School.

The Class was started, and a teacher from Llwydcoed, Mrs. Jean Edwards, was persuaded to be in charge of the Class. At the November 7th meeting it was stated that there were 14 pupils registered, and then the movement met a difficult problem. No more children at three years of age could be accepted, and this became a bitter and endless wrangling. The Director of Education for Glamorgan refused to meet a deputation, and the situation deteriorated. Children were accepted at 3 in the other schools, but at 4 in the Welsh Class, which was subordinated to the quota for the Navigation School.

At the beginning of 1968 — February 23rd, 1968 — meeting, a new note was struck by the Rev. E. Peris Owen, who brought his child 9 miles every day from Troed-y-Rhiw, that a Welsh Nursery Class should be established in one of the Welsh Chapel Vestries. A coffee morning was to be held at Tabernacle Presbyterian Church of Wales on Saturday, 9th March, organised by the Parents' Association of the Welsh Class.

Nothing came of Rev. Peris Owen's idea, though the late Mrs. D. Dolben of Bridgend, organiser for the Glyndwr Trust covering Nursery and Playgroups in Wales, addressed a meeting on 9th April. The number who attended from the Welsh Chapels was few, and the majority of the parents had no close connections with Nonconformity. They had been persuaded from a variety of reasons, and a few from selfish factors. Added to this were two Glamorgan regulations: that their children were not to be admitted till they were 4 years of age, while other Abercynon schools accepted them at 3 years of age; and they argued that Bryntirion housing estate, Ynysboeth, from where many of the children came, was within the mile and a half radius. J. D. Maddox wrote in a letter of 26.3.69: " I also think that the County moved very quickly when I informed Mrs. Lewis, the Headmistress, that I had measured on Thursday, 4th July 1968, from 169 Bryntirion to the Navigation School, and that the distance was 3,018 yards, which was 378 yards more than the 1½ miles, and which would have justified free transport for pupils coming from Bryntirion."

Looking back, Mr. J. D. Maddox felt that " we did not take sufficient time to organise our plans in setting up a Welsh Class in Abercynon. When we launched our campaign in June 1967 we only had a few weeks before the summer holidays, and with the schools breaking up and the large number of people who got away at that time of the year, we were handicapped." Another handicap was that five of the Nonconformist ministers, who were active with the movement, moved away from the district before the end of 1968.

The attendance at the Welsh Class fell away, and the parents who had children in this class had a letter in July 1968 from the County Council Education Department informing them that the Welsh Class could not be retained with the small numbers attending, and that those parents who would like their children to continue in a Welsh Class or School could transfer them to the Pantsionnorton Welsh School. In March 1969 there were 8 pupils from the Welsh Class experiment going to Pontypridd, 5 from Abercynon and 3 from Bryntirion.

This experiment has been dealt with at length as it is a case in point, and shows what are the potentialities for Welsh Chapels in the Mountain Ash area, and the result the influx of English immigrants has had on the society. Welsh is taught as a subject in all the Primary Schools in the area, but it seldom turns out a Welsh-speaking child. It gives him a smattering, enough to follow hymns and to recite the Lord's Prayer in the Welsh language, but not enough to understand fully a sermon. Nonconformity is, therefore, faced in most of the Aberdare Valley areas with a "crisis" and an ever-decreasing population which speaks the Welsh language.

The other influence of the English population was in the militancy of the trade unions. Nonconformity had taken an interest in the conditions of the working class. In the June issue of *Y Gwerinwr* for 1856 a complaint was made by a certain Gwilym Hirwaun (from his nom-de-plume it may be gathered that he was a native of Hirwaun, near Aberdare) against the practice of young girls between 10 and 20 working in the iron works and the coal yards. He maintains that the reason for this is the urge to have more money and profit. Apart from the exploitation of labour, the Industrial Revolution had given rise to several other abuses.

There was the Truck System. The masters of industry had set up shops of their own in conjunction with the works. The system was open to grave misuse, when owners would give food of any quality they liked in return for honest labour. The grievance was acute in the district around Aberdare, and the Rev. David Price, the Independent Minister of Siloa, was one of its strongest opponents. In 1861 he wrote in *Y Diwygiwr* attacking the shops for being unjust, and preventing the worker from taking his earnings to the free market. The Nonconformists in general were opposed to the system of payment in kind.

But though the Nonconformists were sympathetic, and worked for the welfare of the working class, they had no great sympathy with Trade Unionism and strikes. Their objection was that the Unions tended to destroy the liberty and independence of the individual worker. They argued that strikes do not pay. In 1861 a difficult situation arose at the iron works in Abernant when the workers went on strike as a protest against the Truck System. The editor of *Y Diwygiwr* was against the strike, but hoped it would succeed in its intention of abolishing the grievance.

Nonconformity was becoming the "Liberal Party at prayer". Liberalism appealed to Nonconformity because of its indigenous ties of language and sentiment, and because of its radical campaign against the social and political hegemony of the Established Church and the squirearchy. After two decades of intense periodical activity, during which Reform was advocated in agriculture, taxation, tithes, rates and education, Welsh Nonconformity returned in 1868 its first Member of Parliament in the person of Henry Richard, candidate for the industrial constituency of Merthyr, which included Aberdare. He was a former Congregationalist minister. Liberalism became the major party throughout industrial South Wales. Its extent coincided with the strength of Nonconformity, and a pattern developed, Nonconformity with Liberalism, Church with Conservatism.

The great division came with the development of Socialism, and its introduction by many of these new people from England, and the relationship between the working classes and the Nonconformist Chapels became tenuous. Socialism became the creed, and H. R. Niebuhr compares it with the Methodist Revival. The Methodist Revival was a great religious revolution, while Socialism was completely secular in character. It was not "completely secular" in South Wales, though we do not agree that it owed more to "Methodism than Marx". A Marxist writer has put it, "The attempt to suggest that the I.L.P. was founded by a state of Methodist parsons and local preachers is even more widely inaccurate than the attempts to attribute it to the single-handed efforts of Engels and Aveling." In *Essays in Labour History* it states that the "Bradford textile workers owed their socialism no more to the Methodist Church than the peasants of South Italy owe their communism to the Catholic, and if the Socialists succeeded in sweeping whole chapels-ful of the former into the movement by their broad, unsectarian, ethical appeal, the credit is due to them and not the Nonconformist ' Establishment ', which fought the I.L.P. every inch of the way."

Two factors are to be noted.

(1) The ministers of the Aberdare Valley were not, as far as can be ascertained, enthusiastic for Socialism. The warning of F. W. Jowett to clergy in a meeting of the Nonconformist Association was not heeded in the valley : " If you persist in opposing the Labour Movement there will soon be more reason than ever to complain of the absence of working men from your chapels."

(2) Nonconformity as such, except for a few leaders, could not respond to the new movement among the working class. The workers began to conclude that they could best achieve their aspirations through Socialism and not through Nonconformity. The year 1898 may be accepted as a dividing line. The strike of 1898 brought the phase of Lib-Lab period in politics to an end. It was a bitter strike, as a young man from Aberaman describes it: "The forenoon during this strike as we came home from school we saw the strikers on the march. From our streets we could see them tramping wearily up the winding road that crept through the valley. They were covered with dust, to them, perhaps, sacramental dust . . . the march, which had begun as far down the valley as Abercynon, increasing in numbers as it progressed, was organised as a protest against the terms offered by the coal-owners; and its object was to reach Maerdy House, where lived Sir William Thomas Lewis, later to become the first Lord Merthyr. He was a coal-owner, and it was hoped he would meet a deputation" (Edwards, 1956, p. 10).

The result of this strike was the creation of the South Wales Miners' Federation. New voices were heard, Keir Hardie from Scotland became the new leader. His voice was heard at Aberdare. Chapels were refused to them. Mr. W. W. Price, schoolmaster and local historian, was the I.L.P. Secretary at Aberaman when Saron Chapel was refused at the last minute after Bruce Glasier another Scottish enthusiast, was supposed to speak. The same thing happened at Siloa, Aberdare, because it was a political meeting. A week after a meeting was addressed by the Liberal, D. A. Thomas, at the same chapel. Most of the new local leaders were chapel men, A. J. Cook, Arthur Horner and James Winstone. They were the products of the Chapels and the Sunday Schools, but were also English in speech and birth. Socialism and class warfare were the notes of the new industrial gospel. Keir Hardie won a seat in Merthyr Tydfil in 1900, and the political scene changed rapidly. Nonconformity with its Liberalism was outdated. Its struggles — disestablishment, education, land reform, temperance — were not the problems of an industrial community. They were concerned with the conflict of Capital and Labour, low standards of living, fair wages, which Nonconformity was silent upon, and, above everything else, with the world-wide community. Welshness and the Welsh culture was a luxury when the rights of workers for a decent wage and conditions had to be fought for. The Labour leaders found people ready to listen, and the militancy, fervour and religious sayings of their new Member of Parliament, Scot by birth and upbringing, Keir Hardie, were well received.

The working class, and especially the new militant socialists, began to be impatient with the Churches. There was great rejoicing in Aberdare at the return of a Labour Member for Gadlys on the Town Council in 1907. There were three candidates — Rev. J. M. Jones, M.A., Mr. Tysul Davies and Mr. Thomas. The result was: Mr. Thomas (Labour) 793, Mr. Tysul Davies 697, Rev. J. M. Jones, M.A., 599. The old member had lost. It was not the fact that Rev. J. M. Jones lost which gave satisfaction, but rather, according to an article in *Llais Llafur,* to overcome the "hateful spirit" of the Nonconformist ministers towards Labour. Despite disrespectful words uttered about Labour, Mr. Jones had then joined with Mr. T. Davies against the Labour candidate. All the spite of the Bwllfa was against the Socialist candidate. The inexplicable part, according to Iwan Glyn, was that the Rev. J. M. Jones, speaking at Llanelli, gave praise to the I.L.P. branch at Aberdare, but his actions in joining hands with Mr. T. Davies lost him any support which might have come to him from Labour. He asks: "Pa ryfedd fod cynifer o Blaid Annibynnol Llafur, oeddent unwaith yn ffyddloniaid yn yr Eglwys, wedi ymadael?" (It is no wonder that so many of the I.L.P., who were once the faithful in the Churches, have left). (Glyn, *Llais Llafur,* March 30, 1907.)

How the change from religious to political influence affected the life of an individual miner is graphically told by W. J. Edwards in his autobiography, *From the Valley He Came.* He tells of the discussions between workers down the mines at Aberdare, on art, science, religion, philosophy and books — as good as any university lecture room. Then the author goes on to show how, after a meeting with Keir Hardie, despite the protests of his sister Eliza, the symbols of Welsh Nonconformity — Pilgrim's Progress and the Bible — became replaced in the parlour of his home by the Communist Manifesto, *Das Kapital,* and *The Origin of Species.*

The workers were listening, not to the native Welsh Nonconformists, but to the new men who had brought with them the "Socialist Gospel". This gospel became the authentic voice of thousands of people in the valley, and, in time, the majority of people were willing to vote for the party that was largely the creation of the Scot who represented the constituency from 1900 to 1914 in Parliament, J. Keir Hardie. A gap developed between Nonconformity and the new movement, and the relationship between Nonconformity and the Labour Movement was never as close as that between Nonconformity and the Liberal Party in the last quarter of the nineteenth century (Adelman, 1970, p. 5). The Chapel, however, kept a large number of the mining men of the Aberdare Valley as elders and Sunday School teachers, but the writing was on the wall. Howard Williams, the present minister of Bloomsbury Baptist Church, London, remembers, as a boy in Abercynon in the twenties, the vast difference between the religious service conducted by his father at Moriah Baptist Chapel and the meeting he attended after chapel in the near-by Workmen's Hall, addressed by Aneurin Bevan. He was one of the new leaders in the mining areas; a secular Puritan who had discarded the trappings of religion. Brought up in a Sunday School, he had been expelled for his unorthodox views; and his views became much more aggressive than the usual Nonconformist-Liberal politician. Bevan embodied the new influence in the mining valleys of Monmouthshire and Glamorgan — for his sympathy with the Nonconformist way of life was nearly non-existent. Bevan, like many other mining leaders, propagated the values of the English population, and it is no surprise that in the first Welsh Day debate in the Commons in 1944 he argued that there was no special solution for Welsh economic difficulties that was not a solution for the same problems elsewhere in Great Britain. "There is no Welsh problem," he insisted flatly. In the same debate, the Labour member for Wrexham, Robert Richards, a Welsh language enthusiast and historian, expressed what can be called the Welsh Nonconformist value when he said, "Wales is a nation which, in its traditions, history, language and literature, is quite distinct from England. There are many people in Wales who are more concerned about the culture of Wales than about the economic life of Wales" (Williams, 1971, p. 16).

The advent of English and non-Border population meant also a different approach to Sunday. This is not to say that every English-speaking person would be unable to understand the peculiar Nonconformist attachment to Sunday observance, but we argue that the influx of English and Irish people into the Aberdare Valley influenced the Welsh Nonconformist insistence on the keeping of the Sabbath as a holy day. Sunday observance has become a burning issue — a Welsh Nonconformist value — and a cause for heated argument in society at large, with the brewers, clubs, pubs holding out for Sunday opening and a more relaxed attitude to the day. Until the Second World War, Sunday Observance was kept in its strictest sense in Welsh rural areas and among the Chapel members in the Aberdare Valley. We remember in rural Cardiganshire that there were certain things people did in the week which would not be tolerated by parents or society on a Sunday afternoon. Children could not play football after Sunday School, and a good Nonconformist home would not allow its members to read a Sunday newspaper. The shops and pubs were closed, and the only recreation was reading and going for a walk between services. This was not looked upon by the people as any hardship; it was accepted as part of a normal upbringing and of the pattern of village life. It was the typical Welsh Sunday.

Sunday sport was looked upon by Nonconformity as "desecration of the Day of the Lord"; but inroads were made in the Aberdare Valley with the opening of swimming baths and other sporting facilities in the late 50's and early 60's.

I asked in my questionnaire the following question: "Do you agree with Sunday sport?"

	No.	%
Yes	26	36.1
No	37	51.3
Don't know	2	2.7
No answer	7	9.7

The majority of the respondents, that is, 51.3%, opposed organised Sunday sport, which still has not become a regular event in the life of the valley, and represents the expected attitude of middle-aged and elderly Welsh Nonconformists. It is interesting to note that 9 out of 16 teenagers, a 56.2%, felt that there should be Sunday sport and wholeheartedly agreed with it.

In Wales, Sunday observance has become a question of plebiscite with regard to facilities for drinking in public houses. The question and the issue was felt to be irrelevant for so many of the Aberdare Valley inhabitants as the clubs were opened. I grouped both together, rather than make a separation between them. " Do you believe that the Clubs and Pubs should be opened on a Sunday? "

	No.	%
Yes	24	33.3
No	35	48.6
Don't know	4	5.5
No answer	9	12.5

This response would not be typical of the majority of people who would vote in a plebiscite, and the large Nonconformist element is responsible for the untypical majority against the opening of Clubs and Pubs on a Sunday, and represents the prevailing attitude of chapels in the valley to the demand from sections of the community for a more liberal and permissive attitude to Sunday observance.

I also asked the question : " Do you agree with working on a Sunday? " I had the following response :

	No.	%
Yes	26	36.1
No	35	48.6
Don't know	4	5.5
No answer	7	9.7

There are still a majority, a 47.5%, who do not agree with working for money on a Sunday. The ethos of Sunday observance is still stronger than one thinks. It was said of the Rev. William Evans, Tonyrefail, one of the great preachers of Welsh Calvinistic Methodists in Glamorgan in the nineteenth century (" the silver trumpet of Glamorgan "), that he used to go on horseback as much as thirty miles to and from his Sunday engagements, a practice of which one old deacon did not approve. At the close of the day he took him publicly to task with the question : " What is a Sabbath Day's journey? " The reply was staggering : " From the house to Chapel, and from Chapel to the house " (Watcyn-Williams, 1949, p. 7). Though the respondents would not go so far as that reply uttered in the hey-day of Welsh Nonconformity, yet they treasured Sunday as a day free from the toil of everyday working life and had expressed in their response to the question one of the Welsh Nonconformist " values " in the urbanised Aberdare Valley.

This brings me to section 5 of the chapter, that is :

5. *The Breakdown of the Localised Semi-Peasant Culture in the Twentieth Century.*

For the Welsh people, Nonconformity has been not merely a sect within Christianity — like the Anglican Church — but a way of life. One of the fiercest arguments of the nineteenth century and beginning of the twentieth century was over the Disestablishment of the Anglican Church. In Aberdare Valley, Nonconformists can generally be classed as people much involved with the Welsh way of life, its language, culture and traditions. The culture upheld by Nonconformity is a semi-peasant one : that of *penillion singing,* of *noswaith lawen, eisteddfodau,* and *Cymanfa Ganu,* which has to cope with the economics and other sub-systems of an industrial environment. The main result has been that the localised semi-peasant has been severely undermined by urbanisation. To understand this breakdown in the cultural life of Nonconformity we have to discuss urbanisation, as well as the three main agencies for the change from the village set-up and the semi-peasant culture to the larger, more impersonal culture of urbanised life. The three main agencies are mass-media, mass-migration, and mass-production industry.

Urbanisation is a term used to describe the growth of a city or town, and urban, since 1910, has been applied to all places with a population of 2,500 or more. Rural areas, by contrast, are considered to be a form of association resulting from local continuity of residence of people of various occupations. These people live together in a small area centred round the village which is largely dependent on their support for its social and economic organisation. The village usually is accepted to be composed of up to 2,500 inhabitants and not less than 250; figures below this are classed as hamlets.

In the Aberdare Valley, urbanisation has mainly taken place during the last 25 years. Although not villages as far as size, there are still a few settlements which deserve the name, as they embody the characteristics of a village. This was, of course, more true before the last war, but I would argue that Abernant, Cwmdare, Llwydcoed, Cwmaman, Cefnpennar and Penderyn are still villages.

The village is a closely-knit community in which each member is known for his role, or roles (for example, possibly postmaster and deacon), and all are known to each other through more personal family associations. Two factors which united the village were: sharing the same occupation, such as mining, and a common cultural interest, such as language. The decline of the mining industry forced people to leave areas where they had lived for generations, and to seek work elsewhere. Since 1951, only one-third of the population of the Aberdare Valley is shown as employed in mining. In the 1911 census, 65 per cent. of the population of Aberdare Urban District were Welsh only, but by 1921 it was 45 per cent., and in Mountain Ash District the figures were 30 per cent. in 1911 and 26 per cent. ten years later. Today there are only a minority who can still follow a religious service in their native language.

Villages are bound together because they have so much in common — which, of course, includes their religious outlook. The change of industry, drifting away of members leading to the break-up of family ties and traditions, has led to a reduction in the influence of Nonconformity, and a break-down in its culture. Urbanisation means the development from village to town, and town to city, bringing about the inevitable change in living conditions, behaviour and outlook of those who dwell in them. A city has been defined as a population of over 2,500, but today many have as many as 7 or 8 million. Plato declared the desirable size was 5,000; this was the number who could hear the voice of a single orator and so participate in the active political life of his day. This could equally be applied to the minister, and the mere vastness of a modern city is one of the many problems which confront Nonconformity today.

People themselves seem to regard as towns those places in which are assembled the main centres of industries such as gas and electricity, local government offices, libraries, hospitals and medias of social services. Thus, in the Aberdare Valley, Aberdare is regarded as a town, although, in 1951, Penrhiwceibr had a larger population. Emile Durkheim makes a distinction between the social solidarity of the village and the town; the former, he points out, tends to be based on the uniformity of individuals, while the latter stems from the diversity and complementarity which has developed within the division of labour. In the village community it is social relationship which holds people of different tastes and attitudes together; in the town it is interdependence which makes each necessary to the other.

The processes of urbanisation and industrialisation go together, and they have been more rapid today in the Aberdare Valley than in the early part of the nineteenth century.

Industrialisation, as Herbert Frankel put it, makes it necessary: "to repair and maintain, to think of tomorrow, not only of today, to educate and train one's children, to prepare oneself for new activities, to acquire new skills, to search out new contacts, to widen the horizon of one's experience, to invest, to improve, to question the 'dead hand of custom' and the 'heritage of the past'." This effort has brought in its train affluence and a higher standard of living, improved means of communication, the shrinking of the world, and a greater amount of leisure to watch television. Though people may live in villages like Abernant, yet their way of life is urban. They sleep in houses hundreds of years old, but they lead a sort of life that people previously could only lead when they would congregate in large towns, but it means that for the first time in the history of industrial Welsh Nonconformity the social life, based on the small, closely-knit village community, is disappearing. This is an entirely new situation for Nonconformity, for it is called upon to evangelise and to maintain urbanised men and women.

There are a number of elements in our consideration of the mass-media, namely, the motor car, radio, cinema and television.

The motor car was a revolution in itself, and Porthcawl, Barry and other South Wales seaside resorts became Meccas for miners on Sunday. Dr. D. J. Williams, in his autobiography, *Yn Chwech ar Hugain Oed* (1960), describes the life of Ferndale in the Rhondda Valley at the beginning of the century. The chapels were full, but there was no alternative agency to cater for the leisure of the people. It was either to be at home or on the streets, or in attendance at a Sunday service.

The cinema came, the gramophone, and, later, the radio and then television. These had an irresistible fascination. Excursions out into the country, holidays, visits to the cinema, the ownership of some vehicle or machine, and, later on, staying home to watch the television — these were all the order of the day and soon were to become increasingly popular as the years went by. People forsook attendance at public worship for days at the seaside, for a ride in the car, or a serial on television, or Songs of Praise. To make things more difficult, Aberdare Valley witnessed, like many other valleys, mass migration in the difficult years of the 1920s and the 1930s — General Strike of 1926, the depression and the unemployment. Many a chapel congregation was affected, and the people moved away to the London area and the Midlands, never to return to the Aberdare Valley. In the questionnaire I asked the question: " Have you ever been on hard times? "

	No.	%
Yes	34	47.2
No	19	26.3
No answer	19	26.3

The " hard times " meant different events and times to the respondents, though many did experience the General Strike of 1926 and the days of unemployment in the 30's. The General Strike was a catastrophic event, and even 40 years after it the mining community remembered it vividly. Dr. F. Zweig has mentioned it in his study *Men in the Pits*: " Whenever you start a conversation with the miner on the pits, he invariably begins by telling you about the Coal Strike in 1926. The Coal Strike is vividly impressed on their minds, like an event which happened only yesterday. To any troublesome problem you may bring up, the first statement you will hear will be, 'You know that we had a General Strike in 1926, and all the worst troubles in coal-mining started then'" (Zweig, 1948, p. 10). Tragic poverty was witnessed in the mining valleys of the South Wales coalfield during the 20's and 30's. "The situation in South Wales was especially serious, with 60,000 unemployed. There were no alternative forms of employment in the mining valleys and the whole population was sinking hopelessly into deeper and deeper poverty. Hundreds of small shopkeepers were being driven out of business by these conditions" (Hannington, 1967, p. 203). Illness and war and strike would be other factors for hard times, and of the 19 who had not been on hard times, 9 of them were young people under the age of 21, who had been brought up in the Welfare State.

I asked the respondents to be explicit. If so, when?

	No.	%
1. During the Depression	16	22.2
2. During apprenticeship	1	1.3
3. During illness	17	23.6
4. During a strike	9	12.5
5. During the war	6	8.3

Many of my respondents, 22.2%, had witnessed the difficult days of the depression, and 12.5% during a strike, while the others were during the war, or illness, or apprenticeship.

The movement in migration in search of work has meant that a large number of young people has been lost to the life of the Nonconformist Chapels. The mass-production factory has also been a tremendous influence on the rather static life of the valley community.

Mass-production factories would often expect people to work on a Sunday, and the incentive of "double-pay" ensured a 100% attendance. As materialism got hold of people, Sunday became a day to carry out duties that could not be carried out through pressure of work in the week. It became quite a common scene in the 60's in the Aberdare Valley to see washing on the line on a Sunday morning. Often the women who would wash on Sunday worked in factories during the week, and either did their shopping or went on a run in their car on Saturday afternoon, so that Sunday morning took over from the traditional Monday as the day to undertake the family's washing. A prophetic writer of the Edwardian period was not far off in his diagnosis that it was not poverty but affluence which was the real danger. In his *Religion and English Society*, he maintained that people were using wealth for the sake of pleasure (Figgis, 1911, p. 28). There is an element of truth in the popular saying also that this affluence and new leisure activities meant to a great extent an undermining of the traditional Nonconformist culture, particularly in the urban areas of Wales, such as the Aberdare Valley.

The Chapel and Church have been largely unable to meet the more affluent worker in the Aberdare Valley, and to accommodate him in his need for comfort, recreation and fellowship. It is an entirely different proposition if this should be one of the tasks of the Nonconformist Chapel, but we only state that at one time in the past, through the activities of its semi-peasant culture of *eisteddfodau* and *cyfarfodydd diwylliadol,* the Nonconformist Chapels were centres for leisure-time activities. One institution of the working class which has sprung up in the valley, and which is on the increase as well, is the Social Club. It is a trend that even the Working Men's Institutes are converting their premises into drinking clubs.

What one finds on evidence of research carried out by various members of the Department of Industrial Relations of the University College of Cardiff is that attendance at social clubs is higher where church attendance is lower. A kind of encroachment of the world as the Churches retreat. The Social Club can be considered as a social organisation, with its lavish facilities and up-to-date premises, and a quite attractive appeal. It also has the attraction of the freedom of association which it allows. It permits the individual to identify with it — as they do in Chapels. The converted Servicemen's Club in Abercynon was showered with applications in the beginning, and its membership is around 350. The Club permits him to talk with any or none as he chooses, and does not confront him with a highly organised social framework for his activity. Its very freedom reduces the problem of " breaking in " for the individual.

Brian Jackson mentions a number of observations which assist the independence of the Clubs in a working-class community.

It can decide on its own hours, as a Nonconformist Chapel can. This flexibility in time-table is an asset to any organisation. " This allows the club hours to be moulded to the needs of members, and to the local cycle of work and leisure " (Jackson, 1972, p. 46). In working life one has to give one's service in a fixed period of time, so the Club is more flexible : " hours are chosen to suit the members' ' natural breaks ', and not the needs of ' them ' " (Jackson, 1972, p. 46).

This does not mean that the members of a Club can do what they like more than the participating members of a Nonconformist Chapel. Location in society constitutes a definition of rules that have to be obeyed. Social control is one of the most generally used concepts in sociology. It refers to the various means used by a society to bring its recalcitrant members back into line. No society can exist without social control. Even a small group of people meeting but occasionally, as the Elders' meeting or a sub-committee of the Social Club, will have to develop their mechanisms of control if the group is not to dissolve in a very short time. It goes without saying that the instrumentalities of social control vary greatly from one social situation to another.

One of the most devastating means of punishment at the disposal of a human community is to subject one of its members to systematic opprobrium and ostracism. Brian Jackson suggests in *Working-Class Community* that this is one reason why there is less heavy drinking in a Club than in a Pub. " Obviously a member who was habitually unpleasant when he had had too much to drink could be expelled " (Jackson, 1972, p. 50). Another system of social control that exerts its pressures is that of morality, custom and manners, and that is what one had in mind in saying in Chapter 2 that the Nonconformist respectability had become also a part and parcel of the Social Clubs.

Brian Jackson states that there is no crime in the clubs. " A man who burgled a house, stole from a post office, helped set up a bank raid, would get no supporting solidarity here. Members would be just as shocked as the Methodist congregations in the same road " (Jackson, 1972, p. 53). There is a code of conduct :

" It isn't very easy to define right and wrong in the clubs, but it's a very strict difference for all that. It is always wrong to steal money. Violence is always wrong. Theft from workmates or landladies is vicious. Theft from corner shops is utterly wrong. Breaking into the gas meter isn't so much wrong as stupid " (Jackson, 1972, p. 54).

The members of the clubs are, in the main, as any other grouping, law-abiding, with their own methods of social control, and a flexibility of approach and organisation which makes it attractive. But the clubs will not tolerate bad behaviour.

" Only the other week I had the painful job of expelling a member from the club. I hated to do it, but it had to be done. This chap wasn't a very desirable character — anyway, the steward caught him one day behind the bar stealing money. He ran after him and this chap gave him the money back and asked him not to say anything, but somebody else had seen it. We had a committee meeting and expelled him, but we didn't make it a police job because he was a family man. He had a prison record and he'd have got five years " (Jackson, 1972, p. 57).

The life of the club is not based on written rules or abstract situations, but on humanity, compassion, personality and precedent. It is this which has prepared the clubs to be the community centres in the Aberdare Valley and in most other working class areas in the British Isles.

While Nonconformist Chapels were at the centre of Welsh social life during the nineteenth century and the beginning of the twentieth century, the social clubs have largely become the " hubs " of the Valley community. The social activities of the Chapels were lectures, the semi-peasant culture of *eisteddfodau*, amateur concerts (as they still are); while the activities of the clubs are more professional — dancing, darts, concerts, and, in ever-increasing occurrence, bingo. Activities which were condemned by Nonconformity, as Dr. Howard Williams recalls. " The community was, paradoxically, a mixed monasticism. The sins to be avoided at all costs were those which exposed people to the contamination of the world, and the rules of behaviour were the rules of God. The Dance Hall was no place for growing Christians, the lucania billiard hall was thick with smoke and swearing, the Italian shops were not only places of temptation, they flouted the Bible itself by opening on a Sunday, while the pubs were the dwelling-place of the Evil One" (Williams, 1966, p. 13).

The fact remains that today people have more time to enjoy leisure-time activities. In the questionnaire I asked the question: "Do you regard leisure as a good thing for everyone?"

	No.	%
Yes	59	81.9
No	1	1.3
Don't know	5	6.9
No answer	7	9.7

This shows that the old Victorian idea that the ruling class only should enjoy leisure and that the working class should be involved in work still persists to a small degree. There is one who believes that leisure should not be enjoyed by all, a 1.3%, and 5 who don't know, a 6.9%, and 7 who did not answer.

We must remember that there are three typical ways in which people tend to relate their work to their leisure:

(i) The *extension* pattern consists of having leisure activities which are often similar in content to one's working activities, making no sharp distinction between what is considered work and what is considered leisure, and having one's central life interest in work rather than in family or leisure spheres. This pattern seems to be associated with certain work factors: a high degree of autonomy in the work situation, use of most abilities in the work, high — or moral — involvement in the work and intrinsic satisfaction derived from it. Typical occupations which seem to be associated with this pattern are those of a successful businessman, doctors, teachers, ministers of religion, social workers, especially the kind who live and work on the same premises.

(ii) The neutrality pattern consists of having leisure activities which are somewhat different from work, making a distinction between work and leisure, and having one's central life interest in family or leisure rather than in the work sphere. Typical occupations associated with this pattern are those of clerical workers, semi-skilled manual workers, and minor professionals other than social workers.

(iii) With *the opposition* pattern, leisure activities are definitely unlike work; there is a sharp demarcation between work and leisure, and central life interest is in the non-work sphere. The chief function of leisure is recuperation from work, and this pattern is more typical of unskilled manual workers and those in occupations such as mining and steel works.

The validity of these groupings needs to be tested, and question 48: " Do you regard Welsh culture as recreation? " is one to test it. The results were:

	No.	%
Yes	38	52.7
No	11	15.2
Don't know	13	18
No answer	10	13.8

The majority of the respondents regarded the usual activities associated with semi-peasant culture of Nonconformity as recreation; activities like the *Eisteddfod, Cymanfa Ganu, Noson Lawen,* Concerts, *Darlith* (Lecture), *Cyfarfodydd Diwylliadol* (Literary Societies), *Ymryson y Beirdd* (a contest between two teams of poets), *Drama, Poetry Readings.* This response combines the three patterns; the *extension, neutrality,* and *opposition.* A minister of religion, for instance, would regard Welsh culture as part of his Nonconformist ministry, and the majority of the Welsh cultural activities held in the Aberdare Valley in the sixties were held either in chapels or vestries, with the ministers frequently presiding. A clerk, for instance, would find in the Welsh cultural activities an entirely different interest to his work sphere. It would be the neutrality pattern for him, while a miner could take part in these activities and be part of the opposition pattern. There is an annual Eisteddfod held for the miners in South Wales every year at Porthcawl.

The semi-peasant culture, however, has been under severe strain since the 1960s, and it is unable to attract more adherents to its meetings or to compete with the wealthy social club in entertainment and accommodation. Chapel vestries are bleak and bare, the seats are hard, and they are unable to match the comfort of the social clubs near them. The Social Clubs are able to attract professional singing groups, magicians, and all kinds of entertainers, while the Nonconformist Chapels have to depend on local talent, which is often unrehearsed and of an amateurish standard.

The semi-peasant culture of Nonconformity has also, to a large extent, depended on the charismatic influence of the minister of the church. Charisma is a term introduced by Max Weber into the language of the sociologist to mean the power given to influence others. Charisma is derived from the Greek of the New Testament, and can be interpreted as "gift of grace". It denotes social authority that is not based on tradition or legality, but rather on the extraordinary impact of an individual leader. The religious prophet, who defies the established order of things in the name of an absolute authority given to him by divine command, is the prototype of the charismatic leader. Charisma can also appear in the profane areas of life, especially the political one, and reference is often made to the charisma of Napoleon in the nineteenth century and David Lloyd George in the twentieth century. The paradigmatic form of such charismatic authority setting itself up against the established order can be found in Jesus's reiterated assertions that "you have heard it said . . . but I say to you." In this "but" lies a claim rightfully to supersede whatever was regarded as binding before. Typically, then, charisma constitutes a tremendously passionate challenge to the power of predefinition. It substitutes new meanings for old and radically redefines the assumptions of human existence.

Charisma is not to be understood as some work of miracle that occurs without reference to what has happened before or to the social context of its appearance. Nothing in history is free of ties with the past. It is abundantly clear that the *charisma* of personality of the minister dominated the growth of Nonconformity in the second half of the nineteenth century.

The minister became full-time after the 1850s, and the first generation of ministers in the Aberdare Valley were remarkable men. Dr. T. Price (1820-1888) of Calfaria was called upon to mediate in industrial disputes at the Mountain Ash collieries, and edited the following newspapers: *Y Gwron,* 1855-60, *Y Gweithiwr,* 1859-60, and *Seren Cymru,* 1860-75. Dr. David Saunders, one of the finest preachers in Wales, ministered at Bethania Calvinistic Methodist Church from 1857 to 1862, to be followed by Rev.

William James (1836-1908), another remarkable preacher. The Congregationalists had Silyn Evans, and the Unitarians men like John Jones (1802-1863), a pacifist and an educator of rare distinction.

They all possessed remarkable enthusiasm, drive, ability as the Nonconformist charismatic leaders. But invariably charisma becomes what Weber called "routinized", that is, becomes re-integrated into the structures of society in a much less radical form. Prophets are followed by pastors, revolutionaries by administrators. When the great cataclysm of religious revolution is over, as it happened in Welsh Nonconformity after the Revival of 1904-5, men have to settle down to live under what was considered a new order, and which turns out sometimes to be very much like the one that they rebelled against.

Weber regarded charisma as one of the principal moving forces in history, despite his clear insight into the fact that charisma is always a short-lived phenomenon. What would have happened to the Welsh Baptists in the Aberdare Valley without the charismatic figure of Dr. Thomas Price? When he was first ordained as minister of Calfaria Baptist Church, Aberdare, in 1846, there were only 91 members, including a number at Mountain Ash. In 1847 he arranged special missions to Abernant, Heolyfelin and Aberaman with 121 members; 1852 Carmel (English cause) with 58, and, in 1855, Mountain Ash with 89 members.

After Jubilee meetings held in 1862, Calfaria allowed 163 members to form a Church at Bethel, Abernant, and at Ynyslwyd with 31 members; also at Gadlys in 1869 with 49 members. Dr. Price was responsible for building seven chapels, three schools, and forming eight churches. The same pattern can be found in the other Welsh Nonconformist denominations. And even in the "routinization" of charisma, the world is never quite the same again. For *charisma* is a factor that can induce a change in society.

I would argue also that the difference in the ministers of Nonconformity in the twentieth and the nineteenth centuries was due to the fact that *charisma* of *office* took over from personal *charisma*. The charisma of office gave stability to the work done by the men who possessed personal charisma, and their influence was far greater than seemed probable from their numerical strength and extended beyond religion to moral, social, cultural and political spheres.

But with the modern trend to specialisation, emphasis on science and technology, and general secularisation through television in particular, the Nonconformist minister has inevitably lost most of his authority and prestige in the Aberdare Valley. His influence through language, as only a diminishing number of older people speak Welsh, and the breakdown of the localised semi-peasant culture in the twentieth century, grows less every year. The place and function of a minister in Welsh Nonconformity in a mining valley has changed, and the remarkable leaders are not any more attracted to the Nonconformist ministry. Mass media have attracted many of the people who seventy years ago would have been ministers of Nonconformist Churches in the Aberdare Valley, and in South Wales, and could have been in the same tradition as some of the leaders of Nonconformity in its hey-day.

This brings my research to section 6, where I intend to test some of the suppositions that we often hear with the attitudes that were revealed in the questionnaire. The heading is:

6. *Attitudes to the decline of Nonconformity and the Mining Industry.*

It is often said that there is no connection between the decline of the mining industry and the apparent decline of Welsh Nonconformity in the mining valleys of South Wales. I asked in the questionnaire the question: "Do you see a connection between the decline of the mining industry and the apparent decline of Nonconformity?" I was interested in seeing if the hypothesis that I have propounded meant anything to other people, or was it a supposition on the part of the researcher.

26 people answered Yes, giving a 36.1%, while 28 answered No, giving a 38.8%, and 12 didn't know, giving out of 72 a 16.6%, and 6 gave no answer whatsoever, giving an 8.3%. The opportunity of expressing their opinion was also inserted, and 11 responded, and two housewives inserted "no answer". The following are the opinions expressed:

"Numbers have declined because there are more attractive activities available" (18-year-old Abercynon youth).

"Nonconformism has contributed nothing to the decline of the industry" (Barclays Bank employee).

"The collapse of mining has meant people moving to England to find a living. The people remaining are subject to the other attractions of our time" (Aberdare youth).

"Man has emerged and now has opinions" (Barclays Bank employee).

"Since the contraction of the coal industry, many people have left the district to seek coal elsewhere" (Hirwaun Medical Centre attendant, Tower No. 1 Colliery, N.C.B.).

"There was too strong a link between the two" (Tower No. 4 Colliery miner).

"The decline in the mining industry I consider due to the fact that the best seams had been worked. Sport and other activities extract from usual Sunday set-ups" (Retired Darranlas miner).

"Declining because it does not meet modern requirements and not broadminded enough" (Mountain Ash miner). This miner sees the decline of Nonconformity, and does not refer to the run-down in the mining industry.

"Living in times of such rapid change gives a feeling of lack of security and general apathy" (Retired Abercynon Co-operative Department Manager).

"The interest in Nonconformity had begun to decrease before the decline of the coal industry" (Hirwaun youth).

"The chapels were fuller when the mines were open, but the miners have had to move away for work." This is a reference to the mobility of labour, and the necessity, due to the closure of pits, for many miners to travel long distances to other collieries, or to find alternate means of livelihood.

The answers reveal a most interesting awareness of one of the main reasons that we have mentioned for the decline of Nonconformity, namely, mass migration, a fact which is mentioned by more than one, and that nearly 36.1% see a connection between the decline of the one and the other is a revealing attitude on the part of those who answered the questionnaire.

It is often mentioned that Nationalisation is one of the main reasons for the decline of the mining industry, an industry which has also influenced in its early beginnings the structure of Nonconformist Chapels in the Aberdare Valley. In my questionnaire I tested this supposition by formulating the question: "Do you regard nationalisation as being the final blow to the mining industry?" I wanted to test as well the reaction of Nonconformists to an issue which has radically altered the mining industry. This question was based on a quotation found in the *Aberdare Leader* and reported to have been uttered by the organiser of the Penrhiwceibr National Union of Mineworkers' Lodge, but was subsequently denied by him at a confrontation held at the Hall in Penrhiwceibr. Nationalisation is a topic that was widely debated within the South Wales coalfield, and among members of the Labour Party. A number of reasons were always put forward in favour of nationalisation. There are two I am especially concerned with: job-satisfaction and involvement. A. Barratt Brown, in the thirties, published a series of extracts from the writings of his students about their attitude to their work. A colliery screen-hand wrote:

"Coal comes past me on an endless belt, and it is my duty to separate any dirt there may be from the coal. The belt sets the pace at which I must work. I have no feeling of power when working at the machine; on the contrary, I feel dwarfed and I feel that the machine, instead of serving man, has become his master" (Barratt Brown, 1934, p. 85).

Another miner described his attempts to keep pace with underground machinery:

"One machine was vomiting more than I could clean up, while the other had a larger mouth than I could fill. The outcome was a constant worry; I was working always at the top speed without any sense of rhythm. I often wished that all machines and the men who made them were in hell burning" (Barratt Brown, 1934, p. 86).

It was also believed that nationalisation would give the miners an opportunity for involvement in the industry. In the analysis of a Yorkshire mining community by Norman Dennis, Fernando Henriques, and Clifford Slaughter, they came to the conclusion that nationalisation did not alter the fundamental set-up and system of the industry. They maintain that the miner has not experienced a basic change in his status and role in society, a change which goes with a transformation of the relation between the miner and his work. Two reasons are advanced for this. In the first place, the actual changes have been absorbed into the miners' traditional ideology rather than transformed it. Secondly, changes within the mining industry, and no one would dispute that there have been changes, have been unaccompanied by any profound modifications in the general economic framework of which mining is a part, or of the social structure within which miners exist.

" Most miners knew that the first charge on the miner's profits is compensation to the old colliery companies. In the first seven years of nationalisation, despite a loss in the first year, the industry made an overall profit of £90,500,000. However, the compensation bill for the same period was £103,900,000. There was, therefore, an accumulated deficit of £13,400,000. They could see also that many of the members of the National Coal Board, when it was set up, come from outside the mining industry. They saw no change in the local management of the mines when nationalisation took place. In this way they feel often that nationalisation has not altered the situation radically " (Dennis, et al., 1956, pp. 76-77).

There is also the popular view that nationalisation has done much harm, and that it would be better to go back to the days of the private companies. Colin Hurry and his associates numbered 41.7 per cent. of Labour voters in 129 marginal constituencies in 1959 who wanted no more nationalisation (Hurry et al., 1959, p. 23). There is, again, the standpoint of the Nonconformist Churches on questions of labour disputes, industry, trade unionism, and nationalisation. The comment made by Broadus and George Mitchell, who studied the industrial revolution in the American South, applies generally to earlier industrial revolutions in more advanced areas and to the mining areas of Glamorgan :

" The churches have either had nothing to say on the subjects of low wages and long hours in the mills or have distracted attention from economic wrongs by stressing the calamities of individual sinfulness " (Barton, 1965, p. 2). Often the Nonconformist Churches felt that nationalisation was a party political policy, and, therefore, of no concern to them. In my questionnaire on Nationalisation, a Mountain Ash housewife confessed in her answer that "it was hard to say anything about this." Results showed 17 out of 72, giving a 23.5%, answered; they fell into two categories : those that saw nationalisation as the saviour of the mining industry, and the minority who felt that nationalisation could not save the mining industry, as the industry itself was beginning to decline at the end of the Second World War. The following answers will demonstrate the two views :

"Creating too many executive jobs where one would suffice" (Mountain Ash housewife).

"Not the final blow, as it was bound to decline sometime, but it doesn't seem to have helped much" (Mountain Ash housewife).

"Under a private undertaking the mining industry would never survive" (Abercynon Civil Servant).

"The mines were bound to decline as a result of new fuels. Also, the miner demanded nationalisation" (Abercynon schoolboy).

"It is the rest of the country that keeps Wales on its feet" (Barclays Bank employee).

"The mining industry was declining anyway" (Barclays Bank employee).

"It was a dying industry at the end of the war" (Barclays Bank employee).

"Standard of living has gone up" (Attendant at No. 1 Tower Colliery Medical Centre, Hirwaun).

"Too many jobs are created, bringing the profit down" (Hirwaun miner).

"Because it has not worked as envisaged by our forefathers" (Hirwaun miner, referring most probably to the compensation paid, and to the members of the nationalised coal board).

"The pits had been exploited to the limit by private enterprise, and squeezed dry, as were the men, and I was one. Under nationalisation conditions improved" (Darranlas retired miner).

"Nationalisation — good for the mining industry, led to better relations and conditions of work" (Mountain Ash miner).

"Nationalisation is the finest thing that happened to us. Why should the wealth of the country go to a few men?" (Penrhiwceibr miner).

"I think it has brought the industry to its feet by modern management" (C.W.S. Creamery Laboratory Assistant, Trecynon).

"Made for more efficiency. Disposed of overlordship of managers, owners" (Abercynon housewife).

The reasons given have to be considered in relationship to the number who not only expressed an opinion, but who voted on the issue. It was found that 19 out of 72, 13 adults and 6 youths, regarded nationalisation as being the "final blow" to the mining industry, a 26%; while 26 out of 72, 23 adults and 3 youths, regarded nationalisation as not being the final blow, a 36%; and 16 out of 72, 12 adults and 4 youths, didn't know, a 22%, and 6 gave no answer, an 8%. Nationalisation was looked upon by the miners who answered this questionnaire as an answer to the problem of the mining industry. It had a moral and an economic connotation to it.

This account, and this chapter, has been a chronicle of the Consonance and Disconsonance of Industry and Religion. The owners and the workers, the structural similarities, have all influenced the Nonconformist Chapels, and so have the advent of the English and non-Border population, largely to work in the coalfield, in values and ethos. The amazing thing is the persistence of behaviour based on the semi-peasant culture, localized, which has been open to the influence of mass media and mass migration, and by means of psychological and sociological factors, has largely undermined the influence of Nonconformity in a mining valley. We cannot be dogmatic, as the two — the mining industry and Nonconformity — are experiencing difficult conditions. The reactions to failure we have tested in the last section of the chapter, and it leaves us in the position that is very much divided on the connection between the decline of the mining industry and Nonconformity, and whether Nationalisation has given the miner a lease of life or delivered to him a deathly blow. The available sources have been used, and one may ask a number of questions, as they immediately come to one's mind. The view has been put forward that Nonconformity must be aware of the powerful influences exercised upon them by society and industry. At the same time, we believe that much more research is needed in the sociology of Welsh Nonconformity, and what needs to be done will be dealt with in Chapter 7 — Conclusions.

7

CONCLUSIONS
AND THE WAY AHEAD

As was mentioned in Chapter 1, this is a pioneer study in the sociology of Welsh Nonconformity, and while it is obvious that there are some conclusions to be drawn, I am unwilling, because of the nature of the study, to be too definite. The sociologist never uses sentences like " The decline of Nonconformity is due to the decline of the mining industry ". Such a statement is genuinely deterministic and actually avoids stating the conditions under which they may be more or less true.

This does not deter me from stating that this study should be of assistance to the Welsh Nonconformist denominations. But, in common with every science, the sociology of religion has its limits. By definition it is concerned with Man in Society, and its conclusions, therefore, are only valid for wholes. It is not interested in individual cases.

It is true to say, also, that urban areas and industrial areas everywhere present a great problem to Nonconformity and, indeed, to Christianity. Boulard has given us instances of this in France and in Spain among the Roman Catholic Church. The diocese of Bilbao in Spain is the classic example (Boulard, 1960, p. 60). Wickham has shown how the Church of England has never been the Church of the working class in Sheffield. This is not true, as Brennan and his collaborators have shown, in the Swansea area, and it was not true in the Aberdare Valley either. But it is truer in the Aberdare Valley today. Why?

The social and industrial reasons for the decline of Welsh Nonconformity that have been mentioned are many :

1. The change in the mining process from the small team at the coal face to the longwall method of mining which was conducive to the structure of the Nonconformist Chapels has disappeared.

2. The decline in the Welsh language has meant a smaller number of clientele to evangelise and work among.

3. Geographical mobility has meant that the closely-knit community has largely disappeared.

4. The basis of continuity has been threatened in that young men no longer follow fathers into the old local industries, i.e., mining.

5. The new sources of entertainment and instruction outside the Chapel, in the Adult Education Centres, the Social Clubs, has meant that the Nonconformist Chapels are not the social centres for the community.

6. The significance of personalised relationship in the structure of Nonconformity. Charismatic powers aided by revivals strengthened the hold of Welsh Nonconformist ministers on the community, and this phenomenon belongs to the past and not to the present.

The advent of the non-Border population brought other ideas, mostly political, and, in the main, "left-wing ideology". Few Welsh Nonconformist ministers responded to this ideology, for it meant to them a weakening of what they considered to be central to Nonconformity, the furtherance of Liberalism.

The Chapels were not greatly concerned with social problems as distinct from the issues of civil liberties during the nineteenth century. They were certainly co-operative in ethos, but their social critique stopped short of social arrangements, which were largely taken as beyond moralisation. This made them, initially, unresponsive to Socialism when it arrived, quite apart from its English taint and occasional secularism. But just as the Welsh had made "dissent" their own, so they eventually naturalised Socialism. By the First World War the shift was occurring on a large scale from Liberal politics supported by most Chapel-going people and the occasional minister. The political split brought within Nonconformity by the advent of Labour politics prevented any continuing explicit involvement of the Chapels in political life.

These are the reasons I have gathered together and discussed at length in this book. I have also been able to test the sociological findings of other sociologists who have researched in the past. I have shown how Nonconformity in the beginning was suited to the new frontier conditions in the Aberdare Valley, as Trefor Owen pointed out in his study of Glanllyn in Merioneth. Its decentralised structure had fitted the decentralised familism of the Welsh countryside. Nonconformity had adapted itself to the domestic industries in the countryside, as it adapted itself to the mining industry in the Aberdare Valley.

We have also seen that Brennan and his collaborators' axis of Labour with the Free Church was not repeated in the Aberdare Valley. The Chapels and trade unions, as described by Brennan and his collaborators, form a left to right grouping, whereby the hub of the system turns on those who are leaders in the right-wing union and also in the left-wing Chapels, notably the Congregationalists and the Baptists. These two denominations had over 50% working-class leadership. Together, these unions and Chapel leaders dominate all politics, except those of the small Conservative Party, where younger professionals and older business men predominate. It is noticeable that the Trade Union side of the axis leans towards the thrift societies, amenities and sports in its cultural leadership, whereas the Chapel side leans towards choirs, music, temperance and the Y.M.C.A.

Dennis and his collaborators' study of Ashton could be repeated for the culture of the miner in the Aberdare Valley, and Brian Jackson's study of the Social Club has relevance. The work of R. H. Thompson on the four parishes in Birmingham, *The Church's Understanding of Itself*, does precisely what its title suggests : it considers the way in which people view their membership. This is inadequate.

This brings me to the second part of the concluding chapter : the perspectives for research. I have demonstrated the need for more research into other aspects of Nonconformity in an industrial society. There are at least four areas of research that need to be tackled :

Firstly, *the Nonconformist Chapel Structure.*

David Martin's comment on the way that the local group has assisted the decline of the congregation should be tested in the context of Welsh Nonconformity. " Freezing an initially flexible group of Christians into a tight, immovable nucleus is important for the decline of local congregations and their capacity to repel new congregations " (Martin, 1966, p. 133).

Another sociological problem is this: Why are members of the Nonconformist Chapels often unwilling to be so involved when they move to another area? Their loyalties are often local and their primary concern is frequently with holding on to one's position in the group. Is this reluctance one of the main stumbling blocks to unity? Why are the lay-leaders of the Churches much more cautious of unity than the ministers and clergy?

These are questions that need to be looked upon in detail for they influence the whole spectrum of Church life and determine the pattern for the future of Welsh Nonconformity.

Secondly, *Women and Tradition; the Young and Change.*

Amongst the general processes in industrial society, there are two aspects of great importance for the Churches. One is the activity of women in maintaining social continuity and in partly associating that continuity with the Church. The other is the activity of the young in breaking tradition and in partly associating that break with a severance of the umbilical cord of religious practice.

I have indicated some lines for future research on the place of women and young people in the Church. This is why the Sisterhood is such an important organisation in the life of the Church; it is a sub-culture within the Chapel. There are other questions that need to be tackled: Why are women more willing to be involved in the life of the Church than men? It would be worth the trouble to test Abbé Daniel's remark sociologically:

" Women practise more than men " (Boulard, 1960, p. 61).

Margaret Stacey has suggested that women's concern for the Church partly derives from their concern with the protection provided in a stable family. The woman stands to gain most from a stable family, and by extension comes to defend the stability of established institutions as such. This could be right, but it needs to be followed up, and also, in correlation with the part played by other women in other activities, such as Bingo and the life of the Social Clubs. Why are there women from the same home Nonconformist background more involved in Social Club activities than in Chapel activities?

If women are the bearers and sufferers of tradition, then young people are regarded as the source of possible changes. There is no lack of sociological studies on young people, from F. Musgrove's study, *Youth and the Social Order* (London, 1964), to M. Scholfield's study, *The Sexual Behaviour of Young People* (London, 1965). But there are one or two areas which need more research and, in particular, the Sunday School. I have looked upon the Sunday School as Dr. Busia did in his study on Birmingham, for these institutions have been of real importance, and their decline is, therefore, interesting. The various youth cultures are moving down the age-scale; and the age of leaving Sunday School is also earlier than it was.

This poses new problems for the Nonconformist Churches, for the Sunday Schools are usually the nursery for the adult organisation. It also poses the heart-searching dilemma for many a minister when he arranges Confirmation Classes. For the young people who respond are not used to Chapel worship, only Sunday School activities, and though they become members, they are non-activists from the beginning. What has gone wrong? How can this be rectified? These are questions that have to be looked at again.

The place of the Youth Clubs needs also to be considered, and Welsh Nonconformity is challenged to provide facilities for the young people. Is this the reason why the image of Nonconformity is so old-fashioned? Why is it so difficult to run a Youth Club in a Welsh Nonconformist Church, and why are the elders often reluctant to give their support? Dr. Busia and I would stress that it is essential to have the right type of leadership in these Youth Clubs; that the young people have to be trusted with responsibility to run their own affairs, and that there is more chance of success in the Youth Clubs if the Church authorities are unobstrusive.

Thirdly, *the Nonconformist Chapel and Mobility*.

It is a fact that social change has influenced the habits and loyalty of the members who belong to the Nonconformist Chapels. It is necessary to begin by suggesting the different forms of mobility which will be relevant to an enquiry. There is, first, the simple fact of rapid social change. Then there is geographical and social mobility: movement from one place to another on business or at the call of one's profession, and movement from one status grouping to another. Finally, there are the kinds of mobility more directly dependent on technological progress: the impact in particular of the car in allowing physical movement for leisure pursuits, and the impact of mass media. The last — the mass media — results in a combination of perceptual mobility with physical immobility.

Research could be carried out on the influence of mobility on Chapel attendance and Chapel membership. Sometimes Chapel members are glad to have the opportunity of moving, as it gives them a chance to drop the burden of responsibilities which an ever-strained home Church had placed on them in the past. Then there are those Nonconformists who move either in adolescence or in the course of pursuing a career, and the new Chapel is never "quite the same".

The mobility of Chapel members on a Sunday is another factor to be taken into consideration in a study on Mobility and Welsh Nonconformity. Visiting relations, watching sports, going away for the weekend; all these are made easier by the possession of a car. The institutions of Sunday Church and Sunday School, as well as weekday activities, must contend with all the modern alternative avenues for enjoyment and interest.

Fourthly, *The role of the Minister in Welsh Nonconformity.*

I have given an introduction to this subject in the discussion on the charismatic powers of such ministers as Dr. Thomas Price. It is time also that this should be followed through by comparing the role of the minister in nineteenth century Nonconformity with the contention of Paul Halmos that the ministers in our day have lost to other professions part of the tasks that usually were performed by them. The doctors have assumed the functions of secular counsellors, according to Talcott Parsons, as it was easier for them to do this than for others. The doctor has ". . . very important associations with the realm of the sacred " which would help him to inherit the functions of the clergy (Parsons, 1952, p. 445).

A study of this kind needs to go further, and test Halmos's point that the clergy and the doctors are being made redundant by the professions of counselling, namely, the psychiatrists, psycho-analysts, psychologists, and by far the largest group of counsellors, the social workers. Are we, therefore, left with a situation in which the *charisma* is not with a Nonconformist minister in the technological age but with the new counsellors?

These are the areas which need to be looked at in the future, for the only way to preserve the Welsh Nonconformist institutions is to analyse them in research. Welsh Nonconformity is being thrown up for recasting through the demands of other institutions who threaten its challenge. To resist completely the making of necessary modifications is to invite the dead hand of the past to reach out and destroy the institution. Welsh Nonconformity has to look again at its whole ethos, from its worshipping activities to the work of the Sunday School. For the Chapel in an industrial society has to learn to care, and this research has shown that the attitude towards the Chapel is one of neutrality rather than that of apathy. This is the most encouraging note that can be heard in this study, and it is this which should be a spur to the leaders of Welsh Nonconformity to look again at its structures, institutions, ethos and activities in the South Wales valleys.

Mining and industry have also been transformed in new and sometimes unexpected directions. In looking at the diversification and development which have taken place, we have been concerned with the workers themselves, who have made all this possible. It has been said that in the steel industry " men are the most important raw material of all — priceless assets that make great achievements possible ". This is equally true of the mining industry and Welsh Nonconformity as well.

APPENDIX

Table of Population Statistics

Year	Population of Aberdare Parish	Urban District
1801	1,486	
1811	1,781	
1821	2,062	
1831	3,961	
1841	6,471	
1851	14,999	
1861	32,299	
1871	37,774	36,112
1881	35,533	33,804
1891	40,917	38,431
1901		43,365
1911		50,830
1921		55,010
1931		48,880
1939		42,620
1951		40,710
1961		38,970
1966		38,330

REFERENCES

Adelman, Paul, *Gladstone, Disraeli and later Victorian Politics* (London, Longman, 1970).
Arensberg, C. A., and Kimball, S. T., *Family and Community in Ireland* (Cambridge, Mass., Harvard University, 1953).
Barrett Brown, A., *The Machine and the Worker* (London, 1934).
Bell, R. W., *Adroddiad Eglwys y Tabernacl, Abercynon* (Abercynon, Edmunds, 1935).
Bendix, R., Lipset, S. M. (eds.), *Class, Status and Power, a Reader in Social Stratification* (London, Routledge and Kegan Paul Ltd., 1963).
Berger, Peter L., *Invitation to Sociology, A Humanistic Perspective* (London, Penguin, 1971).
Berton, Pierre, *Comfortable Pew* (London, Hodder & Stoughton, 1965).
Boulard, F., *An Introduction to Religious Sociology* (London, Darton, Longmans, Todd, 1960) (translated by Michael Jackson).
Brennan, T., Cooney, E. W., and Pollins, H., *Social Change in South-West Wales* (London, Watts, 1959).
Brothers, J. (Ed.), *Readings in the Sociology of Religion* (Oxford, Pergamon Press, 1967).
Brunner, Emil, *The Divine Imperative* (London, Lutterworth Press, 1947).
Bullock, Alan, *Life and Times of Ernest Bevin* (London, 1960).
Burgess, E. W., " The Determination of Gradients in the Growth of the City ", *Publications of the American Sociological Society*, Vol. 21, 1927.
Busia, K. A., *Urban Churches in Britain* (London, Lutterworth, 1966).
Carter, Harold, *The Towns of Wales* (University of Wales Press, 1965).
Coal Mining Report of the Technical Advisory Committee, March 1945, Cmd. 6610, London, H.M.S.O.
Coates, Ken, and Silburn, Richard, *St. Ann's, Nottingham* (Department of Adult Education, 1967).
Davies, D. Jacob, *Cyfoeth Cwm* (Abercynon, Cyhoeddiadau Modern Cymreig, 1965).
Davies, Elwyn, and Rees, Alwyn D., *Welsh Rural Communities* (Cardiff, University of Wales Press, 1960).
Davies, E. T., *Religion in the Industrial Revolution in South Wales* (Cardiff, University of Wales Press, 1965).
Dennis, N., Henriques, F., and Slaughter, C., *Coal is Our Life* (London, Eyre and Spottiswoode, 1956).
Driver, Christopher, *The Future of the Free Churches* (London, S.C.M., 1962).
Edwards, Wil Jon, *From the Valley I Came* (London, Routledge & Kegan Paul, 1956).
Evans, Benjamin, *Bywgraffiad y diweddar Barch. T. Price, M.A., Ph.D.* (Aberdâr, 1891).
Evans, Eifion, *The Welsh Revival of 1904* (Port Talbot, Evangelical Movement of Wales, 1969).
Evans, Thomas, *The Story of Abercynon* (Cardiff, Western Mail & Echo Ltd., 1963).
Figgis, J. N., *Religion and English Society* (London, Longman, 1911).
Frankenberg, Ronald, *Village on the Border* (London, Cohen and West, 1957).
Gay, John D., *The Geography of Religion in England* (London, Duckworth, 1971).
Halmos, Paul, *The Faith of the Counsellors* (London, Constable, 1966).
Hannington, Wal, *Never on our Knees* (London, Lawrence and Wishart Ltd., 1967).

References

Herberg, W., " Religion in a Secularized Society ", *Readings in the Sociology of Religion* (Ed. Joan Brothers) (Oxford, Pergamon Press, 1967).

Highet, J., *The Churches in Scotland Today* (Glasgow, Jackson, 1950).

idem, " Scottish Religious Adherence ", *British Journal of Sociology* (2) (1953).

Hughes, J., *Methodistiaeth Cymru,* Cyf. iii (Wrexham, Hughes and Son, 1856).

Hurry, Colin, and Associates, *Nationalisation that Survey* (London, 1950).

Jackson, Brian, *Working Class Community: some general notions raised by a series of studies in Northern England* (London, Penguin, 1972).

Jenkins, D. E., in *The Needs of the Church Today,* Pusey House Sermons (London, A. R. Mowbray and Co., 1965).

Jennings, Hilda, *Brynmawr, a Study of a Distressed Area* (London, Allenson and Co. Ltd., 1934).

Jones, R. T., " Y Cylchgrawn ", *Cymro,* November 28th, 1969.

Keating, Joseph, *My Struggle for Life* (London, Simpkin, Marshall, Hamilton, Kent & Co. Ltd., 1916).

Knox, R. Buick, *Voices from the Past* (Llandysul, J. D. Lewis, 1969).

McAllister, Gilbert, *James Maxton: the Portrait of a Rebel* (London, John Murray, 1935).

Martin, David, *A Sociology of English Religion* (London, Heinemann Educational Books Ltd., 1967).

Martin, David (ed.), *A Sociological Year Book of Religion in Britain* (London, S.C.M. Press, 1968, Volume 1).

idem, *A Sociological Year Book of Religion in Britain* (London, S.C.M. Press, 1969, Volume 2).

Mehl, Roger, *The Sociology of Protestantism* (London, S.C.M. Press, 1970).

Mills, C. W., *The Sociological Imagination* (London, Penguin, 1970).

Morgannwg, Dafydd, *Hanes Morgannwg* (Aberdare, Jenkin Howell, 1874).

Owen, Trefor M., " Chapel and Community in Glanllyn, Merioneth ", *Welsh Rural Communities* (Eds. Elwyn Davies and Alwyn D. Rees) (Cardiff, University of Wales Press, 1960).

Parry, R. Ifor, " Crefydd yng Nghwm Aberdâr, a chyfraniad y Bedyddwyr ", Undeb Bedyddwyr Cymru, Aberdâr, Awst 24-27, 1964 (Gol. A. M. Rees) (Clydach, W. Walters, 1964).

idem, " Aberdare and the Industrial Revolution " in *Glamorgan Historian* (Ed. Stewart Williams) (Cowbridge, D. Brown, 1967).

Parsons, Talcott, *The Social System* (London, 1952).

Payne, F. G., *Chwaryddion Crwydrol ac Ysgrifau Eraill* (Dinbych, Clwb Llyfrau Cymraeg, 1943).

Price, W. W., " The History of Powell Duffryn in the Aberdare Valley " (*P.D. Review,* No. 52, October 1942).

idem, " Aberdare, the Queen of the Hills; an Historical Sketch ", *Aberdare Urban District Official Guide* (London, Pyramid Press Ltd., 1956).

Rees, Alwyn D., *Life in a Welsh Countryside* (Cardiff, University of Wales Press, 1951).

Roberts, J. R., " Y Gweinidog yn y Gymdeithas Gyfoes ", *Y Traethodydd,* Hydref 1966, Caernarvon, Cyfrol CXXI, Rhif 521.

Rogues de Fursac, J., *Un Movement Mystique Contemporain; le Reveil Religieux du Pays de Galles, 1904-1905* (Paris, 1907).

Sangster, Paul (ed.), *Sangster of Westminster* (London, Marshall Morgan & Scott, 1960).

Thomas, Gwyn, " Journey from the Rhondda " (*New Statesman,* 26th May 1972).

Thomason, G. F., " The Industrial Challenge to the Church " (*Province,* Winter 1963).

Thompson, R. H. T., *The Church's Understanding of Itself* (London, S.C.M. Press, 1957).
Trist, E. L., Higgin, G. W., Murray, H., Pollock, A. B., *Organizational Choice* (London, Tavistock, 1963).
Valant, Ap, *Cyfeillach Awen* (Merthyr Tydfil, Swyddfa'r *Tyst*, 1885).
Vrijhof, P. H., " What is the Sociology of Religion? " *Readings in the Sociology of Religion* (Ed. Joan Brothers) (Oxford, Pergamon Press, 1967).
Wach, Joachim, *Sociology of Religion* (Chicago, Chicago University Press, 1944).
Watcyn-Williams, Morgan, *From Khaki to Cloth* (Cardiff, Western Mail & Echo Ltd., 1949).
Wendel, Francois, *Calvin* (London, Collins, Fontana Library, 1965, translated by Philip Mairet).
Wickham, E. R., *Church and People in an Industrial City* (London, Lutterworth Press, 1957).
idem, *Encounter with Modern Society* (London, Lutterworth Press, 1956).
Williams, C. R., " The Welsh Religious Revival, 1904-5 (*British Journal of Sociology, 13* (3), September 1952).
Williams, Glanmor (Ed.), *The Making of a Working Class Tradition* (Cardiff, University of Wales Press, 1966).
idem, " Language, Literacy, and Nationality in Wales " (*History*, 1971).
Williams, Howard, *Down to Earth* (London, S.C.M. Press, 1966).
Wright, Ronald Selby, *Asking Them Questions* (London, Oxford University Press, 1963).
Young, David, *A Noble Life. Incidents in the Career of Lewis Davis of Ferndale* (London, Charles H. Kelly, 1899).
Young, M., and Willmott, P., *Family and Kinship in East London* (London, Routledge; Penguin Books, Harmondsworth, 1962).
Zweig, F., *The Worker in an Affluent Society* (London, Heinemann, 1961).
idem, *Men in the Pits* (London, Gollancz, 1948).

INDEX

Aberaman 24, 35, 61, 133
Abercwmboi 35, 36, 42, 59
Abercynon 30, 38, 53, 57, 134, 135-6, 148, 161, 176
  colliery 37, 61, 129, 136
Aberdare (town) 32-36, 192
Aberdare (valley)
  employment figures 48-9
  geography 31-49
  population and languages, 131, 133, 134, 191
  see also specific aspects
Aberdare Coal Company 24
Abernant 34-5, 36, 60, 126, 191, 192
adult education classes 30, 100-101, 209
Anglican Church
  disestablishment 83, 190
  growth and decline 69, 71, 83-5
  internal structure 168, 173

Bacon family 124, 125, 126
baptism of infants 106-7
Baptists
  adult baptism 106-7, 159
  growth and decline 66, 69, 71, 72, 74, 76-7, 159, 201
  internal structure 167
  links with politics 12, 210
betting 63, 161
Bevan, Aneurin 187
bingo 161, 164, 212
bilingualism *see* Welsh language
Birch, James 125-6, 129
Blaendulais Centre 13
Blaengwawr 24, 34, 59, 133
Bryncynon 134

Calvin, John 106
Calvinistic Methodists
  see Presbyterians
chapels and churches
  attendance and membership 47, 73-86, 111-3, 157

growth and decline 24, 26-9, 55, 66-123, 129, 147-60, 209
and mining 24, 27, 28, 50-55, 58, 147-207, 209
ministers 21, 24, 200-202, 209, 211, 213-4
organisation 166-73, 211
present day appeal 113-9, 211-14
religious activities 86-111, 155, 170-72
social and cultural activities 26, 159-60, 190, 195, 197, 199
see also specific denominations
charisma 152, 200-202, 209, 213, 214
Chartism 12
Christadelphians 70
christening 106-7
Christian beliefs today 119-123
Christian socialists 158
Church of England *see* Anglican Church
churches *see* chapels and churches
class conflicts 62, 185, 186
  and politics 51, 168, 185
  and religion 51, 54-5, 168, 185, 186-7
Clifford, Dr. 158
clubs
  drinking and social 45-6, 150, 161-2, 189, 195-9, 209, 210, 212
  Working Men's 45-6, 64-5, 161-2, 195
  youth 212
Coal Industry Social Welfare Organisation 165
collieries
  growth 24, 58-9, 127-9, 174-5
  decline 48-9, 59-60, 136
  management 46, 147-151
  technical development in 58-9, 136-142
  see also mining
Communist Party 53
commuting 28, 144-6

219

Congregationalists
  growth and decline 68-75, 132
  internal structure 167, 168, 176
  links with politics 12, 210
Conservative Clubs 162
Conservative Party 53
Cook, A. J. 150-51, 168, 185
Co-operative movement 45-6
counselling professions 214
Crawshay family 125, 1267-7, 129
Cwmdare 32, 128, 191
Cymanfa Ganu 118, 152, 155, 190
Cymdeithas yr Iaith Gymraeg 52, 178

Darranlas 37, 134
Davies, Rev. Tudwal 158
Davies family (Blaengwawr and Hirwaun) 112, 128, 129, 147
Davies family (Llandinam) 129
death 109-111, 160-61
divorce 121-2
drinking 63-4, 156-7, 161, 166, 189
  see also clubs; public houses

eisteddfodau 25, 190
Elliot, Sir George 128
emotionalism (hwyl) 151-166
Evans, David 147-8
Evans, Rev. D. Silyn 22, 24, 201
Evans, Rev. John 154

factories 27-8, 48-9, 142-6, 194-5
family and kinship 43, 62-3
Forward Movement 154
Fothergill, Richard 126
Free Church Federal Council 11
freedom 122-3
friendship 43-6, 123
funerals 46, 109-111

Gadlys 36, 126, 133
gambling see betting; bingo
General Strike (1926) 12, 72, 137, 193-4
gwrandawyr 79-80

Hardie, J. Keir 51, 185, 187
Harris, Howel 66
Hirwaun 36, 42, 69, 124-5, 127, 136, 142, 143
Homfray family 124, 125, 126, 129

Horner, Arthur 168, 185
Hughes, Emrys 122
Hughes, T. Rowland 117
hwyl (emotionalism) 151-166

immigration 28-9, 48, 70, 124, 129-30, 172, 173-5, 209
Independent Labour Party 153, 184, 186
industrial estates 28, 142-5
industrial relations see trade unions
industrialisation see urbanisation
industries, manufacturing 27-8, 48-9, 142-6, 194-5
iron industry 24, 36, 48, 124-7

James, Rev. William 201
Jews 70
Jenkins, Rev. Joseph 154
Jones, John 201
Jones, Mordecai 128

Kier Hardie, J. 51, 185-187
kinship and family 43, 62-3

Labour Clubs 162
Labour Party
  and mining 52-3, 62, 63, 163, 164
  and Nonconformity 12, 50-54, 168, 184-8, 209-10
  and trade unions 47, 52-3
leisure 159-66, 192, 195, 198-9
Liberalism 12, 52, 183-4, 188, 209
light industry 27-8, 48-9, 142-6, 194-5
Llwydcoed 32, 126, 133, 191

manufacturing industry 27-8, 48-9, 142-6, 194-5
marriage 107-9
mass media 190, 193, 202
Methodist Revivals 66, 151-9, 184, 201
Methodists
  Calvinistic see Presbyterians
  Primitive 70
  Wesleyan
    see Wesleyan Methodists
migration from Aberdare valley 190, 193, 194, 203

INDEX

Miners' Welfare Institutes 164-6
mining
  and Nonconformity 12, 24, 27, 54-5, 69, 166-73, 202-3, 205, 207, 209
  and politics 52-3, 62, 63, 163, 164
  way of life 28, 57-8, 61-5, 136-42
  see also collieries; trade unions
ministers, Nonconformist 21, 24, 200-202, 209, 211, 213-4
Miskin 37, 134, 143
mobility 213 see also immigration; migration
morality 156, 158
Mormons 70
Mountain Ash 32, 36-7, 48-9, 131, 133, 134, 191

National Coal Board 60, 61, 140, 141, 142, 165, 205
National Union of Mineworkers 30, 52-3, 162-3, 164, 185
nationalisation of coal 148, 149, 150, 203-7
Navigation Colliery 60, 128, 174-5
neighbourliness 44-6, 123
Nicholas, Rev. T. E. 122, 158
Nixon, John 128
noson weu 67-8, 172

Overton, George 125

pacifism 122
Paynter, Will 54-5
Penrhiwceibr 38, 134, 143, 148, 157, 192
  colliery 27, 37, 61, 129, 136, 148
  N.U.M. 30, 52-3, 204
Pentecostalism 29, 47, 152, 157, 159
Plaid Cymru 51, 52, 53
political party membership 46
politics and Nonconformism 50-54, 183-88, 209-10
population growth 48, 83-5, 124, 130
Powell, Thomas 128
Presbyterians
  (Calvinistic Methodists)
  growth and decline 66, 68, 69, 70, 71, 77-80, 148, 176
  links with politics 12, 167
  internal structure 167

religious activities 87, 88, 95, 103-6, 135
Price, Rev. David 22, 24, 183
Price, Dr. Thomas 22, 200, 201, 213
Primitive Methodists 70
public houses 44, 157, 189
Pugh, Dr. John 154

recreation see leisure
Rees, Dr. Thomas 130
Reid Committee report 60, 136-42
'religious sociology' movement 18-20
Revivals, Methodist 66, 151-9, 184, 201
Rhigos Industrial estate 28, 142, 145
Roberts, Evan 153-4, 156
Roberts, Rev. Silyn 158
Roman Catholic Church 18-19, 70, 85-6, 107, 109-10, 121, 122, 173

St. John Ambulance Brigade 29, 30, 163, 164
Salvation Army 70
Saunders, Dr. David 200
Scale brothers 126, 129
schools, religious education in 97-100
  see also Sunday schools; Welsh schools
Seiat 86, 101-104, 155, 157, 170
sisterhoods 30, 86, 104-6
social and drinking clubs 45-6, 150, 161-2, 189, 195-9, 209, 210, 212
Solly, Henry 64
strikes 59, 149, 183, 185 see also General Strike
Sunday observance 111-12, 161, 188-90, 213
Sunday schools 38, 68, 86-101, 112, 135, 147, 157, 212

Tappenden brothers 126, 129
Thickens, Rev. John 154
Thomas, D. A. 129, 185
Thomas, Rev. D. R. 122
Thomas, Samuel 128, 129
Thomas, William 128

trade unions
  membership 46-8
  miners' unions 30, 52-3, 162-3, 164, 185
  and Nonconformity 12, 167-8, 169, 183, 210
  and politics 47, 210
Trecynon 66, 68, 142, 143, 159

unemployment 193, 194
Unitarians 66, 69, 167, 168
urban society and religion 12, 55, 56, 186, 208
urbanisation 190-202, 214

village life 190-91

Wayne family 126, 128, 147
Welsh culture and Nonconformity 25, 26, 157-60, 190-95, 199, 207
Welsh language 130-136
  and Nonconformity 48, 53, 135-6, 175-83, 188, 209
Welsh Language Society 52, 178
Welsh Nationalist Party 51, 52, 53
Welsh schools and classes 135, 180-83
Welsh way of life 26, 190
Wesleyan Methodists 12, 47, 69, 70-71, 72, 80-82, 129, 148, 169
Williams, David (Alaw Goch) 128, 129, 147
Williams, Thomas 129
Winstone, James 185
women and religion 63, 121, 155, 211-12
women's role in community 62-3, 143, 161
Working Men's Clubs 45-6, 64-5, 161-2, 195

Ynysboeth Industrial Estate 28, 37, 38, 142, 143, 145
Ynysybwl 37, 38, 61, 129, 136
young people and religion 115-6, 117, 154-5, 211-2 *see also* schools
young people and Welsh language 179-183
youth clubs 212